LIGHT STYLE

LIGHT STYLE

Completely Revised and Updated

The Low Fat, Low Cholesterol, Low Salt Way
to Good Food and Good Health

Rose Dosti and Deborah Kidushim-Allen, R.D.

This revised edition is based on the original *Light Style*
coauthored by Rose Dosti, Deborah Kidushim, and Mark Wolke

HarperSanFrancisco
A Division of HarperCollins*Publishers*

A portion of *Light Style: The New American Cuisine* originally appeared in *Bon Appetit* magazine.

Illustrations are by Heather Preston.

LIGHT STYLE: *The New American Cuisine.* Copyright © 1979 by Rose Dosti, Deborah Kidushim, and Mark Wolke. LIGHT STYLE: *REVISED EDITION.* Copyright © 1991 by Rose Dosti and Deborah Kidushim-Allen.

REVISED EDITION

This revised edition is based on *Light Style: The New American Cuisine* coauthored by Rose Dosti, Deborah Kidushim, and Mark Wolke.

Library of Congress Cataloging-in-Publication Data

Dosti, Rose.
    Light style : the low fat, low cholesterol, low salt way to good
    food and good health / Rose Dosti & Deborah Kidushim.—Rev. ed.
      p. cm.

    Includes bibliographical references and index.
    ISBN 0–06–250241–7 (alk. paper)
      1. Low-fat diet—Recipes.   2. Low-cholesterol diet—Recipes.
    3. Salt-free diet—Recipes.   I. Kidushim-Allen, Deborah.
II. Title.
RM237.7.D67 1991
641.5'63—dc20
                                               90–41780
                                               CIP

---

91 92 93 94 95   MART   10 9 8 7 6 5 4 3 2 1

This edition is printed on acid-free paper that meets the American National Standards Institute Z39.48 Standard.

CONTENTS

Acknowledgments vii
Introduction 1
Appetizers 13
Soups and Stocks 25
Breads 41
Eggs 49
Crêpes 59
Fish and Shellfish 67
Poultry and Game 81
Meats 97
Pasta and Grains 113
Vegetables 125
Salads 141
Salad Dressings 159
Sauces, Condiments, and Specialty Recipes 167
Desserts 189
Beverages 213
Mcnus 221

Modifying Recipes 228
Dining Out 233
Shopping Smart 238
Everyday Food Guide 240
Weight Control 250
Nutrient Counter 256
Alcohol Exchange List 272
Omega-3 Fatty Acids in Selected Seafoods 273
Fiber Content in Foods 274
Vegetable Oil–Fat Comparison 276
Spices, Herbs, and Wines 279
Table of Equivalents 283
Table of Substitutions 284
Metric Conversion Tables 287
Specialty Foods 291
Glossary 297
Bibliography 301
Recipe Index 303

ACKNOWLEDGMENTS

We are grateful to all the people who helped in the preparation of this book. In particular, we would like to acknowledge the generous help of Mo Ezzani, Josie Wilson, Ramona Ponce, and Edwin Smith, who worked in the testing and development of the recipes. We also thank Kathy DeKarr and Marya Dosti for testing many of the recipes and Teresa Salerno for converting the recipes to metric measurements.

Special thanks to Professor Roslyn B. Alfin-Slater, Ph.D., chairman of the Department of Nutritional Sciences at UCLA, for reviewing our manuscript and for her invaluable comments.

In addition, we would like to thank Stephanie Turner, R.D.M.P.H., nutrition writer for the *San Francisco Chronicle.*

ship between diet and disease, and they provide overwhelming evidence for their major conclusions based on seven recommendations:

- Eat a variety of foods.
- Maintain desirable weight.
- Avoid too much fat and cholesterol.
- Eat foods with adequate starch and fiber.
- Avoid too much sugar.
- Avoid too much sodium.
- If you drink alcohol, do so in moderation.

More important, as *Light Style* predicted in 1979, today's recommendations are meant not only for people who have risk factors for chronic diseases—such as those with a family history of obesity or high blood pressure, or those who smoke—but also for people who are healthy. (The new guidelines no longer apply to people with existing diseases or conditions that interfere with normal nutritional requirements, who may need special diet instructions from physicians or registered dietitians.)

In 1979 *Light Style* showed readers how to implement the original guidelines by reducing fat and cholesterol, sodium, sugar, and total calories in recipes, and it is still current in 1990. It taught consumers how to choose and prepare foods in a better, more health-conscious manner—and it still does.

However, to keep *Light Style* as up-to-date as possible, we have added information about the need to increase the intake of complex carbohydrates to provide more fiber in the diet and to lower fat intake in the diet. We have updated the nutrient analyses after each recipe to include protein, carbohydrate, fat, cholesterol, and sodium counts, as well as to indicate the percentage of calories that comes from fat. After each nutrient analysis you will find the "diabetic exchange" (see glossary) for people with diabetes who must carefully calculate simple carbohydrate calories in their diets. We have continued to use the old diabetic exchange, but it can be adapted easily to the current exchange by anyone with diabetes, as well as by individuals following the Weight Watcher's Diet. For the convenience of the readers outside the United States we have added metric conversions to each recipe ingredient.

Also updated and supplemented have been the instructions for modifying your own recipes—something we felt needed extra attention to help our readers become more expert in modifying any recipe.

The Table of Substitutions and the Specialty Foods list also have been updated and supplemented to include the newest products on the market, so that cooking the *Light Style* way becomes easier, faster, and more convenient.

One of the major criticisms of the original *Light Style* book was the exclusive use of fructose as the artificial sweetener. When we wrote the book, fructose seemed to be the best answer for increasing sweetness without adding extra calories, because it contained double the sweetness of sugar gram per gram.

We decided to return to sugar in the most miminal amounts (if at all necessary) and eliminate the use of artificial sweeteners altogether, because artificial sweeteners are not economical and are no longer generally recommended for cooking. Above all, questions about their safety still persist. Those who wish to use sweeteners to sweeten beverages or cereals can follow the equivalency recommendations for several brands on p. 283, if applicable.

Today, sugar is not considered the culprit it was once. The primary problem with sugar is that excess amounts may cause tooth decay. As a simple carbohydrate it contributes only four calories per gram compared to fat, which contains nine calories per gram. Sugar and most foods that contain sugar in large amounts supply calories, but are limited in essential nutrients. Thus they should be used in moderation by most healthy people and sparingly by people with low-calorie needs.

We have also modified the United States Department of Agriculture's (USDA) Daily Food Guide, which we call The Everyday Food Guide, to help you choose foods lower in fat and cholesterol so that less than 30 percent of your total calories come from fat. The guide provides clear standard serving size information to help you meet the RDA (Recommended Dietary Allowances). The new RDA have added vitamin K and selenium to the requirements and also increased the requirement for calcium to meet the growing body needs of teenagers, protect fetuses of pregnant women, and help prevent osteoporosis in the elderly.

We invite you to treat this book as a handbook for nutrition information, recipe modification, and meal planning. The tools are here: the recipes; the scientifically based nutrient anlyses for each recipe; and the charts to help you substitute ingredients and modify recipes. We have provided tips for experimenting with herbs, spices, and wine, as well as information about serving size.

We would like you to use this book as a tool for making life-style changes that will affect the health of your entire family.

Most of all, we hope the book will prove that low-calorie, low-fat, low-salt eating can also be high in flavor appeal.

How do *Light Style* recipes cut calories, sodium, fat, and cholesterol while increasing complex carbohydrates and fiber?

CALORIES

Light Style cuts calories in several ways. When you cut down on fat, you automatically cut down on calories. Fat calories account for roughly 37 to 45 percent of the average American diet. Our recipes strive for the recommended limit of 30 percent fat intake for adults.

Children have higher calorie requirements for growing body needs. Overweight children can be encouraged to eat fewer of the simple carbohydrates (such as candy, cookies, sodas, and pies) and highly processed foods, which contain high amounts of fat and calories. For those children, *Light Style* becomes an effective tool. *Light Style* cooking is also a blessing for the elderly, whose nutrient needs increase, while calorie needs diminish.

Our chapter called Modifying Recipes will show you how *Light Style* cuts calories but not nutrients.

FATS AND CHOLESTEROL

The raging controversy over fat has been somewhat resolved over the last ten years. We now know that high blood cholesterol levels can be reduced by eating fewer saturated fatty acids and less cholesterol. There is even evidence that too much fat in the diet leads to increased risk of breast, prostate, and colon/rectal cancer.

New studies show that omega-3 fatty acids, found in seafood, especially salmon, trout, halibut, tuna, and some vegetable oils, such as canola oil, lower serum cholesterol levels and are especially helpful in inhibiting the formation of blood clots, which can cause heart attacks (see the chart on p. 273).

Monounsaturated fatty acids, such as peanut oil and olive oil, have been found to have a neutralizing effect on serum cholesterol and coronary heart disease risk.

As a result, the recommendation today is to equally divide the intake of polyunsaturated and monounsaturated fat. The American Heart Association and the National Cholesterol Education Committee say the diet should contain less than 30 percent of calories from fat, with less than 10 percent in saturated fat, 10 percent in polyunsaturated fat, and the remaining 10 percent in monounsaturated fat. The *Dietary Guidelines for Americans* recommends that no more than 30 percent of total calories consumed come from fat. Most Americans today eat 37 to 45 percent of their calories in fat daily.

But we are talking about the total amount of fat eaten in one full day. Don't be alarmed if you notice that the percentage of calories from fat in some recipes (especially in the meat, eggs, salad dressing, and dessert chapters) are particularly high. The percentage of calories from fat is high because fat predominates in those recipes. This is especially true when a recipe is low in calories—since each gram of fat has twice the calories of protein or carbohydrates. You will also notice that the recipes in the fruits, vegetables, and grains chapters have lower percentages of calories from fat.

There is a caveat, however. Don't shortchange your diet of nutrients in an attempt to cut fat calories. Many fine foods, such as cheese, nuts, and beef, are high in fat but also high in essential nutrients such as calcium, iron, and zinc.

The *Dietary Guidelines* advise moderation and common sense in eating fat. Try to reduce daily consumption of fat, especially saturated animal fat, which tends to increase blood cholesterol in some people. This is particularly relevant advice for people at risk of heart disease, such as smokers or people with a family history of premature heart disease, high blood pressure, or diabetes.

Light Style teaches readers how to strike for the 30 percent mark by creating recipes filled with ideas on reducing cholesterol and fat.

Our recipes emphasize foods that are naturally low in fat, such as fish, shellfish, poultry (without skin), and lean meats, as well as fruits, vegetables, and grains.

All the dairy products in our recipes contain little or no fat. The recipes teach you how to make your own low-calorie margarine and sauces, which are also lower in fat than their regular counterparts.

All the *Light Style* recipes calling for eggs use egg whites (no cholesterol or fat), commercial egg substitute, or our own egg substitute, made mostly from egg whites. Our chapter on eggs and crêpes will show you how versatile and fat- and cholesterol-free they can be the *Light Style* way.

To cut down on cholesterol, *Light Style* recipes favor the use of highly polyunsaturated and monounsaturated oils. We provide charts comparing vegetable oil fats, a list of omega-3 fatty acids in common foods, and a nutrient counter for meats, cheeses, fish, poultry, and other commonly eaten foods to help you make wise food choices.

In the Vegetable Oil–Fat Comparison chart (p. 276), you will find the count for canola (rapeseed) oil, the oil lowest in saturated and highest in monounsaturated fat. Whenever appropriate we recommend olive oil, not only because it is thought to lower blood cholesterol levels but also because of its wonderful flavor.

For a description of the fats, turn to our glossary.

SUGAR

The *Dietary Guidelines* recommendation to avoid too much sugar cannot be isolated from other dietary recommendations; all are interlocked in building a healthful diet. The *Guidelines* recommend avoiding too much sugar, using fluoridated water, and practicing dental hygiene.

When we give sugar as an ingredient, we try to use as little as possible. *Light Style* recipes rely on fruits and fruit juices for sweetening.

We have eliminated the use of artificial sweeteners because they were not found to be effective in cooking, and they may be unsafe.

Once you've worked with *Light Style* recipes, you will see little reason to use as much sugar as you thought you might need. A little goes a long way. Still, sugar is lower in calories than fat; it has only 4 calories per gram compared with 9 per gram for fat.

SODIUM

Controlling sodium intake is not all that easy. Sodium is found naturally in foods, as well as being added to processed foods, soft drinks, fast foods, water, and even toothpaste.

Sodium is a mineral that is essential to health. The National Research Council of the National Academy of Sciences suggests that a "safe and adequate" range is about 1,100 to 3,300 milligrams for adults (equivalent to ½ to 1½ teaspoons of salt). That's about 1,000 to 3,000 milligrams per day, much lower than the 8,000 to 10,000 milligrams (equivalent to 1½ tablespoons of salt) a day that most Americans consume.

That means throwing away the salt shaker. The food industry, meeting the demands of consumers, is slowly but surely reducing the salt content of soups, salad dressings, cheeses, sauces, cereals, lunch meats, and canned foods, as well as snack food items such as crackers, popcorn, chips, nuts, and pretzels. Still, it's wise to read labels before using canned vegetables, smoked and cured meats, pickles, sauerkraut, and snack goods, such as potato chips, salted nuts, and salted crackers.

If you wish to season your food, you may want to use herb blends without added salt that are now available on the market; users think the blends are effective.

You will not find any added salt in *Light Style* recipes. Instead, we enhance flavors with spices, herbs, fruit juices, fruit, peels, and wine. Whenever regular baking powder and soda is used in recipes we omit the salt, thus keeping the recipe relatively low in sodium.

We offer recipes for condiments, sauces, soups, stocks, and salad dressings, all without salt.

FIBER

The hoopla over fiber in recent years is clouded with confusion. The possible benefits of dietary fiber in preventing colon cancer, heart disease, diabetes, and obesity are under study and not yet fully understood. However, most Americans probably do not eat enough fiber, and although we do not know exactly how much and precisely what types of fiber we need in our diets, a moderate increase is recommended in the *Dietary Guidelines for Americans*.

Fiber, a complex mixture of indigestible organic material found in plant foods, comes in two types: soluble (includes pectins, gums, and mucilages derived from fruits and vegetables, beans, and oats) and insoluble (includes cellulose, hemicellulose, and lignin, which provide bulk to the diet in the form of whole-grain breads and cereals).

Whole grain doesn't just mean bread or cereal. The category also includes brown rice, tortillas, popcorn, scotch barley, bulgur, and whole-wheat pastas.

Oat bran, a soluble fiber food that the food industry is adding to everything from cereals to breakfast drinks, has been found to lower blood cholesterol levels by 6 to 19 percent, resulting in a 2 percent drop in the risk of a first major heart attack.

Unfortunately, however, people who latch onto the fad often do so at the expense of other types of fibers, such as insoluble fiber foods like wheat, fruits, and vegetables, which provide a variety of essential nutrients and can reduce the risk of certain cancers.

The idea is to leave room in the diet for both kinds of fiber. According to the American Cancer Society, the diet should contain 25 to 35 grams of fiber per day, depending on one's weight. That's equivalent to 1 ounce of fiber cereal, two slices of whole-wheat bread, ½ cup peas, and one apple with the skin (see the chart on fiber content in common foods on p. 274).

Throughout *Light Style* you will find recipes for vegetable dishes, breads, and fruit dishes containing complex carbohydrates. All the recipes tell you how much fiber they contain.

THE RECIPES

Light Style is a valuable guide for light eating because more than 250 recipes in the book contain about half the calories, fat, cholesterol, and salt found in comparable dishes.

Light Style teaches you how to modify any recipe to suit your personal needs. The recipes in the book are the examples you will need to apply to your own recipes, as well.

All our recipes have been tested several times at hospitals, restaurants, and homes. They have been prepared by experienced chefs and by home cooks who have never cooked before. We have given the recipes a final home-test to make sure that even the novice cook finds them foolproof. All the recipes have been simplified to make use of the most basic home equipment.

In *Light Style* we have emphasized the eclectic cuisine most Americans cook at home. You will find plain and fancy recipes to suit your life-style, whether you entertain or cook for a family or just for yourself.

Following each recipe is an analysis of the amount of total calories, fats, cholesterol, sodium, carbohydrates, protein, and fiber per serving, as well as the percentage of calories from fat. The analyses were prepared by Computrition Laboratory in Chatsworth, California.

Because no two sources listing nutrient values of foods contain identical nutrient counts, allow for a variance of 5 to 10 percent in values.

SPECIAL RECIPES

Light Style contains recipes for low-sodium, low-calorie, low-cholesterol, and low-fat sauces, stocks, catsup, egg substitute, mustard, and salad dressings. You can make your own at a fraction of the cost of the commercial types, as well as keeping the quality and quantity controls in your own hands.

MENUS

Having a party? Calling the neighbors in for Sunday TV football lunch or supper? Going Mexican, Italian, or Chinese tonight? The menus, with nutrient analyses, will help you plan any occasion with an eye for health and good taste.

MODIFYING RECIPES

We decided to give special attention to helping you modify any recipe in your repertoire. A sample recipe in the Modifying Recipes chapter will give you the formula you'll need to make the necessary changes to reduce calories, fat, cholesterol, and sodium in any recipe.

DINING OUT

As more Americans eat meals away from home, the challenge of applying good nutrition increases. The Dining Out chapter helps you make wise selections whether you dine at a restaurant, fast food establishment, salad bar, supermarket deli, or breakfast counter. We even provide a chart showing how fast foods fare in the calories, fats, cholesterol, and sodium departments.

SHOPPING SMART

The Shopping Smart chapter will help you fill your shopping cart with foods that are low in fat, sugar, and sodium and get the most nutrition from the meat, bread and cereal, dairy, and fruit and vegetable counters. It also shows you how to be a smart label shopper at the frozen food counter and snack rack.

EVERYDAY FOOD GUIDE

The Everyday Food Guide gives recommendations for serving sizes considered nutritionally adequate for adults. The guide is based on the United States Department of Agriculture Daily Food Guide, which helps you choose foods that will provide your total intake of calories, with less than 30 percent fat. The operative word is *total*: some recipes may be higher in fat content than others, but it is the total day's intake over several days that counts.

The Everyday Food Guide also lists the foods in order of highest fat intake, for quick referral. By following the food guide's serving size recommendations, you will be providing your body with a safe margin of baseline nutrients needed for good health.

WEIGHT CONTROL

Maintaining a healthy body weight is the best preventive health tool you can employ to reduce the fat, cholesterol, sugar, and salt in your diet. The charts and formulas for maintaining a healthy weight and the ideas for ways to reach your healthy weight will, we hope, motivate you to reduce or maintain your weight.

NUTRIENT COUNTER

The Nutrient Counter lists in household measures the amounts of calories, sodium, fat, and cholesterol in commonly used foods. We have also included the fiber content of commonly used foods, a chart listing the omega-3 fatty acid content for commonly consumed fish, a fat comparison chart for different cooking oils, and a chart comparing fat and cholesterol in fast foods.

SPICE AND HERB CHART

What a difference ten years make in the way people use herbs and spices! Our updated Spice and Herb Chart is indicative of the trend toward the use of and familiarity with the abundant herbs and spices available in markets today. *Light Style* recipes will give you a good idea of how fresh herbs and spices are incorporated successfully into saltless dishes. Feel free to use the chart to help you concoct your own herb and spice combinations.

TABLE OF SUBSTITUTIONS

The Table of Substitutions is your tool for modifying recipes accurately. It contains conversions for herbs and spices as well as for numerous ingredients commonly used in *Light Style* recipes.

TABLE OF MEASUREMENT EQUIVALENTS

The table of liquid and solid measures in both standard and metric units will help you make conversions in American and foreign recipes using the metric system.

SPECIALTY PRODUCTS

The updated list of special brand-name products used in the book includes a brief description of the product and tells where to find it.

GLOSSARY

We've updated the glossary to help you better understand nutrition terms used in the book.

APPETIZERS

Appetizers have moved into prime time on many household and entertaining menus over the last ten years. Some wise parents work fruits, vegetables, and dairy products into family meals through appetizers, especially when there are growing children who might not get enough of these foods at meal times.

In this chapter you'll find an exciting array of low-calorie, low-fat, no-salt appetizers that will suit most any party situation. Our appetizers range from elbow-to-elbow party-time goodies that make a meal to elegant sit-down dinner appetizers.

Many of the appetizers, such as meatballs, pizza, and dips, can be made well in advance and stored in either the freezer or the refrigerator until ready to use. Enjoy.

—————— DIPS ——————

CRAB DIP

1 pound [450 g] cooked crab meat (fresh or frozen)
1 cup [225 g] low-fat cottage cheese
2 tablespoons low-calorie Mayonnaise (p. 179)
1 tablespoon Dijon Mustard (p. 182)
1 tablespoon fresh lemon juice
   Thin lemon slices, twisted
   Parsley sprigs

Combine crab meat, cottage cheese, mayonnaise, mustard, and lemon juice in a blender container and blend until smooth. Serve garnished with twists of lemon and parsley sprigs. Makes 2 cups.

NOTE: Canned crab has a very high sodium content. We suggest that those watching their salt intake use only fresh or frozen Alaskan king crab meat.

Each 1 tablespoon serving contains about:

> 26 calories; 181 mg sodium; 8 mg
> cholesterol; tr fat; tr carbohydrate;
> 4 g protein; 0 fiber. 32% calories
> from fat.
> Exchanges: ½ meat

GUACAMOLE

Excellent on baked potatoes or as a salad dressing.

> *1 large avocado*
> *2 tablespoons fresh lemon juice*
> *1 clove garlic, minced*
> *1 small tomato, peeled and chopped*
> *2 green onions, chopped*
> *¼ green bell pepper, minced, or ½ teaspoon chopped green*
> *   chili pepper*
> *½ teaspoon chili powder*
> *1 tablespoon minced cilantro (fresh coriander)*
> *Pepper to taste*

Cut avocado in half and remove pit. Scoop out pulp into a bowl and mash with a fork. Add lemon juice, garlic, tomato, green onions, green pepper, chili powder, cilantro, and pepper and mix well. Makes about 1¼ cups.

Each 1 tablespoon serving contains about:

> 27 calories; 3 mg sodium; 0 cholesterol;
> 2 g fat; 2 g carbohydrate; tr protein;
> tr fiber. 31% calories from fat.
> Exchanges: ½ fat

SEAFOOD DIP

> *½ cup [115 g] low-calorie sour cream*
> *½ cup [115 g] low-fat plain yogurt*
> *½ cup [76 g] shredded cooked crab meat (fresh or frozen)*
> *¼ teaspoon Worcestershire sauce*
> *2 cloves garlic, minced*
> *3 tablespoons fresh lemon juice*

Combine sour cream, yogurt, crab meat, Worcestershire sauce, garlic, and lemon juice and mix well. Serve with cut raw vegetables, such as carrots, zucchini, jicama, green and red peppers, snow peas, and green beans. Makes about 1½ cups.

NOTE: Canned crab has a very high sodium content. We suggest that those watching their salt intake use only fresh or frozen Alaskan king crab meat.

Each 2 tablespoon serving contains about:

> 30 calories; 106 mg sodium; 9 mg
> cholesterol; 2 g fat; 2 g carbohydrate;
> 3 g protein; 0 fiber. 45% calories from
> fat.
> Exchanges: ¼ meat

SKINNY DIP

¼ cup [58 g] low-calorie Mayonnaise (p. 179)
2 cups [68 g] low-fat plain yogurt
4 green onions, chopped
2 tablespoons fresh lemon juice
2 cloves garlic, minced
1 (10-ounce) [285 g] package frozen chopped spinach,
*   thawed, drained, and squeezed dry*

Combine mayonnaise, yogurt, onion, lemon juice, and garlic. Let stand 30 minutes, to allow flavors to blend. Fold in spinach. Serve with cut raw vegetables, such as carrots, cauliflowerets, zucchini, celery, green or red bell peppers, jicama, and green beans. Makes 2½ cups.

Each 1 tablespoon serving contains about:

> 16 calories; 15 mg sodium; 1 mg
> cholesterol; tr fat; 1 g carbohydrate;
> tr protein; tr fiber. Tr calories
> from fat.
> Exchanges: negligible

APPETIZER ARTICHOKES

6 large artichokes
Water
2 tablespoons coriander seeds
Juice of 2 lemons
Curry Mayonnaise (p. 180), Drawn Margarine (p. 170),
Vinaigrette (p. 165)

Trim rough outer leaves from artichokes. Cut stems even with bottoms. Place artichokes upright in a pan in which they fit snugly. Add water to cover, coriander seeds, and lemon juice and bring to a boil. Reduce to a simmer, cover, and cook until outer leaves pull off easily, about 40 minutes. Let cool. Hold cooked artichokes upright under a steady stream of cold water. Leaves will open out, exposing choke and center leaves. Pull out center leaves with fingers. Using a spoon, scrape out remaining choke fibers and small leaves. Fill centers with 2 tablespoons Curry Mayonnaise, or chill and serve with Drawn Margarine or Vinaigrette. Makes 6 servings.

1 artichoke without sauce contains about:

> 44 calories; 30 mg sodium;
> 0 cholesterol; tr fat; 10 g
> carbohydrate; 3 g protein; 2 g
> fiber. Tr calories from fat.
> Exchanges: 1B vegetable

CHAMPAGNE MEATBALLS

1 pound [450 g] lean ground beef sirloin
Freshly ground pepper to taste
1 tablespoon minced onion
1 teaspoon minced garlic
1 tablespoon egg substitute, or 1 egg white
½ cup [115 g] low-calorie grape jelly
¼ cup [225 g] Catsup (p. 182)
½ cup [119 ml] Champagne or dry white wine

In a mixing bowl, mix together beef, pepper, onion, garlic, and egg substitute or egg. Form mixture into 36 (1-inch) [2½ cm] balls, set aside. In a skillet, combine grape jelly, Catsup, and Champagne and simmer, uncovered, 5 minutes to blend flavors. Add meatballs and simmer, uncovered, 30 minutes, stirring often. Makes 36 meatballs.

NOTE: Meatballs may be stored in the freezer before or after cooking. To cook from raw frozen state, thaw slightly, then cook as directed. To heat from cooked frozen state, thaw slightly and place in a 350°F [177°C] oven about 15 minutes, or until heated through.

Each meatball contains about:

> 24 calories; 10 mg sodium; 8 mg
> cholesterol; tr fat; 1 g carbohydrate;
> 3 g protein; 0 fiber. 33% calories
> from fat.
> Exchanges: ¼ meat

CHICKEN PACIFICA

1 tablespoon Low-Calorie Margarine (p. 185)
½ cup [119 ml] Low-Calorie Russian Dressing (p. 166)
1½ tablespoons low-calorie apricot jelly
3 whole chicken breasts, skinned, boned, and cut in 1-inch
[2½ cm] cubes

In a small saucepan, melt margarine over low heat. Add dressing and apricot jelly and blend thoroughly. Heat through. Place chicken cubes in a baking dish and cover with dressing-jelly mixture. Marinate chicken, refrigerated, 3 to 6 hours. One hour before cooking, remove chicken from refrigerator and allow to come to room temperature. Leave chicken in pan used for marinating and place in a 350°F [177°C] oven for 20 minutes, or until lightly browned. Remove meat from marinade and serve with wood picks. Makes about 50 pieces.

Each piece contains about:

> 22 calories; 30 mg sodium; 9 mg
> cholesterol; tr fat; tr carbohydrate;
> 3 g protein; 0 fiber. 26% calories
> from fat.
> Exchanges: ⅛ meat

MELON WITH PORT

This can double as a dessert.

> 1 large honeydew or melon of choice
> ½ cup [119 ml] port wine
> Fresh mint sprigs

Cut melon in half, remove and discard seeds. Using a melon scoop, carve balls from melon flesh and place them in a bowl. Pour wine over melon balls and chill several hours for flavors to blend. Serve in sherbet dishes and garnish with mint sprigs. Makes 6 servings.

Each ½ cup serving contains about:

> 50 calories; 11 mg sodium; 0 cholesterol;
> tr fat; 11 g carbohydrate; tr protein;
> 1 g fiber. 2% calories from fat.
> Exchanges: 1 fruit

PIZZA

> 1 envelope active dry yeast
> ¾ cup [178 ml] lukewarm water (105° to 115°F)
> ½ teaspoon sugar
> 2 cups [285 g] sifted unbleached flour
> 1½ teaspoons vegetable oil or olive oil
> 1 tablespoon yellow cornmeal
> 1 cup [237 ml] Italian Tomato Sauce (p. 173)
> ¾ cup [225 g] shredded mozzarella cheese
> ½ cup [40 g] sliced mushrooms
> ½ onion, sliced in rings
> ½ green bell pepper, sliced in rings
> ½ red bell pepper, sliced in rings
> 1½ tablespoons grated Parmesan cheese (optional)

Dissolve yeast in lukewarm water. Add sugar and let yeast mixture stand 10 minutes. Measure flour into a mixing bowl. Add yeast mixture and stir in thoroughly. On a lightly floured board, knead about 5 minutes, or until soft and pliable. Form dough into ball and place in a lightly greased bowl. Turn ball to grease top, cover bowl, and let rise in a warm place about 2 hours, or until doubled in bulk.

Grease a 14-inch [36 cm] pizza pan or 11-by-17-inch [28-by-43 cm] baking sheet with ½ teaspoon of the oil. Sprinkle pan evenly with cornmeal. Punch down dough and roll out on a lightly floured board into a 14-inch [36 cm] circle to fit pizza pan or a rectangle to fit baking sheet. Place dough in pan and pat and stretch it to fit the pan, pinching up a rim around the edges. Pierce dough in several places with a fork. Spread Italian Tomato Sauce over the crust and let it rest about 10 minutes. (At this point, pizza may be frozen for up to 1 week; thaw before proceeding with recipe.) Cover crust with a layer of mozzarella cheese. Arrange mushrooms, onions, and green and red peppers over cheese. Brush vegetables with remaining teaspoon of oil. Sprinkle with Parmesan cheese. Bake at 450°F [232°C] about 25 minutes, or until browned. Serve at once. Cut into 8 portions. Makes 8 servings.

NOTE: If you do not want to make a crust, use Boboli or pita bread.

Each serving with Parmesan cheese contains about:

> 168 calories; 60 mg sodium; 9 mg cholesterol;
> 4 g fat; 27 g carbohydrate; 7 g protein;
> 2 g fiber. 21% calories from fat.
> Exchanges: 1 bread, 1 vegetable

PIZZA CANAPES

Prepare dough as directed for Pizza. Divide dough into 14 portions. Roll each portion into a circle about 2 inches [5 cm] in diameter. Place canapes on baking sheet and top as directed in recipe. Bake at 450°F [232°C] for 15 minutes.

SCALLOPS DEJONGHE

2 tablespoons Low-Calorie Margarine (p. 185)
2 cloves garlic, minced
1 cup soft French Bread (p. 46) crumbs without crust
¾ pound [340 g] scallops or cleaned shrimp
1 tablespoon sweet Marsala wine
* Lemon wedges*
* Parsley sprigs*

In a mixing bowl, cream margarine with garlic. Add crumbs, stirring well to form a paste. Place scallops in 6 individual scallop shells or flameproof ramekins or in a nonstick baking pan. Spread crumb mixture over scallops. Sprinkle with Marsala and broil 4 inches [10 cm] from source of heat until browned, about 10 minutes. Garnish with lemon wedges and parsley sprigs. Makes 6 servings.

Each serving contains about:

> 78 calories; 116 mg sodium; 18 mg
> cholesterol; 2 g fat; 3 g carbohydrate;
> 12 g protein; tr fiber. 23% calories
> from fat.
> Exchanges: 3 meat, ¼ bread

SEAFOOD COCKTAIL

*½ pound [225 g] each cooked lobster meat, crab meat, and
    cleaned shrimp (about 12)
    Seafood Cocktail Sauce (p. 186)
    Lemon wedges*

Cut lobster and crab into 1-inch [2½ cm] pieces. Arrange lobster, crab, and
shrimp on a serving platter or on a bed of shaved ice. Serve with Seafood
Cocktail Sauce and garnish with lemon wedges. Makes 6 servings.

Each serving lobster (2 pieces) without sauce contains about:

> 37 calories; 144 mg sodium; 27 mg
> cholesterol; tr fat; tr carbohydrate;
> 8 g protein; tr fiber. Tr calories from
> fat.
> Exchanges: ¼ meat

Each serving crab meat (2 pieces) without sauce contains about:

> 26 calories, 124 mg sodium; 15 mg cholesterol;
> tr fat; tr carbohydrate;
> 6 g protein; tr fiber.
> Tr calories from fat.
> Exchanges: ¼ meat

Each serving shrimp (2 pieces) without sauce contains about:

> 36 calories; 30 mg sodium; 20 mg cholesterol; tr fat;
> tr carbohydrate; 9 g protein; tr fiber. Tr calories
> from fat.
> Exchanges: ¼ meat

SIRLOIN TERIYAKI

*1 pound [450 g] top beef sirloin, cut in ½-inch [1½ cm]
cubes*

*1 (10½-ounce) [300 g] can water-packed mandarin orange
sections, drained*

¾ cup [178 ml] low-sodium soy sauce

Thread sirloin cubes on 12 presoaked bamboo skewers or small metal
skewers alternately with mandarin orange sections. Arrange in a single
layer in a shallow dish. Pour soy sauce over skewers and marinate, refrigerated, 1 hour. Place under broiler or on a barbecue grill and cook to desired
doneness. Makes 12 servings.

Each skewer contains about:

> 72 calories, 99 mg sodium; 27 mg
> cholesterol; 3 g fat; 3 g carbohydrate;
> 9 g protein; 0 fiber. 33% calories
> from fat.
> Exchanges: 1 meat

STUFFED MUSHROOMS

12 large mushrooms (1½ to 2 inches [4 to 5 cm] in diameter)

¾ pound [340 g] lean ground beef sirloin

2 cloves garlic, minced

¼ cup [59 ml] fresh lemon juice

¼ teaspoon pepper

  Pinch dried thyme

1 bay leaf

1½ teaspoons ground coriander

2½ teaspoons chopped cilantro (fresh coriander)

1½ teaspoons low-calorie margarine

⅛ teaspoon paprika

½ cup [119 ml] dry white wine

Remove stems from mushrooms. Set caps aside and chop stems. In a skillet,
combine meat, chopped stems, and garlic and cook over medium heat until
meat is browned and crumbly. Add lemon juice, pepper, thyme, bay leaf,
coriander, and cilantro. Cook until flavors are blended, about 5 minutes.

While meat mixture is cooking, melt margarine in a skillet and add
paprika, wine, and mushroom caps. Cover and cook over medium heat

until mushrooms are just tender, about 7 minutes. Stuff caps with meat mixture and place on a greased baking sheet. Broil 2 inches from source of heat 5 minutes or until golden. Makes 12 servings.

Each stuffed mushroom contains about:

> 44 calories; 18 mg sodium; 14 mg cholesterol;
> 2 g fat; 2 g carbohydrate; 5 g protein;
> tr fiber. 34% calories from fat.
> Exchanges: ½ meat

STUFFED CHERRY TOMATOES

1½ cups [340 g] low-calorie Cream Cheese (p. 185)
¼ cup [30 g] grated carrot
¼ cup [30 g] finely chopped celery
2 tablespoons finely chopped green bell pepper
2 tablespoons finely chopped red bell pepper
¾ teaspoon Herb Blend (p. 184)
  Pinch garlic powder
  Dash hot pepper sauce
48 cherry tomatoes
2 tablespoons sesame seeds, toasted*

Combine Cream Cheese, carrot, celery, green and red peppers, Herb Blend, garlic powder, and hot pepper sauce in a bowl. Stir until well mixed. Cut a shallow slice off stem end of each cherry tomato. Remove seeds and pulp, leaving shells intact. Fill each tomato shell with a teaspoonful of cheese mixture. Sprinkle with sesame seeds. Makes 48 stuffed tomatoes.

* To toast sesame seeds, place in a dry pan over medium heat and heat, shaking pan gently, until golden.

Each stuffed tomato contains about:

> 14 calories; 17 mg sodium, 2 mg
> cholesterol; tr fat; 1 g carbohydrate;
> 1 g protein; tr fiber. 38% calories from
> fat.
> Exchanges: ¼ B vegetable

TORTILLA SALAD

6 corn tortillas
1½ tablespoons safflower oil
3 tablespoons red wine vinegar
2 tablespoons chopped cilantro (fresh coriander)
1 small sweet white onion, chopped
1 large tomato, diced
½ avocado, diced (optional)

Cut each tortilla into 4 triangular pieces. Place the tortilla triangles on a baking sheet and put under the broiler for about 1 minute on each side, or until crisp. In a bowl, combine oil, vinegar, and cilantro. Add tortillas, onion, tomato, and avocado, if desired, and toss to coat well. Makes 6 servings.

Each serving with avocado contains about:

> 138 calories; 58 mg sodium;
> 0 cholesterol; 7 g fat;
> 17 g carbohydrate; 3 g protein;
> 2 g fiber. 44% calories from fat.
> Exchanges: 1 bread, 1 fat

Each serving without avocado contains about:

> 111 calories; 57 mg sodium;
> 0 cholesterol; 4 g fat;
> 16 g carbohydrate; 3 g protein;
> 2 g fiber. 30% calories from fat.
> Exchanges: ½ bread, ½ fat

SOUPS AND STOCKS

Making your own soups and stocks will remove the guesswork and worry over excess fat and sodium often present in commercial brands. And the cost of homemade stocks and soups beats that of most found in a can, salted or not.

A saltless soup, however, needs all the help it can get from the herb and spice department, and these recipes show you how it's done.

Set aside ample time for preparing soups and stocks, and be prepared to store them properly in the freezer.

Plan on extra-large jars with tight-fitting lids for storage, especially if you want to have stock on hand for steaming vegetables, cooking pasta and rice, or making sauces. We suggest freezing the stocks in pint-size freezer containers for convenient handling when large quantities are called for, or in an ice-cube tray when stocks are used only as a seasoning in a sauce. You can store stocks or soups safely for up to a week in the refrigerator or four months in the freezer.

There are excellent frozen stocks available in markets (see the Specialty Products list on p. 292) if time is at a premium, as it might be in working families.

A few tips about trimming fat and cholesterol in soups:
- Use polyunsaturated or monounsaturated fat instead of saturated animal fat.
- Use skim or low-fat dairy products instead of the regular counterpart.
- Rid the soup of fat by chilling it long enough for the fat to coagulate on the surface, then scoop it off.

ALBONDIGAS SOUP

½ pound [225 g] ground lean beef
½ teaspoon pepper
2 tablespoons chopped parsley
2 cloves garlic, minced
1 tablespoon egg substitute, or 1 egg white
4 tablespoons chopped cilantro (fresh coriander)
1 teaspoon dried oregano
3 tablespoons long-grain rice
1 small onion, minced
1 teaspoon vegetable oil
1½ quarts [1½ L] low-sodium Beef Stock (p. 37)
  1 cup [115 g] peeled and diced tomatoes, preferably Italian
    plum
6 medium carrots, sliced
2 cups [300 g] sliced celery
1 cup [450 g] corn kernels (fresh or frozen only)

Combine ground beef, pepper, parsley, garlic, egg substitute or egg, 1 tablespoon of the cilantro, oregano, and rice. Form into meatballs about 1 inch [2½ cm] in diameter; set aside.

In a large saucepan, sauté the onion in oil until tender. Add stock and tomatoes and bring to a boil. Add carrots and celery. Drop meatballs into boiling stock. Add corn, reduce heat to low, cover, and simmer 30 minutes. Stir in remaining cilantro and serve. Makes 8 servings.

Each 1 cup serving contains about:

> 156 calories; 71 mg sodium; 29 mg
> cholesterol; 6 g fat; 16 g carbohydrate;
> 8 g protein; 2 g fiber. 22% calories
> from fat.
> Exchanges: 1 meat, 1 B vegetable

CHICKEN SOUP KLARA

⅓ bunch parsley
½ bunch dill
   Tops of 2 parsley roots
1 pound [450 g] chicken pieces
3 leeks, cut in ½-inch [1½ cm] pieces
1 onion, cut in wedges
1 clove garlic, minced
3 parsley roots, peeled and diced
4 carrots, cut in halves
3 stalks celery, sliced
2 quarts [2 L] low-sodium Chicken Stock (p. 38)

Tie parsley, dill, and parsley root tops into a bouquet garni. Place in a large kettle with chicken, leeks, onion, garlic, parsley roots, carrots, celery, and stock. Bring to a boil, reduce heat, and simmer, partially covered, over low heat 1½ hours, removing froth from surface as needed. Discard bouquet garni. Chill soup until fat coagulates on surface, then lift off fat. Skin and bone chicken pieces, cut meat into cubes and return to pot. Reheat to serving temperature. Makes 16 servings.

Each ½ cup serving contains about:

      82 calories; 44 mg sodium, 25 mg cholesterol;
      2 g fat; 6 g carbohydrate; 9 g protein;
      1 g fiber. 24% calories from fat.
      Exchanges: ½ meat, ½ vegetable

CHINATOWN SOUP

1½ quarts [1½ L] low-sodium Chicken Stock (p. 38)
2 cups [202 g] firmly packed coarsely chopped spinach
¼ cup [30 g] chopped green onion
1 teaspoon minced ginger root
½ cup [76 g] julienne-cut cooked pork roast or chicken
⅛ teaspoon white pepper
4 ounces [115 g] cooked crab meat or lobster meat, diced
1 egg white, lightly beaten
1 teaspoon cornstarch
1 tablespoon water

Bring chicken stock to a boil. Add spinach and return to a boil. Reduce heat and simmer 1 minute. Add green onions, ginger, pork, and pepper and simmer 2 to 3 minutes longer. Add meat of choice and heat through. Add egg white to simmering soup in a slow, steady stream and cook until egg white sets. Mix cornstarch with water until smooth and stir into soup. Cook and stir until soup is transparent. Serve at once. Makes 6 servings.

Each 1 cup serving contains about:

> 52 calories; 233 mg sodium; 20 mg
> cholesterol; 2 g fat; 1 g carbohydrate;
> 8 g protein; 1 g fiber. 32% calories from
> fat.
> Exchanges: ½ meat, 1 vegetable

CONSOMMÉ MADRILÈNE

1 cup [150 g] each thinly sliced celery, leeks, and carrots
6 whole peeled tomatoes
1 teaspoon dried thyme
½ bay leaf
1 sprig parsley
1 green bell pepper, sliced
¼ cup [60 g] sliced canned pimiento, drained
8 peppercorns
¼ cup [59 ml] dry Sherry
½ cup [76 g] thinly sliced turnip
2 quarts [2 L] low-sodium Beef Stock (p. 37)
2 egg whites, beaten
   White pepper to taste (optional)

Combine celery, leeks, carrots, tomatoes, thyme, bay leaf, parsley, green pepper, pimiento, peppercorns, Sherry, and turnip in a large saucepan. Add stock and egg whites. Bring to a boil, reduce heat, cover, and simmer for 1½ hours; do not allow to boil. Strain through fine cheesecloth into a bowl. Add pepper to taste. Consommé should be clear. Makes 8 servings.

Each 1 cup serving contains about:

> 22 calories; 24 mg sodium; 0 cholesterol;
> tr fat; 5 g carbohydrate; 1 g protein;
> 0 g fiber. 7% calories from fat.
> Exchanges: negligible

FRENCH ONION SOUP

1 tablespoon low-calorie margarine
6 medium onions, thinly sliced
1 tablespoon arrowroot
2 tablespoons water
2 quarts [2 L] low-sodium Beef Stock, heated (p. 37)
½ cup [119 ml] dry white wine
  Pepper to taste
1½ tablespoons Cognac (optional)
1 tablespoon grated Parmesan cheese (optional)

Melt margarine in a saucepan. Add onions, cover, and cook over low heat 15 minutes. Uncover, increase heat to medium, and cook, stirring frequently, until onions are tender and golden, about 40 minutes. Dissolve arrowroot in water and add to pan with stock. Bring to a boil, then reduce heat to a simmer. Add wine and pepper, partially cover, and cook for 30 minutes. When ready to serve, stir in Cognac and sprinkle with Parmesan cheese, if desired. Makes 8 servings.

Each 1 cup serving with cheese contains about:

> 59 calories; 33 mg sodium; 0 cholesterol;
> 1 g fat; 11 g carbohydrate; 2 g protein;
> 1 g fiber. 18% calories from fat.
> Exchanges: 1 B vegetable

HEARTY MINESTRONE

The next day, add some leftover meat and you've got a nutritious meal-in-a-dish.

> ½ cup [76 g] Great Northern beans, soaked overnight in
> water and drained
> 1 tablespoon olive oil
> 1 clove garlic, minced
> 1 cup [150 g] thinly sliced onions
> 1 cup [180 g] diced carrots
> 1 cup [225 g] diced celery
> ½ cup [65 g] diced peeled potatoes
> 2 cups [260 g] diced zucchini
> 1 cup [150 g] diced green beans
> 3 cups [300 g] shredded cabbage
> 1½ quarts [1½ L] low-sodium Beef Stock (p. 37)
> 4 Italian plum tomatoes, peeled, or 1 (8-ounce) [225 g] can
> low-sodium canned tomatoes, with their liquid
> 1 teaspoon dried basil
> ½ cup [60 g] elbow macaroni
> ¼ cup [30 g] freshly grated Parmesan cheese (optional)

Put beans in a saucepan and add water to cover by 2 inches [5 cm]. Bring to a moderate boil, cover, and cook until beans are tender, about 40 minutes. Let stand in cooking liquid until ready to use.

While beans are cooking, heat oil in a large kettle. Add garlic and onions and cook over medium heat until the onions are tender and golden but not browned. Add the carrots and cook, stirring frequently, for 3 minutes. Repeat this procedure with the celery, potato, zucchini, and green beans, cooking each vegetable for 3 minutes. Add the cabbage. Cook, stirring occasionally, about 5 minutes. Add stock, tomatoes with their liquid, and basil. Cover and simmer for at least 3 hours.

About 15 minutes before the soup is done, drain beans and add with macaroni to soup. Just before removing from heat, swirl in Parmesan cheese if desired. Makes 10 servings.

Each ½ cup serving without Parmesan cheese contains about:

> 104 calories; 24 mg sodium; tr cholesterol;
> 1 g fat; 18 g carbohydrate; 4 g protein;
> 3 g fiber. 8% calories from fat.
> Exchanges: 1 vegetable

LOBSTER BISQUE

1 small carrot, sliced
1 medium onion, chopped
2 peppercorns
1 bay leaf
   Pinch dried thyme
1 sprig parsley
6 cups [1½ L] Fish Stock (p. 38)
¾ cup [178 ml] dry white wine
1 pound [450 g] uncooked small lobster tails
2 tablespoons low-calorie margarine
3 tablespoons arrowroot
1 cup [225 g] nonfat milk
1 cup [225 g] evaporated nonfat milk
2 tablespoons dry Sherry
   Paprika

Combine carrot, onion, peppercorns, bay leaf, thyme, parsley, and stock in a 4-quart [4 L] saucepan. Bring to a boil, add wine and lobster, reduce heat, and simmer 10 minutes. Remove lobster tails. Continue simmering cooking liquid 35 minutes, then strain through a fine sieve and set aside. When lobster tails are cool enough to handle, remove meat from shells and dice coarsely; set aside.

Melt margarine in the same saucepan and stir in arrowroot until smooth. Gradually add strained cooking liquid. Bring to a boil, reduce heat, and simmer 10 minutes. Gradually stir in milks and Sherry. Add reserved lobster meat and heat through. Sprinkle with paprika. Makes 10 servings.

Each ½ cup serving contains about:

> 110 calories; 242 mg sodium; 34 mg cholesterol;
> 2 g fat; 11 g carbohydrate; 12 g protein;
> 1 g fiber. 16% calories from fat.
> Exchanges: 1 meat

PEA SOUP

1 pound [450 g] green split peas
1 tablespoon low-calorie margarine
4 leeks, coarsely chopped
1 quart [1 L] water
   Bouquet Garni (p. 181)
   White pepper to taste
   Heart of small head Boston or butter lettuce, shredded
7 tablespoons evaporated nonfat milk
1 tablespoon finely chopped parsley
1½ tablespoons dry Sherry
   Parsley sprigs

Soak peas in warm water to cover 2 hours. Drain and set aside. Melt margarine in a large saucepan and sauté leeks about 15 minutes, or until tender. Add peas, water, Bouquet Garni, and pepper and bring to a simmer. Cover and cook 1 to 1½ hours, or until peas are tender. Drain and reserve liquid and puree vegetables. Return pureed vegetables and liquid to pot and bring to a boil. Add lettuce and cook 1 minute. Remove from heat and stir in milk, parsley, and Sherry. Return to heat and bring to a gentle simmer. Garnish with parsley sprigs. Makes 16 servings.

Each ½ cup serving contains about:

> 116 calories; 107 mg sodium; 1 mg
> cholesterol; 2 g fat; 19 g carbohydrate;
> 7 g protein; 2 g fiber. 6% calories
> from fat.
> Exchanges: 1 meat

POTATO AND LEEK SOUP

1 tablespoon low-calorie margarine
4 leeks, cut in ½-inch [1½ cm] slices
1 onion, diced
4 potatoes, peeled and diced
4 cups [1 L] low-sodium Chicken Stock (p. 38)
1½ cups [237 ml] evaporated nonfat milk
½ cup [119 ml] nonfat milk
   Pepper to taste

Melt margarine in a large saucepan. Add leeks and onion and cook, covered, until vegetables are tender, stirring occasionally. Add potatoes and stock and simmer, covered, for 40 minutes. Add milks and heat to serving temperature. Season with pepper. Makes 12 servings.

NOTE: For a smooth soup, place soup with vegetables in a blender container or food processor and blend until smooth. Return puree to pot and add milks and pepper. Heat just to serving temperature.

Each ½ cup serving contains about:

> 61 calories; 33 mg sodium; 1 mg cholesterol;
> tr fat; 12 g carbohydrate; 3 g protein;
> 1 g fiber. 6% calories from fat.
> Exchanges: 1 bread

VEGETABLE SOUP

7 cups [1¾ L] low-sodium Chicken Stock (p. 38)
1 cup [237 ml] low-sodium tomato juice
½ cup [50 g] thinly sliced cabbage
¼ cup [45 g] chopped onion
3 medium carrots, chopped
3 leeks, sliced
1 cup [225 g] chopped celery
¼ cup [85 g] chopped green bell pepper
1 (10-ounce) [285 g] can low-sodium tomatoes with their
*   liquid, or 3 medium tomatoes, peeled*
½ cup [225 g] lima beans (fresh or frozen)
⅛ teaspoon ground cloves
½ cup [225 g] shelled peas (fresh or frozen)
½ cup [225 g] corn kernels (fresh or frozen)

Place chicken stock and tomato juice in a large kettle. Add cabbage, onion, carrots, leeks, celery, green pepper, tomatoes, lima beans, and cloves. Bring to a boil, reduce heat, partially cover, and simmer 45 minutes. Add peas and corn and simmer 15 minutes. Makes 8 servings.

Each 1 cup serving contains about:

> 57 calories; 52 mg sodium; 0 cholesterol;
> tr fat; 12 g carbohydrate; 2 g protein;
> 3 g fiber. Tr calories from fat.
> Exchanges: 1 B vegetable

COLD SOUPS

CHILLED BERRY SOUP

1¾ [414 ml] cups water
½ cup [119 ml] rosé wine
¼ cup [50 g] sugar
2 tablespoons fresh lemon juice
1 stick cinnamon
4 cups [806 g] fresh or unsweetened frozen strawberries,
  thawed, or berries of choice
1 teaspoon cornstarch
1 tablespoon water
½ cup [119 ml] evaporated nonfat milk

Combine 1¾ cups [414 ml] water, wine, sugar, lemon juice, and cinnamon stick in a saucepan. Bring to a boil and simmer, uncovered, 15 minutes, stirring occasionally. Meanwhile, rinse, hull, and puree berries. Add pureed berries to wine mixture and simmer 10 minutes, stirring frequently. Remove cinnamon stick. Dissolve cornstarch in 1 tablespoon water and stir into berry mixture. Simmer 2 minutes longer. Remove from heat and let cool. Stir milk into berry mixture. Serve chilled or at room temperature. Makes 8 servings.

Each ½ cup serving contains about:

> 63 calories; 21 mg sodium; 1 mg cholesterol;
> tr fat; 14 g carbohydrate; 1 g protein;
> 2 g fiber. 4% calories from fat.
> Exchanges: 2 fruit

CHILLED CROOKNECK SOUP

4 crookneck squash, sliced
1 medium carrot, sliced
1 large onion, chopped
1 leek, white part only, chopped
2 cloves garlic, minced
¼ teaspoon ground cumin
¼ teaspoon ground nutmeg
3 cups [710 ml] low-sodium Chicken Stock (p. 38)
    Dash hot pepper sauce
2 tablespoons low-fat plain yogurt
    Chopped chives

Combine squash, carrot, onion, leek, garlic, cumin, nutmeg, and stock in a large saucepan. Bring to a boil, reduce heat, cover, and simmer 15 minutes until tender (overcooking will discolor vegetables). Add hot pepper sauce. Puree soup in blender. Chill thoroughly. Garnish each serving with 1 teaspoon yogurt and chives. Makes 6 servings.

   NOTE: If a thinner soup is desired, add chicken stock to desired consistency.

Each ½ cup serving contains about:

> 30 calories; 13 mg sodium; 0 cholesterol;
> tr fat; 6 g carbohydrate; 1 g protein;
> 2 g fiber. 8% calories from fat.
> Exchanges: 1 vegetable

GAZPACHO ANDALUZ

1 large cucumber, peeled, seeded, and cut up
1 small onion, cut up
4 medium tomatoes, peeled and cut up
2 cloves garlic, pressed
1 cup [237 ml] low-sodium Chicken Stock (p. 38)
2 cups [473 ml] low-sodium vegetable cocktail juice
1 tablespoon fresh lemon juice
2 tablespoons red wine vinegar
2 teaspoons Worcestershire sauce
2 tablespoons each chopped parsley, onion, cucumber,
    cilantro (fresh coriander), and green bell pepper

Combine cucumber, onion, tomatoes, garlic, stock, juice, lemon juice, vinegar, and Worcestershire sauce in a blender container and blend until coarsely chopped. Cover and chill 1 hour. Place parsley, cilantro, and green pepper in small individual bowls. Place gazpacho in a chilled serving bowl on the table and surround with the condiments. Ladle soup into chilled bowls and let each diner add condiments as desired. Makes 6 servings.

Each ¾ cup serving contains about:

> 35 calories; 40 mg sodium; 0 cholesterol;
> tr fat; 12 g carbohydrate; 0 protein;
> tr fiber. 6% calories from fat.
> Exchanges: 1 vegetable

——————— STOCKS ———————

BEEF OR VEAL STOCK

2½ pounds [1125 g] beef or veal bones with meat on them
2 medium carrots, chopped
2 large onions, chopped
3 quarts plus 2 cups [3½ L] water
   Bouquet Garni (p. 181)

Brown meat bones in a 400° [204° C] to 450°F [232°C] oven for 30 minutes. Transfer to stockpot and add carrots, onions, and water and bring to a boil. Add Bouquet Garni, reduce heat to low, cover partially, and simmer about 5 hours, removing froth from surface as necessary. Add boiling water if liquid evaporates below level of ingredients.

   Strain stock through a fine sieve into a bowl and let stand 15 minutes. Carefully remove fat that rises to the surface, or place stock, uncovered, in refrigerator until fat coagulates on top and can be lifted off. Store in tightly covered jar in refrigerator up to 1 week, or freeze up to 4 months. Makes 1½ to 2 quarts [1½ to 2 L].

Each cup stock contains about:

> 22 calories; 18 mg sodium; 2 mg cholesterol;
> tr fat; tr carbohydrate; tr protein;
> 0 fiber. 0 calories from fat.
> Exchanges: negligible

CHICKEN OR TURKEY STOCK

*3 pounds [1⅓ kg] chicken or turkey bones with meat on
    them*
2 medium carrots, chopped
2 large onions, chopped
3 quarts [3 L] water
    Bouquet Garni (p. 181)

Combine chicken, carrots, onions, and water in a stockpot. Bring to a boil
and add Bouquet Garni. Reduce heat to low, cover partially, and simmer
about 2 hours, removing froth from surface as necessary. Add boiling water
if liquid evaporates below level of ingredients.

Strain stock through a fine sieve into a bowl and let stand 15 minutes.
Carefully remove fat that rises to the surface, or place stock, uncovered, in
refrigerator until fat coagulates on top and can be lifted off. Store in tightly
covered jar in refrigerator up to 1 week, or freeze up to 4 months. Makes 1½
to 2 quarts [1½ to 2 L].

Each cup stock contains about:

> 26 calories; 16 mg sodium, tr cholesterol;
> tr fat; 0 carbohydrate; tr protein;
> 0 fiber. 0 calories from fat.
> Exchanges: negligible

FISH STOCK

2 pounds [900 g] fish bones
1 quart [1 L] water
2 large onions, chopped
2 sprigs parsley
1 large carrot, chopped
    Bouquet Garni (p. 181)

Place fish bones and water in a saucepan and bring to a boil. Add onions,
parsley, carrot, and Bouquet Garni. Skim any froth that forms on the
surface. Reduce heat, partially cover, and simmer 30 minutes. Strain
through fine sieve. Store in tightly covered jar in refrigerator up to 1 week,
or freeze up to 4 months. Makes 1 quart [1 L].

Each ½ cup stock contains about:

> 15 calories; 13 mg sodium; tr fat; tr
> cholesterol; 0 carbohydrate; tr protein;
> 0 fiber. 0 calories from fat.
> Exchanges: negligible

BREADS

Over the last decade, the common misconception that bread, a complex carbohydrate (starch), is fattening has been dispelled. Most people know that bread is an excellent source of many important vitamins and minerals.

Whole-grain breads are also a good source of insoluble fiber, which helps promote regular elimination and may help reduce the risk of colon cancers. Oat bran, a type of soluble fiber, is thought to reduce cholesterol levels in the blood.

So it makes sense to include grains from both types of fiber in the diet.

According to the USDA portion size recommendations, your diet should include six or more daily servings from the bread group, which includes cereals, rice, and other grains, in addition to bread.

The bread recipes given here (including a recipe for Oat Bran Muffins on p. 44) are exceptionally low in calories, fat, cholesterol, sugar, and salt. We have found that we can eliminate salt altogether in bread at no cost to flavor, if we prepare the bread the *Light Style* way. Try it and you'll see.

Some breads will, incidentally, make wonderful gifts from your kitchen at holiday time. Our favorite is Ramona's Whole Wheat Bread, which has only 70 calories a slice, 30 milligrams sodium, and hardly any fat. It's so rich you won't miss slathering it with butter or anything else. It's almost a dessert in itself!

CLOUD BISCUITS

2 cups [285 g] unbleached flour
4 teaspoons baking powder
½ cup [115 g] low-calorie margarine
3 tablespoons egg substitute, or 1 egg white
½ cup [115 g] nonfat milk

In a large mixing bowl, sift together flour and baking powder. With a pastry blender, cut in margarine until the mixture resembles coarse crumbs. Combine egg substitute or egg and milk and add to flour mixture all at once. Stir until dough is just moistened; do not overmix.

Turn dough out on a lightly floured board and knead *gently* with heel of one hand, about 20 strokes in all. Roll dough out ¾-inch [2 cm] thick, flouring board as needed. Dip a 2-inch [5 cm] biscuit cutter in flour and cut straight down through dough without twisting. Repeat until all dough is cut, dipping the cutter in flour each time. Place circles on an ungreased baking sheet ¾ inch [2 cm] apart for crusty biscuits or close together for ones with soft sides. Chill, covered with plastic wrap, 1 to 3 hours. Bake at 450°F [232°C] for 10 to 14 minutes, or until biscuits are golden. Serve with low-calorie jam or jelly. Makes about 20 biscuits.

NOTE: For drop biscuits, increase milk to ½ cup [115 g] plus 1½ tablespoons and omit the kneading. Drop rounded tablespoons of dough onto baking sheet about ¾ inch [2 cm] apart and bake as directed.

Each biscuit contains about:

> 67 calories; 123 mg sodium; 0 cholesterol;
> 2 g fat; 9 g carbohydrate; 2 g protein;
> tr fiber. 33% calories from fat.
> Exchanges: 1 bread

OAT BRAN MUFFINS

1½ cups [45 g] dry bran flakes cereal
½ cup [119 ml] apple juice
3 tablespoons egg substitute, or 1 egg white
½ cup [119 ml] nonfat milk
1 (6-ounce) [178 ml] can apple juice concentrate
3 tablespoons vegetable oil
1 large banana, mashed
½ cup [85 g] dried figs, snipped finely
2 tablespoons honey, or ¼ cup [50 g] brown sugar, packed
1½ cups [215 g] oat flour, whole-wheat flour, or all-purpose flour*
½ cup [45 g] dry oatmeal
1 teaspoon cinnamon
1½ teaspoons baking soda
2 teaspoons baking powder

Combine bran flakes in a bowl with apple juice. Mix to moisten the flakes evenly. Add egg substitute or egg white, milk, apple juice concentrate, oil, banana, figs, and honey. Mix well. In a small bowl combine flour, oatmeal, cinnamon, baking soda, and baking powder. Add to bran mixture and mix well. Line a muffin tin with paper liners. Spoon batter into paper-lined muffin cups. Bake at 350°F [177°C] for 20 minutes. Makes 12 large muffins.

*Note: fiber content will alter depending on the type of flour you use.

Each muffin contains about:

> 187 calories; 216 mg sodium; 0 cholesterol;
> 4 g fat; 35 g carbohydrate; 4 g protein; 4 g fiber. 20% calories from fat.
> Exchanges: 2 bread, 1 fat

CORN BREAD

2 cups [285 g] sifted unbleached flour
2 cups [305 g] yellow cornmeal
¼ cup [50 g] sugar
2 tablespoons baking powder
½ cup [115 g] low-calorie margarine
1 cup [255 ml] plus 2 tablespoons egg substitute, or 6 egg whites
1½ cups [356 ml] nonfat milk

In a mixing bowl, combine flour, cornmeal, sugar, and baking powder and mix well. With a pastry blender, cut margarine into dry ingredients until mixture resembles coarse crumbs. In a small bowl, beat egg substitute or egg whites with milk. Add to dry ingredients and stir with a fork until just blended. Pour into a greased 13-by-9-inch [33-by-23 cm] baking pan. Bake at 400°F [205°C] for 25 minutes. Makes 24 servings.

Each 2-by-2-inch [5-by-5 cm] slice Corn Bread contains about:

> 109 calories; 141 mg sodium; 0 cholesterol;
> 2 g fat; 18 g carbohydrate; 3 g protein;
> 1 g fiber. 19% calories from fat.
> Exchanges: 1 bread, ½ fat

GARLIC BREAD

2 tablespoons low-calorie margarine
1 clove garlic, pressed
1 teaspoon fresh lemon juice
6 slices French Bread (p. 46), toasted on 1 side
  Paprika
1 tablespoon grated Romano cheese (optional)
1 tablespoon chopped parsley

Melt margarine in a saucepan and add garlic and lemon juice. Spread garlic-margarine mixture on untoasted side of each bread slice. Sprinkle with paprika and cheese. Place bread slices, buttered side up, on a broiler rack and broil 3 inches [8 cm] from source of heat about 3 minutes or until golden. Sprinkle with parsley. Makes 6 servings.

Each slice Garlic Bread with cheese contains about:

> 82 calories; 67 mg sodium; 1 mg cholesterol;
> 2 g fat; 13 g carbohydrate; 2 g protein;
> 1 g fiber. 27% calories from fat.
> Exchanges: 1 bread, ½ fat

FRENCH BREAD

½ cup [119 ml] nonfat milk
1 cup [237 ml] boiling water
1 envelope active dry yeast
¼ cup [59 ml] warm water (105° to 115°F) [41° to 46°C]
1½ tablespoons low-calorie margarine
1 tablespoon plus 2 teaspoons sugar
4 cups [570 g] sifted unbleached flour
2 tablespoons cornmeal
1 egg white, beaten
1 tablespoon cold water

Scald the milk in a saucepan and add boiling water. Cool to lukewarm (about 85°F) [30°C]. Meanwhile, dissolve yeast in warm water. Let stand 10 minutes, then stir in margarine and milk mixture. Combine sugar and flour in a mixing bowl. Make a well in center and add cooled milk-yeast mixture. Stir thoroughly, but do not knead; the dough will be soft. Form into a ball, cover, and let rise in a warm place, or until doubled in bulk.

Punch down dough and divide into 2 portions. Form each portion into a long loaf on a floured board. Dust bottom of loaves with cornmeal. Place loaves on a greased baking sheet or one lined with parchment paper. Make several ¼-inch-[½ cm] deep slits across tops of loaves. Let rise in a warm place until almost doubled in bulk. Place in oven over a pan of simmering water and bake at 400°F [205°C] for 15 minutes. Reduce heat to 350°F [177°C] and bake for 30 minutes, or until golden and crisp. About 5 minutes before loaves are done, mix egg white with cold water and brush on loaves, then finish baking. Makes 2 loaves, 16 slices each.

BREAD STICKS

Prepare dough as for French Bread in the preceding recipe. After first rising, roll out half the dough into an 18-by-8-inch [46-by-20 cm] rectangle ½-inch [1½ cm] thick on a lightly floured board. Cut into 9, 8-by-2-inch [20-by-5 cm] strips. Roll each strip into a rope. Hold rope up by one end until stretching stops, then cut in half to make 2 ropes. Place on baking sheet. Repeat with other strips and remaining half of dough. Brush ropes with eggwhite glaze and sprinkle with caraway, sesame, cumin, or dill seeds. Let rise in a warm place until barely doubled in bulk, about 20 minutes. Bake at 400°F [205°C] over a pan of simmering water about 15 minutes or until golden and crisp. Makes 32 bread sticks.

Each slice or stick of French Bread contains about:

> 52 calories; 10 mg sodium; 0 cholesterol;
> tr fat; 12 g carbohydrate; 1 g protein;
> 1 g fiber. 0 calories from fat.
> Exchanges: 1 bread

NOTE: To make bread cubes, dice baked French Bread into ½-inch [1½ cm] cubes. To toast, bake at 350°F [177°C] about 7 minutes, or until golden. To make dry bread crumbs, dry bread in 350°F [177°C] oven 5 minutes or use stale bread. Grind in blender or food processor, or crumble by hand. To make soft bread crumbs, crumble French Bread by hand.

RAMONA'S WHOLE-WHEAT BREAD

This outstanding low-sodium, low-calorie wheat bread developed by Ramona Ponce, a hospital chef, is so rich that adding a smidgen of butter or anything else to it would be like gilding the lily.

> *2 envelopes active dry yeast*
> *1½ cups [355 ml] warm water (105° to 115°F) [41° to 46°C]*
> *¾ cup [178 ml] nonfat milk*
> *2½ tablespoons sugar*
> *5 tablespoons low-calorie margarine*
> *⅓ cup [79 ml] low-calorie maple syrup*
> *3½ cups [454 g] whole-wheat flour*
> *3½ cups [454 g] unbleached flour, sifted*
> *1 tablespoon poppy seeds or wheat germ*

Dissolve yeast in warm water in a large mixing bowl. Let stand 10 minutes. Combine milk, sugar, and margarine in a saucepan and heat, stirring, until sugar dissolves and margarine melts. Blend in maple syrup. Stir warm milk mixture into yeast mixture until smooth. Add 1 cup [140 g] whole-wheat flour and 1 cup [140 g] unbleached flour to yeast mixture and stir until smooth. Stir remaining whole-wheat and unbleached flour into batter and knead 10 minutes, or until smooth and elastic. Form dough into a ball and place in a lightly greased bowl. Turn dough ball to grease top side and cover bowl with plastic wrap. Let rise in a warm place until doubled in bulk, about 1½ hours.

Punch dough down and divide into 2 portions. Form each into a loaf and place in greased 8-by-5-by-3-inch [20-by-13-by-8 cm] loaf pans. Brush lightly with water and sprinkle with poppy seeds. Let rise in a warm place about 1½ hours, or until almost doubled in bulk. Bake at 400°F [205°C] for 20 to 25 minutes. Cool on wire racks. Makes 2 loaves, or 25 slices each.

RAMONA'S ROLLS

Prepare dough as for Ramona's Whole-Wheat Bread. After first rising, shape the dough into balls to fill 48 greased muffin tin wells about a third full. Let rise until doubled in bulk, about 45 minutes. Brush with water and sprinkle with poppy seeds. Bake at 400°F [205°C] for 15 to 18 minutes. Makes 48 rolls.

Each slice or roll contains about:

> 71 calories; 21 mg sodium; 0 cholesterol;
> tr fat; 14 g carbohydrate; 2 g protein;
> 2 g fiber. 11% calories from fat.
> Exchanges: 1 bread

EGGS

In the last decade, the most striking news about eggs has been that they may not be as high in cholesterol as previously thought. Reports from independent egg producers show that eggs contain 200 milligrams of cholesterol each, instead of 275 milligrams, as estimated by the USDA. So if you have no medical reason to limit your egg intake, go ahead and enjoy three or four a week.

The major ingredient in our egg dishes is the egg white, which has no cholesterol or fat. All you have left is the protein and minerals, which will get you by if you are preparing a frittata, omelet, soufflé, or quiche.

We give a recipe for an ingredient we call egg substitute, which is nothing more than egg whites with some coloring from a real egg. You can, however, use commercial egg substitute for convenience; refer to the Nutrient Counter to calculate the calories and other nutrients in it. You will note that commercial egg substitute contains not only more calories than its homemade equivalent but also more sodium.

Otherwise, you're home free with these stunning egg dishes that will be easy to incorporate into low-cholesterol, low-fat, low-calorie meal plans once you get used to using only the whites of eggs. Have fun.

Special note: Most of these egg dishes are very low in calories. Only a small amount of margarine or oil was used for preparation or to enhance flavor. However, the percentage of calories from fat is above 30 percent. This is because each gram of fat contains 9 calories, whereas each gram of protein or carbohydrate contains 4 calories.

OMELETS

FRITTATA

Leave out the feta and Romano cheeses if you are on a sodium-restricted diet.

> ¾ cup [180 g] egg substitute, or 4 egg whites
> 1½ cups [340 g] low-fat cottage cheese
> ½ cup [115 g] feta cheese
> 3 tablespoons grated Romano cheese, optional
> ⅛ teaspoon pepper
> 6 zucchini, about 1½ pounds [675 g], shredded
> 1 tablespoon vegetable oil

Combine egg substitute, cottage cheese, feta cheese, Romano, if desired, and pepper. Blend well. Stir in zucchini. Place oil in 12-by-7-inch [30-by-18 cm] or 9-by-9-inch [23-by-23 cm] baking pan. Pour zucchini-cheese mixture into baking pan and bake at 350°F [177°C] for 45 to 50 minutes or until set. Pour off any excess oil, cut into squares to serve. Makes 16 servings.

Each serving with Romano and feta cheeses contains about:

> 55 calories; 159 mg sodium; 6 mg cholesterol; 3 g fat;
> 2 g carbohydrate; 6 g protein; tr fiber. 44% calories
> from fat.
> Exchanges: 1 vegetable, ¼ milk

HERB OMELET

Endless variations are possible using this omelet as a base. A nourishing, easy to prepare, and economical main dish.

> 6 tablespoons egg substitute, or 2 egg whites
> 1 teaspoon minced parsley
> ¼ teaspoon each dried thyme and tarragon
> 2 teaspoons chopped shallots
> ⅛ teaspoon white pepper
> 1 teaspoon low-calorie margarine
> Filling of your choice

Combine egg substitute or egg whites, parsley, thyme, tarragon, shallots, and pepper in a bowl and beat until well blended. Melt margarine in a nonstick 7- or 8-inch [18- or 20 cm] omelet pan or skillet. Pour egg mixture into the pan and cook over medium heat, lifting the edges as they set so the uncooked portions flow underneath to cook. Continue to cook until the center is dry and set. Top omelet with 2 tablespoons filling of your choice and fold in half. Slide onto serving plate. Makes 1 serving.

Each omelet without filling contains about:

> 104 calories; 215 mg sodium; 1 mg cholesterol; 5 g fat; 2 g carbohydrate; 12 g protein; tr fiber. 44% calories from fat.
> Exchanges: 2 meat

CHEESE OMELET

Prepare omelet as for Herb Omelet. Fill with 2 tablespoons shredded low-fat Cheddar or Gouda cheese, or low-fat ricotta or cottage cheese. See Nutrient Analysis for Herb Omelet.

2 tablespoons cheese contains about:

> Ricotta or Cottage Cheese
>
> 124 calories; 230 mg sodium; 1 mg cholesterol; 5 g fat; 3 g carbohydrate; 12 g protein; tr fiber. 40% calories from fat.

> Low-fat Cheddar or Gouda
>
> 161 calories; 333 mg sodium; 16 mg cholesterol; 9 g fat; 3 g carbohydrate; 15 g protein; tr fiber. 59% calories from fat.
> Exchanges: ¼ milk

FLORENTINE OMELET

Prepare omelet as for Herb Omelet, omitting herbs and shallots. Fill with 2 tablespoons Creamed Spinach (p. 130).

Each omelet contains about:

> 111 calories; 253 mg sodium; 1 mg cholesterol; 5 g fat; 3 g carbohydrate; 13 g protein; 2 g fiber. 44% calories from fat.
> Exchanges: ¼ milk, 2 meat

ORIENTAL OMELET

Prepare omelet as for Herb Omelet, omitting herbs and shallots. Fill with 2 tablespoons Chinese Stir-Fry Vegetables (p. 129).

Each omelet contains about:

> 105 calories; 219 mg sodium;
> 1 mg cholesterol; 5 g fat;
> 3 g carbohydrate; 12 g protein;
> tr fiber. 44% calories from fat.
> Exchanges: 1½ meat, 1 vegetable

SPANISH OMELET

Prepare omelet as for Herb Omelet, omitting herbs and shallots. Fill with 2 tablespoons Spanish Sauce (p. 174).

Each omelet contains about:

> 105 calories; 249 mg sodium;
> 1 mg cholesterol; 5 g fat;
> 3 g carbohydrate; 12 g protein;
> tr fiber. 45% calories from fat.
> Exchanges: 2 meat

OMELET SUPREME

1 teaspoon low-calorie margarine
3 mushrooms, thinly sliced
3 green onions, chopped
2 slices tomato, chopped
¼ teaspoon dried basil
   Pinch pepper
6 tablespoons egg substitute, or 2 egg whites, beaten
1 tablespoon ricotta cheese (made from partially skimmed milk)
1 teaspoon dry white wine

Melt margarine in a nonstick 7- or 8-inch [18- or 20 cm] omelet pan or skillet. Add mushrooms, green onions, and tomato and sauté until tender. Remove vegetables from pan and set aside. Combine basil, pepper, and egg substitute or egg whites and pour into pan. Cook over medium heat, lifting the edges as they set so the uncooked portions flow underneath to cook. Continue to cook until the center is almost dry and set. Top with mushroom mixture and then ricotta cheese. Sprinkle the filling with wine and fold omelet in half. Slide onto serving plate. Makes 1 serving.

Each omelet contains about:

142 calories; 238 mg sodium; 6 mg cholesterol;
6 g fat; 7 g carbohydrate; 15 g protein;
1 g fiber. 40% calories from fat.
Exchanges: 2 meat, ¼ vegetable

——————— SOUFFLÉS* ———————

MUSHROOM SOUFFLÉ

3 tablespoons low-calorie margarine
1 shallot or small onion, chopped
1½ pounds [675 g] mushrooms, finely chopped
1½ tablespoons arrowroot
1¼ cups [355 ml] nonfat milk
  Pinch cayenne pepper
  Pinch ground nutmeg
¾ cup [180 g] egg substitute
5 egg whites
1 teaspoon white vinegar

Melt 1 tablespoon of the margarine in a saucepan. Add shallot and mushrooms and cook over medium heat until mushrooms are tender. Remove mushrooms from pan, drain, and set aside. Melt remaining 2 tablespoons margarine in the same saucepan. Add arrowroot and cook until smooth. Gradually add milk and cook, stirring, until thickened and smooth, about 5 minutes. Stir in cayenne and nutmeg. Add mushroom mixture to milk mixture and bring to a boil. Remove from heat and stir in egg substitute, a little at a time, until well blended. Let cool slightly. Beat egg whites with vinegar until stiff. Stir about one quarter of the egg whites into the milk mixture to lighten it, then gently fold in remaining whites. Turn into a greased 1-quart soufflé dish and bake at 375°F [190°C] for 30 minutes, or until golden and puffy. Serve at once. Makes 8 servings.

* See dessert chapter for sweet soufflés.

Each ½ cup serving contains about:

> 97 calories; 148 mg sodium; 1 mg cholesterol;
> 3 g fat; 10 g carbohydrate; 8 g protein;
> 1 g fiber. 30% calories from fat.
> Exchanges: 1 meat

SPINACH SOUFFLÉ

3 tablespoons low-calorie margarine
1 tablespoon chopped shallots or green onion
1 cup [100 g] chopped fresh spinach, or ½ (10-ounce)
    [285 g] package frozen chopped spinach, thawed, drained,
    and squeezed dry
1½ tablespoons arrowroot
1¼ cups [296 ml] nonfat milk, heated
    Dash each cayenne pepper and ground nutmeg
¾ cup [215 g] plus 3 tablespoons egg substitute
5 egg whites
1 teaspoon white vinegar

Melt 1 tablespoon of the margarine in a saucepan. Add shallots and sauté until golden. Add spinach and cook until moisture from spinach evaporates. (If using frozen spinach, measure 1 cup and add to pan. Reserve remainder for another use.) Set spinach mixture aside. Melt remaining 2 tablespoons margarine in a separate saucepan. Add arrowroot and stir until smooth. Gradually add hot milk and cook, stirring, until smooth and thickened. Stir in cayenne and nutmeg and bring to a boil. Remove from heat and stir in egg substitute a little at a time, until well blended. Add spinach mixture to sauce. Let cool slightly. Beat egg whites with vinegar until stiff. Stir about one-quarter of the egg whites into the milk mixture to lighten it, then gently fold in remaining whites. Turn into a greased 1-quart [1 L] soufflé dish and bake at 375°F [190°C] for 30 minutes, or until golden and puffy. Serve at once. Makes 8 servings.

Each ½ cup serving contains about:

> 80 calories; 160 mg sodium; 1 mg cholesterol;
> 3 g fat; 5 g carbohydrate; 7 g protein;
> tr fiber. 36% calories from fat.
> Exchanges: 1 meat, 1 vegetable

CALIFORNIA QUICHE

1 medium sweet white onion, halved and thinly sliced
2 teaspoons low-calorie margarine
½ pound [225 g] mushrooms, sliced
1 teaspoon fresh lemon juice
1½ teaspoons flour
½ cup [115 g] egg substitute, or 3 egg whites
1 cup [237 ml] evaporated nonfat milk
  Dash ground nutmeg
  Pepper to taste
1 cup [115 g] shredded low-fat Jarlsberg or Cheddar cheese
  Quiche Crust (following recipe)*
2 tablespoons grated Romano cheese (optional)
  Dash paprika

Melt margarine in a skillet and sauté onion until tender. Add mushrooms and cook over medium heat until tender, about 3 minutes. Stir in lemon juice, cover, and simmer 2 minutes. Sprinkle with flour and cook, stirring constantly, until mushroom liquid has thickened. Set aside.

Beat egg substitute or egg whites lightly and add milk, nutmeg, pepper, and cheese, blending well. Spread mushroom mixture in Quiche Crust and pour in egg mixture. Sprinkle with Romano cheese (without touching pastry) if desired, and paprika. Bake at 350°F [177°C] for 35 to 40 minutes, or until custard is set and knife inserted near center comes out clean. Cool about 10 minutes before serving. Makes 10 entrée servings.

NOTE: To reheat, place in 350°F [177°C] oven for 10 to 15 minutes.

* To make Quiche without crust, place ½ tablespoon oil in baking dish, then add mushroom-cheese mixture.

QUICHE CRUST
¾ cup [105 g] unbleached flour
3 tablespoons vegetable oil
1½ tablespoons nonfat milk

Place flour in a mixing bowl. Combine oil and milk and add to flour all at once. Mix quickly with a fork until mixture forms into a ball. Roll dough out between sheets of wax paper to a 12-inch [30 cm] circle. Line an 8- or 9-inch

[20- or 23 cm] pie plate with the pastry and crimp edges. Pierce dough in several places with fork. Bake at 450°F [232°C] for 10 minutes or until golden. Cool before filling.

Each entrée serving contains about:

> 160 calories; 173 mg sodium; 15 mg
> cholesterol; 9 g fat; 12 g carbohydrate;
> 9 g protein; 1 g fiber. 48% calories
> from fat.
> Exchanges: 1 meat, 1 vegetable

ZUCCHINI QUICHE

Sauté 2½ cups [324 g] sliced zucchini and 1 onion, thinly sliced, in 1 tablespoon vegetable oil until crisp but tender. Drain well, then place in Quiche Crust. Prepare egg-milk mixture as directed in California Quiche, substituting ½ teaspoon Herb Blend (p. 184) for the nutmeg. Pour over zucchini mixture and proceed according to directions for California Quiche. Makes 10 entrée servings.

Each entrée serving contains about:

> 182 calories; 175 mg sodium;
> 15 mg cholesterol; 10 g
> fat; 14 g carbohydrate;
> 9 g protein; 1 g fiber.
> 49% calories from fat.
> Exchanges: 1 meat, 1 vegetable

CRÊPES

In trying to come up with exciting, novel party dishes that are also low in calories, fat, cholesterol, sodium, and sugar, we found that the crêpe was tailor-made for the job.

There are about 39 calories in each crêpe prepared the *Light Style* way with nonfat milk and egg whites. Fill them to suit the occasion and your budget.

There is one hitch. You have to make the crêpes yourself. If you've never made crêpes before, this is your chance to start practicing. It isn't difficult; once you're used to it, you'll fly through the procedure.

You can store crêpes in the freezer for several months, or up to a week in the refrigerator. Stack them between sheets of wax paper, and you have an easy-to-use supply on hand for any party event or for a simple family meal using fillings from a leftover meal.

—————— FILLED CRÊPES ——————

CRÊPES DIVAN

Mornay Sauce (p. 172)
1 teaspoon Worcestershire sauce
*½ pound [225 g] fresh asparagus, cooked and chopped, or 1
    (10-ounce) [285 g] package frozen cut asparagus, cooked*
2 cups [302 g] shredded cooked turkey meat
6 Feather Crêpes (p. 63)
Dash ground nutmeg

In a mixing bowl, combine half of the Mornay Sauce, the Worcestershire sauce, asparagus, and turkey and mix well. Spoon ¼ cup [60 g] of mixture in a strip down the center of the unbrowned side of each crêpe. Fold the sides over the filling so they overlap and place seam side down, in a shallow nonstick baking dish in a single layer. Pour remaining Mornay Sauce over crêpes. Sprinkle with nutmeg and bake at 325°F [163°C] for 20 minutes. Makes 6 servings.

Each serving contains about:

206 calories; 193 mg sodium; 45 mg cholesterol;
6 g fat; 15 g carbohydrate; 21 g protein;
1 g fiber. 23% calories from fat.
Exchanges: 2 meat, ½ bread

CRÊPES FLORENTINE

1¼ cups [285 g] Creamed Spinach (p. 130)
6 Feather Crêpes (p. 63)
½ cup [119 ml] Béchamel Sauce (p. 169)
1 tablespoon grated Parmesan cheese

Spoon about 3 tablespoons of the Creamed Spinach in a strip down the center of the unbrowned side of each crêpe. Fold the sides over the filling so they overlap and place seam side down in a shallow nonstick baking pan in a single layer. Spoon Béchamel Sauce over crêpes and sprinkle with cheese. Bake at 350°F [177°C] for 8 minutes, or until heated through. Place under a broiler for 30 seconds to brown tops. Makes 6 servings.

Each serving contains about:

86 calories; 130 mg sodium; 2 mg cholesterol;
2 g fat; 12 g carbohydrate; 5 g protein;
3 g fiber. 24% calories from fat.
Exchanges: 1 bread, 1 vegetable

CRÊPES ST. JACQUES

½ pound [225 g] raw scallops, cooked Alaskan king crab
    meat, or cooked and cleaned shrimp
    Mornay Sauce (p. 172)
6 Feather Crêpes (p. 63)
2 tablespoons evaporated nonfat milk
1 tablespoon toasted slivered almonds*

Place scallops in skillet with 1 inch water. Bring to boil, reduce heat, and simmer, covered, 2 minutes. Drain and halve scallops. (If using cooked crab meat or shrimp omit this step.) Stir scallops into one-half of the Mornay Sauce. Spoon about ¼ cup [60 g] of the filling in a strip down the center of the unbrowned side of each crêpe. Fold the sides over the filling so they overlap, and place seam side down in a shallow nonstick baking dish in a single layer. Stir milk into remaining sauce and spoon over crêpes. Cover pan with aluminum foil and bake at 375°F [190°C] for 15 minutes. Uncover and bake 5 to 10 minutes longer, or until sauce bubbles. Remove from oven and sprinkle with almonds. Makes 6 servings.

NOTE: Although shrimp is low in calories and fat, it is high in cholesterol. If you are on a cholesterol-restricted diet, use scallops or crab meat.

*To toast almonds, place in a skillet over medium heat and cook, stirring frequently, until golden.

Each serving contains about:

> 164 calories; 218 mg sodium; 22 mg cholesterol;
> 5 g fat; 15 g carbohydrate; 14 g protein;
> tr fiber. 28% calories from fat.
> Exchanges: 2 meat, ½ bread

RATATOUILLE CRÊPES

2 cups [450 g] Ratatouille (p. 134)
8 Feather Crêpes (p. 63)
½ cup [115 g] low-fat plain yogurt (optional)

Spoon ¼ cup [60 g] Ratatouille in a strip down the center of the unbrowned side of each crêpe. Fold the sides over the filling so they overlap and place seam-side down in a shallow nonstick baking dish in a single layer. Cover pan with aluminum foil and bake at 375°F [190°C] for 20 minutes, or until heated through. Top each crêpe with 1 tablespoon yogurt, if desired. Makes 8 servings.

Each serving without yogurt contains about:

> 81 calories; 30 mg sodium; 1 mg cholesterol;
> 2 g fat; 12 g carbohydrate; 4 g protein;
> 1 g fiber. 23% calories from fat.
> Exchanges: ½ bread, 1 vegetable

CRÊPE BATTERS

FEATHER CRÊPES

1 cup [140 g] unbleached flour
1½ cups [355 ml] nonfat milk
3 tablespoons egg substitute, or 1 egg white, beaten
2 teaspoons vegetable oil

In a mixing bowl, combine flour, milk, and egg substitute or egg white. Beat with a rotary beater or wire whisk until blended. Chill batter. Lightly grease a 6-inch [15 cm] nonstick skillet or crêpe pan with some of the oil and place over medium heat until pan is hot. Remove pan from heat and spoon in about 2 tablespoons of the batter. Lift and tilt the skillet to spread the batter evenly over the pan bottom. Return pan to medium heat and cook crêpe until lightly browned on underside. Turn crêpe out onto paper toweling. (Crêpe will slide easily from pan when done.) Repeat until all crêpes are cooked, greasing skillet as necessary. Makes about 18 crêpes.

Each crêpe contains about:

> 37 calories; 15 mg sodium; 0 cholesterol;
> tr fat; 6 g carbohydrate; 2 g protein;
> tr fiber. 17% calories from fat.
> Exchanges: ½ bread

FEATHER WHEAT CRÊPES

Proceed as directed for Feather Crêpes, substituting 1¼ cups [175 g] whole-wheat flour for the unbleached flour, increasing nonfat milk to 1¾ cups [414 ml], and substituting low-calorie margarine for the vegetable oil. Makes about 18 crêpes.

Each crêpe contains about:

> 43 calories; 17 mg sodium, 1 mg cholesterol;
> tr fat; 7 g carbohydrate; 2 g protein; 1 g
> fiber. 16% calories from fat.
> Exchanges: ½ bread

FEATHER CRÊPE CUPS

1 cup [140 g] all-purpose flour
1½ cups [355 ml] nonfat milk
½ teaspoon sugar
3 tablespoons egg substitute, or 1 egg white
3 tablespoons low-calorie margarine

In a mixing bowl, combine flour, milk, sugar, and egg substitute or egg white. Beat until blended. Melt ⅛ teaspoon of the margarine in a 6-inch [15 cm] nonstick skillet or crêpe pan placed over medium heat. Remove from heat and spoon in about 1 tablespoon of batter. Lift and tilt skillet to spread batter evenly into a 5-inch [13 cm] circle. Return pan to heat. Brown crêpe on one side only and slip onto paper toweling. (Crêpe will slide easily from pan when done.) Continue until all crêpes are cooked, using ⅛ teaspoon margarine for cooking each crêpe.

Invert 18 custard cups on baking sheets. Grease outside of cups with remaining margarine. (You may need to make the crêpe cups in batches, depending on the number of custard cups you have.) Place a crêpe, browned side up, onto each custard cup. Press crêpe lightly to fit cup. Bake at 375°F [190°C] until crisp, about 20 to 25 minutes. Use a knife tip to remove crêpes from cups. Cool and stack, wrapped in plastic wrap, until ready to use. Makes 18.

Each crêpe cup contains about:

> 41 calories; 39 mg sodium; 0 cholesterol;
> 1 g fat; 6 g carbohydrate; 2 g protein;
> tr fiber. 24% calories from fat.
> Exchanges: ½ bread

BLUEBERRY-CHEESE BLINTZES

2¼ cups [320 g] whole-wheat or unbleached flour
1¼ cups [296 ml] nonfat milk
½ to ¾ cup [119 to 178 ml] water
¾ cup [178 ml] unsweetened orange juice
¼ cup [85 g] plus 2 tablespoons egg substitute, or 2 egg whites
1 tablespoon vegetable oil
2 teaspoons low-calorie margarine
Blueberry-Cheese filling (following recipe)

In a food processor or blender, combine flour, milk, water, orange juice, egg substitute, and oil. Beat until well blended and smooth. Chill batter for 30 minutes. Lightly grease a 6-inch [15 cm] nonstick skillet or crêpe pan with a little of the margarine and place over medium-high heat until pan is hot. Remove from heat and spoon in about 3 tablespoons of the batter. Lift and tilt the skillet to spread the batter evenly. Return pan to heat and cook crêpe until lightly browned on the underside. Turn crêpe out onto paper toweling (it will slide easily from pan when done). Repeat until all the crêpes are cooked, greasing skillet as necessary. Makes 20 crêpes.

BLUEBERRY-CHEESE FILLING

1½ cups [340 g] low-fat ricotta cheese or cottage cheese
1 tablespoon sugar
½ teaspoon ground cinnamon
1 tablespoon low-calorie margarine
1 cup [151 g] fresh or frozen, unsweetened and thawed blueberries, dried thoroughly
¾ cup [340 g] low-fat vanilla or blueberry yogurt

Mix ricotta cheese, sugar, and cinnamon together. Place a spoonful of filling on each crêpe, fold the ends, and roll up. Melt margarine in a nonstick skillet and sauté the crêpes until golden. Place crêpes on a hot serving platter. Top with blueberries and 1 tablespoon yogurt. Makes 10 servings.

Each 2 blintz serving contains about:

169 calories; 31 mg sodium; 14 mg cholesterol;
4 g fat; 23 mg carbohydrate; 8 g protein; 4 g fiber (with whole-wheat flour). 18% calories from fat.
Exchanges: 1 milk, 1 bread

FISH AND SHELLFISH

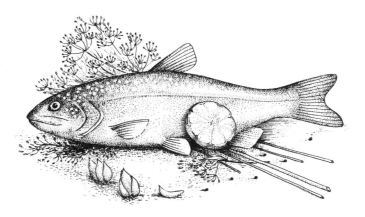

Fresh fish markets have grown by leaps and bounds since 1979, making fish accessible to more people than ever before.

And that should tell you something about the status of fish in the diet today.

The health benefits of fish are well documented. Fish is highly nutritious and low in calories (about 100 calories per 4 ounces for most fish), and compared to most meats it is lower in fat (1–3% fat content in white-fleshed fish), higher in polyunsaturated fats, and somewhat lower in cholesterol. And fish has yet another nutritional asset. Fish oils in salmon, bluefish and sable, albacore tuna, trout as well as all seafood, contain omega-3 fatty acids, highly polyunsaturated fats that have been shown to lower blood cholesterol in humans. They also have been shown to inhibit the formation of blood clots, which can cause heart attacks.

Check the Omega-3 Fatty Acid Chart on p. 273 for fish high in these fatty acids and low in fat when making out your shopping list. Our Nutrient Counter will give you the latest score on shellfish.

Some fish and shellfish are higher in sodium and cholesterol content than others, so people with special sodium and cholesterol requirements should check the Nutrient Counter to avoid problems.

Cooking fish and shellfish can be a bugaboo. But a little practice will go a long way in adding this important food to your menu. The thing to remember is not to overcook fish, or it will become rubbery. Grilling, baking, and broiling with some liquid added for moisture are especially suitable methods for cooking fish.

A rule of thumb is to cook a 1-inch-thick fish for 10 minutes—but no gauge is better than your eyes, fingers, and nose for assessing doneness. Cook the fish until the flesh becomes opaque and flakes easily when touched with a fork. Use two spatulas when transferring fish from oven to platter, to prevent breaking.

You'll improve the texture, flavor, and vitamin content of fish if you buy it fresh or flash frozen on board ship. Deal only with a reputable market. You should also use your nose to test freshness. If the fish smells like clean ocean air it's fresh. If the odor is "fishy," pass.

—————————— FISH ——————————

CLASSIC SOLE

2 tablespoons olive oil, or less
3 or 4 shallots, finely minced
½ pound [225 g] mushrooms, sliced
⅓ cup [79 ml] dry white wine
  Juice of 1 lemon
6 (4-ounce) [115 g] fish fillets, such as sole, haddock,
  halibut, or snapper (about 1½ pounds) [675 g]
¾ cup [178 ml] Sauce Velouté (p. 176)
6 asparagus spears, cooked and kept warm (p. 127)

Heat olive oil in a large skillet. Add shallots and mushrooms and sauté 2 minutes. Add 2 tablespoons of the wine and sauté 1 minute longer, or until mushrooms are tender. Remove mushroom mixture from skillet; set aside and keep hot.

Add remaining wine, lemon juice, and fillets to skillet and cook until fillets are tender, about 3 minutes on each side. Place fillets on a heated platter and top with Sauce Velouté. Arrange asparagus spears and mushrooms over fish. Makes 6 servings.

Each serving with sauce contains about:

>   199 calories; 210 mg sodium; 51 mg cholesterol;
>   5 g fat; 16 g carbohydrate; 22 g protein;
>   1 g fiber. 24% calories from fat.
>   Exchanges: 3 meat

DILLY TROUT IN A POUCH

6 (4-ounce) [115 g] lake trout, split and cleaned
White pepper to taste
6 fresh sprigs dill or fennel, or 1½ teaspoons dill weed
2 shallots, minced
3 tablespoons dry sherry
½ cup [119 ml] Fish Stock (p. 38)
2 teaspoons low-calorie margarine
6 lemon slices
Lemon wedges

Rub each trout inside and out with pepper. Place a sprig of dill or fennel or some of the dill weed in each cavity. Cut out 6 (6-inch) [15 cm] circles of aluminum foil. Fold each circle in half and pinch the corners to make a "boat" shape. Fit each trout into a foil boat and sprinkle with shallots. Mix together Sherry and stock and pour over each trout. Dot each with bits of margarine and top with a lemon slice. Bring edges of foil up to completely enclose fish and pinch foil together securely. (The shape of the pouch should resemble a turnover.) Place trout pouches in a baking dish and bake at 450°F [232°C] for 25 minutes or until trout are tender when tested with a fork.

To serve, place pouches on a serving platter, and with scissors cut open tops of pouches so that each diner may lift out the trout easily. Garnish with lemon wedges. Makes 6 servings.

Each serving contains about:

> 125 calories; 43 mg sodium; 54 mg cholesterol;
> 4 g fat; 2 g carbohydrate; 20 g protein;
> tr fiber. 20% calories from fat.
> Exchanges: 4 meat

MARINE KEBABS

Serve this colorful kebab over a bed of rice for a complete meal.

½ pound [225 g] scallops
12 cherry tomatoes
¼ pound [115 g] swordfish, cut in 1-inch cubes
1 green bell pepper, cut in small squares
1 onion, cut in 6 wedges
¼ pound [115 g] halibut, cut in 1-inch cubes
1 tablespoon olive oil
1 tablespoon fresh lemon juice
Lemon wedges
Tartar Sauce (p. 187), optional

Alternately thread scallops, cherry tomatoes, swordfish, green pepper, onion, and halibut on each of 6 metal skewers. Combine olive oil and lemon juice. Brush kebabs with some of the oil-lemon mixture and place on rack in a broiler pan. Broil 4 inches [10 cm] from source of heat about 4 minutes on each side, basting often. Arrange on serving platter and garnish with lemon wedges. Serve with Tartar Sauce, if desired. Makes 6 servings.

Each skewer without sauce contains about:

97 calories; 72 mg sodium; 27 mg cholesterol;
2 g fat; 5 g carbohydrate; 15 g protein;
tr fiber. 16% calories from fat.
Exchanges: 3 meat

POACHED SEA BASS

Court Bouillon (following recipe)
6 (4-ounce) [115 g] sea bass, salmon, haddock, whitefish,
other fish fillets or steaks (about 1½ pounds) [675 g]
1 tablespoon chopped parsley
Lemon wedges

Place Court Bouillon in a large skillet and heat to a simmer. Place fish in Court Bouillon, cover, and simmer until fish becomes creamy white and flakes easily when tested with a fork, about 12 to 15 minutes. Carefully remove fish to a heated serving platter. Sprinkle with parsley and garnish with lemon wedges. Makes 6 servings.

NOTE: Chill fish and serve with Dill Sauce (p. 188).

Each serving contains about:

> 92 calories; 64 mg sodium; 39 mg cholesterol;
> 2 g fat; 0 carbohydrate; 17 g protein;
> 0 fiber. 20% calories from fat.
> Exchanges: 3 meat

COURT BOUILLON

¾ cup [178 ml] dry white wine
¾ cup [178 ml] water
½ small onion, sliced
½ stalk celery, cut up
½ carrot, sliced
1 sprig parsley
1 bay leaf

Combine wine, water, onion, celery, carrots, parsley, and bay leaf in a large saucepan. Bring to a boil, reduce heat, and simmer, covered, 15 minutes. Strain through a fine sieve or cheesecloth. Makes 1½ cups [355 ml].

Each ½ cup contains about:

> 3 calories; 5 mg sodium; 0 cholesterol; 0 fat;
> tr carbohydrate; tr protein; 0 fiber.
> 0 calories from fat.
> Exchanges: negligible

SOLE AMANDINE

6 (4-ounce) [115 g] sole, perch, or haddock fillets
(about 1½ pounds) [675 g]
Flour
2 tablespoons plus 1 teaspoon low-calorie margarine
Juice of 1 lemon
1 clove garlic, minced
2 tablespoons [30 g] slivered almonds, chopped
¼ cup [59 ml] dry white wine
1 tablespoon chopped parsley
White pepper to taste

Dust fish lightly with flour. Heat 2 tablespoons of the margarine in a skillet. Add fillets and sauté about 2 to 3 minutes on each side, or until fish becomes creamy white and flakes easily when tested with a fork. Remove fish to a heated serving platter and sprinkle with lemon juice.

Melt remaining 1 teaspoon margarine in skillet placed over medium heat. Add garlic, almonds, and wine and cook, stirring briskly, for 30 seconds or until light brown in color. Spoon sauce over fish and sprinkle with parsley and pepper. Makes 6 servings.

NOTE: Whole trout may be used in place of fillets.

Each serving contains about:

> 143 calories; 133 mg sodium; 50 mg
> cholesterol; 5 g fat; 5 g carbohydrate;
> 20 g protein; 1 g fiber. 30% calories
> from fat.
> Exchanges: 3 meat

SWORDFISH PIQUANT

1 tablespoon low-calorie margarine
1 tablespoon olive oil
4 large cloves garlic, minced or pressed
  Juice of 1 lemon
6 (4-ounce) [115 g] swordfish steaks, 1 inch [2½ cm] thick
  (about 1½ pounds) [675 g]
2 tablespoons chopped parsley
2 lemons, cut in wedges
  Paprika

Melt margarine and olive oil in a saucepan over low heat. Add garlic and lemon juice and heat briefly to blend flavors. Brush half of the margarine-garlic mixture on one side of each swordfish steak. Place, basted side up, on a broiler pan and broil 4 inches [10 cm] from source of heat about 6 minutes. Turn steaks over, brush with remaining margarine-garlic mixture, and broil 6 minutes on second side, or until fish flakes easily with a fork. Place on a heated platter and garnish with chopped parsley, lemon wedges, and paprika. Makes 6 servings.

NOTE: Add 1 teaspoon anchovy paste to the margarine-garlic mixture for variation.

Each serving contains about:

> 148 calories; 132 mg sodium; 37 mg cholesterol;
> 7 g fat; 1 g carbohydrate; 19 g protein; tr fiber.
> 42% calories from fat.
> Exchanges: 4 meat

SOLE VERONIQUE

A modern variation on a classic theme cuts calories drastically.

> 2 shallots or green onions (white part only), minced
> 2 tablespoons low-calorie margarine
> 6 (4-ounce) [115 g] fillets of sole (about 1½ pounds)
>   [675 g]
> ½ cup [119 ml] dry white wine
> ¼ cup [59 ml] water
> 1½ teaspoons arrowroot
> ¼ cup [59 ml] plus 1 teaspoon nonfat milk
> ¼ cup [59 ml] evaporated nonfat milk
> ½ cup [180 g] small seedless green grapes
> 2 tablespoons egg substitute, or 1 egg white, beaten
>   White pepper to taste
> 2 tablespoons slivered almonds, toasted* (optional)

Sauté shallots in 1 tablespoon of the margarine in skillet until tender. Add fish fillets, wine, and water. Cut a circle of wax paper the size of the skillet, grease one side, and place it grease-side down over fish. Bring liquid to a boil, reduce heat, and simmer, covered, until fish is tender when tested with a fork, about 12 to 15 minutes. Carefully transfer fillets to a heated serving platter.

In a small saucepan, melt remaining 1 tablespoon margarine. Mix arrowroot with 1 teaspoon nonfat milk and stir into margarine until smooth. Gradually add ¼ cup [59 ml] *each* nonfat milk and evaporated nonfat milk and bring to a boil. Reduce heat and cook, stirring, until thickened and smooth. Stir ¼ cup [59 ml] of the hot sauce into egg substitute, then return to sauce in pan. Cook and stir until blended. Add grapes and heat through. Season to taste with pepper. Spoon sauce over fish. Sprinkle with toasted slivered almonds, if desired. Makes 6 servings.

* To toast almonds, place in a dry pan over medium heat and heat, stirring, until golden.

Each serving with almonds contains about:

> 158 calories; 154 mg sodium; 51 mg cholesterol;
> 5 g fat; 8 g carbohydrate; 21 g protein;
> 1 g fiber. 28% calories from fat.
> Exchanges: 4 meat

CRAB-STUFFED SOLE

2 tablespoons low-calorie margarine
2 tablespoons dry white wine
2 tablespoons fresh lemon juice
6 (4-ounce) [115 g] fillets of sole (about 1½ pounds)
[675 g]
¾ cup [178 ml] Sauce Velouté (p. 176)
¼ pound [115 g] shredded Alaskan king crab meat (fresh or frozen)
1 tablespoon chopped parsley

Melt margarine in a large skillet. Add wine and lemon juice. Place sole in skillet and simmer, covered, 3 minutes or until fish becomes creamy white and flakes easily when tested with a fork. Combine ¼ cup [60 g] of the Sauce Velouté and the crab meat in a small saucepan and heat through. Place 1 tablespoon of the crab meat mixture in the center of each fillet. Roll up jellyroll fashion and secure with wood picks. Arrange stuffed rolls in a nonstick baking pan. Pour remaining Sauce Velouté over fish. Bake at 350°F [177°C] 10 minutes. Sprinkle with parsley. Makes 6 servings.

NOTE: Canned crab meat has a very high salt content. We suggest that those watching their salt intake use only fresh or frozen Alaskan king crab meat.

Each serving with sauce contains about:

> 150 calories; 125 mg sodium; 57 mg cholesterol;
> 4 g fat; 5 g carbohydrate; 22 g protein; tr
> fiber. 25% calories from fat.
> Exchanges: 4 meat

WHITEFISH À LA PORT

1 tablespoon honey
½ cup [119 ml] port wine or dry Sherry
  Juice of 2 lemons
1 teaspoon dill weed, or 1 sprig fresh dill, minced
6 (4-ounce) [115 g] whitefish, snapper, or sea bass fillets
  (about 1½ pounds) [675 g]
  Parsley or dill sprigs
  Paprika

Blend together honey, port, lemon juice, and dill in a small bowl. Brush fish with mixture, reserving some for basting. Broil fillets 4 inches from source of heat, basting often with marinade, 3 minutes on each side, or until fish is creamy white and flakes easily when tested with a fork. Garnish with parsley and dust with paprika. Makes 6 servings.

Each serving contains about:

> 121 calories; 44 mg sodium; 35 mg
> cholesterol; 1 g fat; 8 g carbohydrate;
> 21 g protein; 0 fiber. 10% calories from fat.
> Exchanges: 4 low-fat meat

SHELLFISH

SOLE MEUNIÈRE

The classic sauce used in this recipe is quick, tasty, and simple to make. It is also excellent with veal, chicken, or any fish.

> 1 tablespoon low-calorie margarine
> 1 clove garlic, minced
> ½ pound [225 g] mushrooms, sliced
> 2 tablespoons dry white wine
> 1 tablespoon vegetable oil
> 1 tablespoon flour
>   Pepper to taste
> 1 pound [450 g] fillet of sole, cut into 6 portions
> ¼ cup [59 ml] nonfat milk
> 1 tablespoon chopped parsley
> 2 teaspoons fresh lemon juice
>   Lemon wedges

Melt 1 tablespoon of the margarine in a skillet. Add garlic and mushrooms and sauté about 2 minutes. Add wine and sauté until mushrooms are tender and liquid is almost absorbed; set aside and keep hot.

In another skillet, heat remaining margarine and oil. Season flour with pepper. Dredge sole steaks lightly in seasoned flour mixture, then dip in milk. Place in the skillet and cook about 1 minute on each side. Remove to a heated platter. Spoon mushrooms over sole and sprinkle with parsley and lemon juice. Garnish with lemon wedges. Makes 6 servings.

Each serving contains about:

> 159 calories; 129 mg sodium;
> 64 mg cholesterol; 6 g fat;
> 8 g carbohydrate; 22 g
> protein; tr fiber. 33% calories
> from fat.
> Exchanges: 3 meat

LIME-LACED LOBSTER TAILS

Note the low, low calories.

> *6 (6-ounce) [180 g] lobster tails*
> *¼ cup [59 ml] fresh lime or lemon juice*
> *2 cloves garlic, minced*
> *⅛ teaspoon paprika*
> *⅛ teaspoon white pepper*
> *1 teaspoon finely chopped parsley*

With scissors, snip off the soft undercovering of each lobster tail. Remove the meat from the shell and clean and reserve shells. Cut meat in small pieces and place in a shallow dish. Combine lime juice, garlic, paprika, pepper, and parsley. Pour over lobster and marinate in the refrigerator for 1 hour.

Remove meat from marinade, reserving marinade for basting. Stuff meat back into shells. Place shells on a broiler pan and broil 4 inches [10 cm] from source of heat about 10 minutes, basting often with reserved marinade. Makes 6 servings.

NOTE: 6 ounces [180 g] of lobster includes the shell.

Each serving contains about:

> 90 calories; 210 mg sodium; 85 mg cholesterol;
> 2 g fat; 1 g carbohydrate; 17 g protein; 0 fiber.
> 2% calories from fat.
> Exchanges: 3 meat

PICNIC LOBSTER

> *6 (1-pound) [450 g] live lobsters*
> *Drawn Margarine (p. 170), or Seafood Cocktail Sauce*
> *(p. 186)*
> *Lemon wedges*

Add enough water to a large kettle so the lobsters will be completely immersed when you plunge them. Bring water to a rolling boil. Immerse live lobsters in water head first, and allow the water to return to a boil. Reduce heat and simmer about 20 minutes, or until lobster shells are bright red. Drain. Serve with small bowl of Drawn Margarine or Seafood Cocktail Sauce and lemon wedges. Cut lobsters on underside, separating shell from meat. Use lobster fork or shellfish fork to pick out meat. Makes 6 servings.

Each lobster without sauce contains about:

> 137 calories; 512 mg sodium, 72 mg
> cholesterol; 4 g fat; 2 g carbohydrate;
> 21 g protein; 0 fiber. 26% calories from fat.
> Exchanges: 3 meat

SCALLOPS IN CIDER

½ cup [119 ml] Fish Stock (p. 38)
½ cup [119 ml] unsweetened apple cider
2 teaspoons minced shallots
¼ teaspoon dried tarragon
½ pound [225 g] mushrooms, thinly sliced
1½ pounds [675 g] scallops or cleaned shrimp
Pepper to taste
1 tablespoon chopped parsley

Combine stock, cider, shallots, tarragon, mushrooms, and scallops in a skillet and sprinkle with pepper. Bring to a boil, reduce heat, and simmer, uncovered, 4 minutes or until scallops are tender. With a slotted spoon, remove scallops and mushrooms to a heated serving platter. Bring pan liquid to a boil and boil 3 to 4 minutes, or until liquid is reduced by one-third. Spoon pan liquid over scallop mixture and sprinkle with parsley. Makes 6 servings.

Each serving contains about:

> 122 calories; 185 mg sodium, 37 mg
> cholesterol; 1 g fat; 7 g carbohydrate;
> 20 g protein; tr fiber. 8% calories from fat.
> Exchanges: 4 meat

SCALLOPS MARCUS

A squeeze of lemon juice over the scallops keeps them creamy white.

2 tablespoons low-calorie margarine
2 tablespoons dry white wine
1 clove garlic, minced
1 sprig parsley, finely chopped
1½ pounds [675 g] scallops
2 tablespoons fresh lemon juice
Lemon wedges

Melt margarine in a small saucepan. Add wine, garlic, and parsley and blend thoroughly. Sprinkle scallops with lemon juice and place in a baking dish. Pour margarine-wine mixture over scallops and bake at 350°F [177°C] for 15 minutes. Garnish with lemon wedges. Makes 6 servings.

Each serving contains about:

> 119 calories; 230 mg sodium; 37 mg cholesterol; 3 g fat; 4 g carbohydrate; 19 g protein; 0 fiber. 21% calories from fat.
> Exchanges: 4 meat

GRILLED SALMON

> 1 tablespoon olive oil
> Juice of ½ lemon
> 1 bunch fresh dill
> 6 (4-ounce) [115 g] salmon steaks (about 1½ pounds) [675 g]
> Dill Sauce (p. 188)

Combine olive oil and lemon juice. Brush over salmon. Place 3 sprigs of dill on each salmon steak, and tie it on the steak with a piece of string. Place fish on a hot grill. Grill about 5 minutes on each side or until fish flakes easily with a fork. Remove fish from grill. Cut string and remove the dill. Serve with dill sauce.

Each serving (without sauce) contains about:

> 159 calories; 64 mg sodium; 54 mg cholesterol; 6 g fat; tr carbohydrate; 21 g protein; 0 fiber. 30% calories from fat.
> Exchanges: 3 meat

POULTRY AND GAME

Poultry has come up in the world in ten short years. Today, you will find poultry breasts boned and skinned, cut into scallops, dressed, seasoned, and ready to cook, if not already cooked.

Our *Light Style* recipes will give you an idea of how versatile poultry can be, while remaining low in fat and cholesterol.

Light cooking and eating means removing the skin from chicken or other birds to reduce fat and cholesterol by at least a third; imaginative seasonings will compensate for the lack of salt. It means keeping portions moderate to avoid too many calories. It means using light cooking methods—baking, barbecuing, broiling, grilling, poaching, and sautéeing with a minimum of fat to avoid excess fat and extra calories. It means quick cooking and easy preparation.

As a bonus, all the recipes calling for chicken breasts are interchangeable with turkey or other meat cutlets. You can substitute one fowl for another in any recipe.

We cover the gamut from poultry to serve the kids (Oven-Fried Chicken, p. 91) to poultry that is ideal at a party (Chicken alla Marsala, p. 85).

CHICKEN

BARBECUED CHICKEN

3 whole chicken breasts (about 1½ pounds [675 g] boned
weight), skinned, boned, and split
1½ teaspoons Worcestershire sauce
¼ cup [59 ml] water
½ cup [119 ml] Catsup (p. 182)
¼ cup [59 ml] unsweetened pineapple juice
1 tablespoon brown sugar
Pepper to taste
2 tablespoons low-calorie margarine, melted

Pound chicken breasts into thin cutlets between sheets of wax paper with a mallet. In a saucepan, combine Worcestershire sauce, water, Catsup, pineapple juice, brown sugar, and pepper. Bring to a boil, reduce heat, and simmer 10 minutes. Combine sauce and margarine in a shallow baking dish. Coat chicken cutlets with mixture and marinate for 15 minutes, turning occasionally to coat all sides. Grill over charcoal or broil 3 minutes on each side, or bake at 350°F [177°C] for 15 minutes. Makes 6 servings.

NOTE: This sauce is also delicious on ground beef patties and pork chops.

Each serving contains about:

> 180 calories; 138 mg sodium; 73 mg
> cholesterol; 5 g fat; 7 g carbohydrate;
> 27 g protein; tr fiber. 25% calories
> from fat.
> Exchanges: 3 meat

CHICKEN CASHEW

3 whole chicken breasts (about 1½ pounds [675 g] boned
   weight), skinned, boned, and split
2 tablespoons low-calorie margarine
2 cloves garlic, minced
1 teaspoon minced ginger root
2 tablespoons unsalted cashews
2 teaspoons fresh lemon juice
½ pound [225 g] asparagus spears, cooked (p. 127)

Cut meat into ¼-inch [½ cm]-wide strips. Melt margarine in a large skillet
and add garlic, ginger, cashews, lemon juice, and chicken. Cook, tossing
gently, until golden, about 5 minutes. Garnish with asparagus spears. Makes
6 servings.

Each serving contains about:

> 187 calories; 120 mg sodium; 73 mg
> cholesterol; 7 g fat; 4 g carbohydrate;
> 29 g protein; 1 g fiber. 30% calories
> from fat.
> Exchanges: 3 meat

CHICKEN MARENGO

3 whole chicken breasts (about 1½ pounds [675 g] boned
   weight), skinned, boned, and split
1 tablespoon olive oil
1½ cloves garlic, finely minced
2 shallots, finely chopped
2½ cups [592 ml] low-sodium Chicken Stock (p. 38)
5 medium tomatoes, peeled and chopped
1½ medium onions, cut in wedges
1 pound [450 g] mushrooms, sliced
1 bay leaf
1 tablespoon Herb Blend (p. 184)
1 tablespoon chopped parsley or fresh oregano, chopped
¼ cup [59 ml] dry Sherry

Pound chicken breasts into thin cutlets between sheets of wax paper with
a mallet. In skillet add oil. Add chicken, garlic, and shallots, and sauté until
chicken is golden brown, 3 to 4 minutes on each side. Remove chicken and
set aside. Add stock, tomatoes, onions, mushrooms, bay leaf, and Herb

Blend to skillet. Bring to a boil, reduce heat, and simmer 7 to 10 minutes. Return chicken to skillet, add Sherry, and heat through. Sprinkle with parsley. Makes 6 servings.

Each 3 ounce serving contains about:

> 224 calories; 73 mg sodium; 74 mg
> cholesterol; 6 g fat; 13 g
> carbohydrate; 20 g protein; 1 g fiber.
> 24% calories from fat.
> Exchanges: 3 meat, 1 vegetable

CHICKEN ALLA MARSALA

3 whole chicken breasts (about 1½ pounds [675 g] boned
*   weight), skinned, boned, and split, or 1½ pounds veal*
*   scallops*
¼ cup [35 g] flour
*   Pepper to taste*
3 tablespoons low-calorie margarine
¼ cup [60 g] minced shallots
1 clove garlic, minced
½ pound [225 g] mushrooms, sliced
½ cup [119 ml] sweet Marsala wine

Pound chicken breasts into thin cutlets between sheets of wax paper with a mallet. Mix together flour and pepper and dredge chicken lightly in seasoned flour, shaking off excess. In a skillet, melt 2 tablespoons of the margarine and sauté shallots, garlic, and mushrooms until vegetables are tender. Remove vegetables and set aside. Melt remaining 1 tablespoon margarine in same skillet, add chicken and sauté 2 to 3 minutes on each side, or until golden. Add Marsala and reserved mushroom mixture and cook 1 minute longer or until tender. Remove chicken and mushrooms from skillet with a slotted spoon and arrange on a heated platter. Bring liquid remaining in pan to a brisk boil and cook until reduced to a thin, syrupy glaze. Pour glaze over chicken and mushrooms. Makes 6 servings.

Each serving contains about:

> 200 calories; 137 mg sodium;
> 72 mg cholesterol; 6 g fat;
> 7 g carbohydrate; 28 g protein;
> 1 g fiber. 28% calories from fat.
> Exchanges: 3 meat

ENCHILADAS SUIZA

*2 whole chicken breasts, boned and skinned (1 pound
[450 g] boned weight)*
1 cup [237 ml] low-sodium Chicken Stock (p. 38)
6 corn tortillas
Suiza Sauce (following recipe)
2 tablespoons low-calorie sour cream
Chopped green onions

Place chicken breasts in skillet and add chicken stock. Bring to a boil, reduce heat, cover, and simmer 10 to 15 minutes, or until chicken breasts are tender. Remove chicken breasts from stock, cool and shred meat. Set aside.

Heat tortillas on ungreased griddle until piping hot and softened. Dip tortilla in Suiza Sauce. Place about 2 tablespoons shredded chicken in center of each tortilla and fold over once. Place on serving platter. Repeat with remaining tortillas and filling. Pour remaining Suiza Sauce over enchiladas. Garnish each enchilada with 1 teaspoon sour cream and sprinkle with green onions. Makes 6 servings.

SUIZA SAUCE

*4 tomatoes, peeled, or 1 (1-pound) [450 g] can low-sodium
tomatoes, drained*
1 large onion, chopped
1 teaspoon corn oil
1 cup [237 ml] evaporated nonfat milk

Combine tomatoes and onion in a blender container and blend until smooth. Heat oil in a skillet and add tomato mixture. Bring to a boil, reduce heat to low, and simmer, uncovered, 30 minutes or until slightly thickened, stirring occasionally. Stir in milk gradually. Heat through.

Each enchilada with sauce contains about:

> 210 calories; 149 mg sodium; 52 mg
> cholesterol; 4 g fat; 24 g carbohydrate;
> 20 g protein; 2 g fiber. 17% calories
> from fat.
> Exchanges: 2 meat, ½ bread, 1 B vegetable

LEMON CHICKEN

*3 whole chicken breasts (about 1½ pounds [675 g] boned
weight), skinned, boned, and split*
2 tablespoons low-sodium Soy Sauce (p. 187)
*2 tablespoons gin, vodka, or other high-proof alcoholic
beverage, optional*
1 tablespoon Chinese-style sesame seed oil
*½ teaspoon ginger juice**
2 teaspoons arrowroot or cornstarch
1 tablespoon water
1½ to 2 tablespoons fresh lemon juice
1 teaspoon grated lemon peel
¼ cup [59 ml] low-sodium Chicken Stock (p. 38)

Mix together the Soy Sauce and gin, rub the mixture over the chicken and let it marinate in the refrigerator about 1 hour, turning occasionally. Remove chicken from marinade and dice. Heat oil and ginger juice in a saucepan or wok over moderately low heat. Add chicken and cook, stirring constantly, until golden, about 3 minutes. Remove chicken with a slotted spoon and set aside. Dissolve arrowroot in water and add to pan. Stir until smooth. Stir in lemon juice, lemon peel, and stock. Cook over low heat, stirring, until thickened. Add reserved chicken and heat through. Makes 6 servings.

* To extract juice from ginger, place a 1-inch [2 ½ cm] piece of ginger root in a garlic press and squeeze. Use more ginger as needed to make ½ teaspoon juice.

Each serving contains about:

> 179 calories; 90 mg sodium; 73 mg
> cholesterol; 5 g fat; 4 g carbohydrate;
> 28 g protein; tr fiber. 28% calories
> from fat.
> Exchanges: 3 meat

CHICKEN-MUSHROOM SAUTÉ

3 whole chicken breasts (about 1½ pounds [675 grams]
  boned weight), skinned, boned, and split
2 tablespoons low-calorie margarine
¾ cup [178 ml] dry white wine
2 cloves garlic, minced
1 pound mushrooms, sliced
½ teaspoon paprika
¼ cup [35 g] flour
2 teaspoons fresh lemon juice
1 tablespoon finely chopped parsley
  White pepper to taste
1 teaspoon arrowroot

Pound chicken breasts into thin cutlets between sheets of wax paper with a mallet; set aside. Heat 1 tablespoon of the margarine in a skillet. Add ½ cup [119 ml] of the wine, garlic, and mushrooms and cook until mushrooms are tender. Remove mushrooms with a slotted spoon and keep hot; reserve liquid in pan.

Mix together paprika and flour and dredge chicken lightly in the mixture. Add remaining 1 tablespoon margarine, lemon juice, parsley, and white pepper to reserved pan liquid, and heat until margarine melts. Add chicken and cook until tender, about 2 to 3 minutes on each side. Remove chicken and mushrooms with a slotted spoon and arrange on a heated serving platter; reserve pan liquid. Dissolve arrowroot in remaining ¼ cup [59 ml] wine and add to pan liquid. Stir over low heat until thickened. Pour sauce over chicken and mushrooms. Makes 6 servings.

Each serving contains about:

> 203 calories; 116 mg sodium; 73 mg
> cholesterol; 5 g fat; 9 g carbohydrate;
> 29 g protein; 1 g fiber. 24% calories
> from fat.
> Exchanges: 3 meat, 1 vegetable

CHICKEN ORIENTAL

1 tablespoon safflower oil

2 cloves garlic, minced

3 chicken breast halves, skinned, boned, and cut into 1-inch [2½ cm] cubes

2 cups [450 g] chopped celery

½ pound [225 g] mushrooms, sliced

½ pound [225 g] bean sprouts

1 teaspoon minced ginger root or ½ teaspoon ground ginger

⅛ teaspoon pepper

½ teaspoon cornstarch

1 tablespoon water

2 tablespoons low-sodium Soy Sauce (p. 187)

3 cups Steamed Rice (p. 122)

Heat oil in a hot skillet or wok until oil smokes. Add the garlic and stir-fry for 10 seconds. Add the chicken and stir-fry until cooked (about 4 minutes). Add celery, mushrooms, bean sprouts, ginger, and pepper and sauté until celery is tender—about 5 minutes—stirring frequently. Dissolve cornstarch in water; then mix in soy sauce. Push aside chicken and vegetables and stir cornstarch mixture into juices. Cook, stirring frequently, until mixture thickens. Divide into 6 equal portions and spoon each serving over ½ cup [38 g] rice. Makes 6 servings.

NOTE: Add chopped red pepper for added color.

Each ½ cup serving with ½ cup rice contains about:

> 220 calories; 76 mg sodium; 35 mg cholesterol; 4 g fat; 31 g carbohydrate; 15 g protein; 2 g fiber. 16% calories from fat.
> Exchanges: 3 meat, ½ vegetable, 1 bread

CHICKEN PICCATA

3 whole chicken breasts (about 1½ pounds [675 g] boned
   weight), skinned, boned, and split, or 1½ pounds [675 g]
   of veal scallops
¼ cup [35 g] flour
   Pepper to taste
1 tablespoon olive oil
1 tablespoon low-calorie margarine
¾ cup [178 ml] low-sodium Chicken Stock (p. 38)
1½ tablespoons fresh lemon juice
6 paper-thin lemon slices

Pound chicken into thin cutlets between sheets of wax paper with a mallet. Mix together flour and pepper and dredge chicken lightly in seasoned flour, shaking off excess. Heat oil in a skillet and sauté chicken 2 to 3 minutes on each side, or until golden. Remove chicken and set aside. Add ½ cup [119 ml] of the stock and lemon juice to skillet, bring to a boil, and boil 1 to 2 minutes. Return chicken to skillet and place 1 lemon slice on each cutlet. Cover and simmer 7 to 10 minutes, or until chicken is tender. Remove chicken with a slotted spoon and place on a heated serving platter; reserve pan liquid. Surround chicken with cooked lemon slices. Add remaining ¼ cup [59 ml] stock to pan liquid and cook over medium-high heat until reduced to a thin syrupy glaze. Remove from heat and blend in remaining 1 tablespoon margarine, stirring until margarine melts. Pour sauce over chicken. Makes 6 servings.

Each serving contains about:

> 199 calories: 87 mg sodium; 73 mg cholesterol;
> 6 g fat; 4 g carbohydrate; 27 g protein;
> tr fiber. 23% calories from fat.
> Exchanges: 3 meat

CHICKEN TARRAGON

1 (3-pound) [1⅓ kg] chicken
1 clove garlic, split
   Pepper to taste
½ teaspoon dried tarragon, or 2 large sprigs fresh tarragon
¾ cup [178 ml] low-sodium Chicken Stock (p. 38)
   Tarragon Sauce (p. 177)

Rub outside and cavity of chicken with garlic. Season inside and out with pepper and sprinkle cavity with dried tarragon, or if using sprigs, place them in cavity. Moisten chicken with stock with a baster. Place chicken on rack in a roasting pan and bake at 350°F [177°C] for 50 minutes to 1 hour. Remove from oven, cool slightly, and remove and discard skin. Carve and serve with Tarragon Sauce. Makes 6 servings.

Each serving with sauce contains about:

> 155 calories; 125 mg sodium; 60 mg
> cholesterol; 7 g fat; 5 g carbohydrate;
> 27 g protein; tr fiber. 25% calories
> from fat.
> Exchanges: 3 meat

OVEN-FRIED CHICKEN

> *3 whole chicken breasts (about 1½ pounds [675 g] boned*
> *weight), skinned, boned, and split*
> *3 tablespoons egg substitute, or 1 egg white*
> *1 tablespoon water*
> *1 teaspoon Herb Blend (p. 184)*
> *¾ cup [45 g] dry French Bread crumbs (p. 47)*
> *2 tablespoons low-calorie margarine, melted*
> *1 tablespoon fresh lemon juice*

Pound chicken into thin cutlets between sheets of wax paper with a mallet. Lightly beat egg substitute or egg white with water. Mix Herb Blend with bread crumbs. Dip cutlets in egg mixture, then in seasoned bread crumbs. Cover and chill 1 hour.

Arrange chicken cutlets in a nonstick baking dish and drizzle each one with melted margarine and lemon juice. Bake at 350°F [177°C] for 20 to 25 minutes, or until golden. Makes 6 servings.

Each serving contains about:

> 191 calories; 128 mg sodium; 73 mg cholesterol;
> 5 g fat; 5 g carbohydrate; 28 g protein;
> tr fiber. 26% calories from fat.
> Exchanges: 3 meat, 1 bread

TURKEY DIVAN

1 (1½-pound) [675 g] turkey breast
½ pound [225 g] broccoli spears, cooked
¾ cup [178 ml] Sauce Abel (p. 176)
    Paprika
1 tablespoon minced parsley
1 tablespoon grated Parmesan cheese (optional)

Place turkey breast in a roasting pan and roast at 325°F [163°C] for 40 minutes or until a meat thermometer inserted in the thickest part of breast registers 180°F [82°C]. Cool slightly, then slice. Divide broccoli into 6 equal portions and arrange the portions in a nonstick baking pan. Cover each broccoli portion with a 3-ounce [85 g] serving of turkey. Pour a generous tablespoon of Sauce Abel over each serving and sprinkle with paprika. Bake at 325°F [163°C] for 8 minutes, or until heated through. Garnish with parsley and sprinkle with Parmesan cheese, if desired. Makes 6 servings.

Each serving with sauce and cheese contains about:

149 calories; 86 mg sodium; 43 mg cholesterol;
5 g fat; 6 g carbohydrate; 20 g protein;
1 g fiber. 32% calories from fat.
Exchanges: 3 meat, ½ vegetable

ROAST TURKEY WITH ROYAL GLAZE

1 cup [237 ml] Low-Calorie Russian Dressing (p. 166)
3 tablespoons low-calorie apricot jelly
1 (12-pound) [5½ kg] turkey
    Apple-Onion Stuffing (following recipe)

Combine Russian Dressing and apricot jelly in a small saucepan and stir over low heat until well blended. Place turkey in a baking dish and pour marinade over. Cover and refrigerate several hours or overnight, turning occasionally. Remove turkey to roasting pan, breast side up; reserve marinade. Stuff cavity with stuffing. (Any remaining stuffing may be placed in a baking dish to bake separately at 350°F [177°C] for 20 minutes.) Cover turkey loosely with foil and roast at 350°F [177°C] until meat thermometer registers 180°F [82°C], basting with reserved marinade every 30 minutes. Remove foil about 20 minutes before turkey finishes roasting to brown. Makes 20 servings.

Each serving of white or dark meat contains about:

> 110 calories; 70 mg sodium; 72 mg
> cholesterol; 3 g fat; 7 g carbohydrate;
> 17 g protein; tr fiber. 26% calories
> from fat.
> Exchanges: 3 low-fat meat

APPLE-ONION STUFFING

2 tablespoons low-calorie margarine
1 cup [181 g] chopped onions
1 shallot, minced
1 cup [225 g] chopped celery
7 cups [400 g] French Bread cubes (p. 47; about 14 slices)
¾ cup [124 g] raisins, plumped
3 cups [450 g] diced unpeeled apples
¼ cup [4 tablespoons] minced parsley
½ cup [60 g] chopped pecans
¼ teaspoon paprika (optional)
1¼ to 1½ cups [296 to 355 ml] low-sodium Turkey Stock
  (p. 38)

Melt the margarine in a large skillet. Add onions, shallot, and celery and sauté until onions are golden. Add bread cubes, raisins, apples, parsley, pecans, and paprika and mix well with a fork. Add just enough stock to make a moist stuffing. Use to loosely stuff turkey (½ cup per pound of bird), or place in a nonstick baking pan, cover, and bake at 350°F [177°C] for 20 minutes. If stuffing dries out while baking, drizzle with more turkey stock. Makes 8 cups.

Each ¼ cup serving contains about:

> 63 calories; 17 mg sodium; 0 cholesterol;
> 2 g fat; 1 g carbohydrate; 2 g protein;
> 1 g fiber. 28% calories from fat.
> Exchanges: 1 bread

TURKEY TETRAZZINI

An excellent do-ahead party dish.

¼ cup [60 g] low-calorie margarine
3 tablespoons flour
1½ teaspoons arrowroot
1½ teaspoons water
2½ cups [592 ml] low-sodium Chicken Stock (p. 38)
½ cup [119 ml] evaporated nonfat milk
1 (6-ounce) [180 g] can low-sodium tomato paste
1 cup [225 g] diced celery
4 cloves garlic, minced
½ pound [225 g] mushrooms, sliced
2 cups [60 g] shell macaroni, cooked
1 (1½-pound) [675 g] turkey breast, or 3 chicken breasts
(1½ pounds [675 g] boned weight), skinned, boned,
cooked, and diced
½ cup [60 g] grated low-sodium, low-fat Cheddar cheese

Melt margarine in a large saucepan. Add flour and stir until smooth. Dissolve arrowroot in water and stir into flour mixture until smooth. Stir in stock, milk, tomato paste, celery, garlic, and mushrooms. Cook over low heat until celery has softened slightly, about 10 minutes. Stir in cooked macaroni and turkey and turn mixture into a casserole. Cover and place in the refrigerator overnight to blend flavors. When ready to bake, remove from refrigerator, bring to room temperature, sprinkle with grated cheese, and bake at 350°F [177°C] for 1 hour. Makes 12 servings.

NOTE: Casserole may be covered with aluminum foil and frozen before baking. Thaw, sprinkle with cheese, and bake as directed.

Each ½ cup serving contains about:

201 calories; 147 mg sodium; 48 mg
cholesterol; 7 g fat; 14 g carbohydrate;
21 g protein; 1 g fiber. 30% calories
from fat.
Exchanges: 2 meat, ¼ bread

GAME

CORNISH GAME HENS
WITH HERB–CORN BREAD STUFFING

6 Cornish game hens
1 onion, cut in 6 wedges
2 small carrots, cut in thirds
6 sprigs parsley
6 teaspoons low-calorie margarine
  Pepper to taste
  Herb–Corn Bread Stuffing (following recipe)

Stuff each hen cavity with an onion wedge, carrot piece, and parsley sprig. Rub 1 teaspoon margarine on each bird and sprinkle with pepper to taste. Place birds in a roasting pan and bake at 350°F [177°]C for 25 minutes, or until tender. Remove from the oven. Serve with Herb–Corn Bread Stuffing. Makes 6 servings.

Each game hen (without skin) with ½ cup dressing contains about:

> 244 calories; 128 mg sodium; 59 mg
> cholesterol; 6 g fat; 15 g carbohydrate;
> 21 g protein; 2 g fiber. 25% calories
> from fat.
> Exchanges: 3 meat, 1 bread

HERB–CORN BREAD STUFFING
Excellent for game birds or turkey.

2 tablespoons low-calorie margarine
1 large onion, chopped
3 celery stalks, chopped
3 cups [180 g] crumbled Corn Bread (p. 44)
1 cup [45 g] French Bread cubes (p. 47; about 1½ slices)
2 egg whites, lightly beaten
½ teaspoon pepper
1 teaspoon Herb Blend (p. 184)
¼ teaspoon freshly grated nutmeg
*2 tablespoons sesame seeds, toasted**
1 cup [237 ml] low-sodium Chicken Stock (p. 38)

In a large skillet, melt margarine. Add onion and celery and sauté until onion is golden. Add Corn Bread, bread cubes, egg whites, pepper, Herb Blend, nutmeg, and sesame seeds and mix well. Add stock and toss gently until bread is moistened. Place stuffing in a nonstick baking dish, cover, and bake at 350°F [177°C] for 20 minutes. (Or stuff fowl, allowing ½ cup [115 g] stuffing for each pound.) If stuffing appears dry while baking, add a little more stock. Makes 8 servings.

* To toast sesame seeds, put them in a dry skillet and place over low heat, shaking now and then, until seeds are golden.

Each ½ cup serving contains about:

> 90 calories; 110 mg sodium; 0 cholesterol;
> 4 g fat; 12 g carbohydrate; 3 g protein;
> 1 g fiber. 35% calories from fat.
> Exchanges: 1 bread, ½ fat

MEATS

Meat is an excellent source of iron in an easily absorbable form, as well as zinc, protein, and vitamins B6 and B12. The body's need for protein is smaller than you might think, so a little goes a long way. A 3-ounce serving of meat provides up to 50 percent of the RDA for protein.

Because meat is such a good nutritional buy, the USDA has seen fit in the last few years to remind consumers that there is danger in eliminating meat from the diet. Meat contains many essential vitamins and minerals as well as protein, fat, and cholesterol. The USDA recommends eating lean meat to avoid too much cholesterol and fat.

The USDA has recently changed the grading title of very lean "Good" grade to "Select" grade to make it more appealing to consumers concerned about fat and cholesterol levels in meat. Select grade meat is not widely available yet, but you can be your own selector by looking for cuts of meat that are lean, trimming all visible fat, and learning how to use less tender (and more lean) meats. You can cook lean, less expensive cuts of meat by stewing or other slow methods that retain moisture, or you can shave, dice, or even coarse-grind the meat for use in stir-fry dishes.

In recent years, pork, too, has changed its image; it has become a leaner meat, thanks to new raising methods. Lamb and veal have grown in favor over recent years, as well. We include them among our recipes for variety.

Some tips:

- Purchase lean meats closely trimmed of fat, or trim them yourself at home to save on cost.
- Choose one of beef's "skinniest" cuts: top round, top loin, round tip, eye of round, sirloin, or tenderloin. A 3-ounce cooked serving of the leaner cuts contains under 8 grams of total fat and fewer than 3 grams saturated fat.
- For every 3 ounces of cooked beef, start with 4 ounces of uncooked meat.

- Keep lean beef lean by broiling or roasting on a rack.
- Avoid frying.
- Use a nonstick skillet to sauté or brown meat.
- Marinate with spices, wine, or lemon juice instead of oil.
- Cook stews, chili, and meat sauce the day before and refrigerate. Skim off any coagulated fat.
- Partially freeze meat and poultry to facilitate slicing thinly for stir-frying.
- Avoid salting foods until you taste them. Salt delays browning in meat and can draw out moisture and dietary iron.

BEEF

BEEF BROCHETTE

½ *cup [119 ml] dry red wine*
1 *tablespoon Dijon Mustard (p. 182)*
  Pepper to taste
1½ *pounds [675 g] top sirloin, cut in 1-inch [2½ cm] cubes*
24 *each cherry tomatoes, whole button mushrooms, and pearl onions*

In a bowl, combine wine, mustard, and pepper. Add meat, cover, and refrigerate for at least 5 hours or overnight. Alternately thread meat, tomatoes, mushrooms, and onions on 6 skewers. Broil to desired doneness. Makes 6 servings.

Each serving contains about:

> 233 calories; 68 mg sodium; 80 mg
> cholesterol; 8 g fat; 9 g carbohydrate;
> 29 g protein; 2 g fiber. 33% calories
> from fat.
> Exchanges: 3 meat

BEEF TACOS

Taco stands dot the streets of southern California, and for good reason. People of all ages love these nutritious, easy-to-eat Mexican sandwiches. Here's a *Light Style* version.

6 corn tortillas

½ pound [225 g] ground lean beef, or 1 cup [225 g]
  chopped cooked roast beef

½ teaspoon each chili powder and ground cumin

⅛ teaspoon onion powder
  Pepper to taste

½ small iceberg lettuce, shredded

1 tomato, diced

6 tablespoons grated low-sodium, low-fat Cheddar cheese

6 tablespoons Guacamole (p. 15)

6 tablespoons Spanish Sauce (p. 174)

Loosely fold each tortilla in half. Place a wedge of foil inside each folded tortilla to allow for filling. Secure with wood picks, if necessary. Place on a baking sheet and bake at 450°F [232°C] until toasted, about 7 to 10 minutes. Discard foil and wood pick.

In a skillet, sauté ground beef with chili powder, cumin, onion powder, and pepper until browned. Gently fill openings in tortillas with 3 table-spoons *each* meat, shredded lettuce, and diced tomato, and 1 tablespoon cheese. Top each taco with 1 tablespoon *each* Guacamole and Spanish Sauce. Makes 6 servings.

Each taco contains about:

> 218 calories; 158 mg sodium; 30 mg
> cholesterol; 11 g fat; 19 g carbohydrate;
> 12 g protein; 3 g fiber. 48% calories
> from fat.
> Exchanges: ½ meat, ½ bread, ½ vegetable, 1½ fat

CHATEAUBRIAND

1 (2-pound) [900 g] beef tenderloin, trimmed of fat
  Garlic powder, lemon juice, and freshly ground pepper to
  taste
  French Provincial Sauce (p. 171)

Season tenderloin on both sides with garlic powder, lemon juice, and pepper. Place on a broiler rack and broil until meat is done as desired. Turn during broiling to cook both sides. To serve, thinly slice tenderloin on bias and arrange on a heated serving platter. Serve with French Provincial Sauce. Makes 10 servings.

Each 3 ounce serving without sauce contains about:

162 calories; 48 mg sodium; 57 mg
cholesterol; 6 g fat; 3 g carbohydrate;
20 g protein; tr fiber. 38% calories
from fat.
Exchanges: 3 meat

CHINESE BEEF WITH PEA PODS

Serve this classic Chinese beef dish with steamed rice, broccoli, and a fruit
dessert for a glamorous, yet nutritiously low-fat, low-sodium meal.

1 tablespoon safflower oil
4 cloves garlic, minced
1½ pounds [675 g] beef tenderloin, cut into ¼-inch [½ cm]
    strips
¾ pound [340 g] pea pods (snow peas)
1 teaspoon grated ginger root
2 tablespoons low-sodium Soy Sauce (p. 187)
1 tablespoon arrowroot or cornstarch
    Steamed Rice (p. 122, optional)

Heat ½ tablespoon of the oil in a hot skillet or wok until oil smokes. Add half
the garlic and stir-fry 10 seconds. Add meat and stir-fry until brown. With a
slotted spoon, remove meat to a bowl and set aside. Pour any juice remaining in skillet into a separate bowl and reserve. Add remaining ½ tablespoon
oil to hot skillet, heat until oil smokes, and add remaining garlic. Stir-fry 10
seconds. Add pea pods and stir-fry until they turn a bright green color and
are crisp but tender. Dissolve arrowroot in reserved pan juices. Push pea
pods to side of skillet and add arrowroot mixture, ginger, and Soy Sauce.
Cook and stir until smooth. Return meat to skillet and heat through. Serve
over steamed rice, if desired. Makes 8 servings.

NOTE: Omit oil if using a nonstick wok.

Each serving contains about:

183 calories; 59 mg sodium; 55 mg cholesterol;
9 g fat; 6 g carbohydrate; 19 g protein;
1 g fiber. 45% calories from fat.
Exchanges: 3 meat, ½ B vegetable

ROAST BEEF AU JUS

1 (3- to 4-pound) [1⅓ to 1¾ kg] sirloin tip or boned roast
  Pepper to taste
3 cloves garlic, slivered
1 tablespoon low-calorie margarine
½ cup minced shallots
¾ cup [178 ml] dry red wine
1½ cups [355 ml] low-sodium Beef Stock (p. 37)
1 tablespoon minced parsley

Sprinkle roast all over with pepper. With a sharp, pointed knife blade make incisions in several places in meat and insert slivers of garlic into openings. Place in a roasting pan and roast at 325°F [163°C] until meat thermometer registers 155°F [68°C] for medium, or done as desired. Remove from oven. Drain pan juices and chill until surface fat coagulates, then scoop out, leaving a clear broth; set aside.

In a small skillet, melt margarine and sauté shallots until glazed but not brown. Add reserved pan juices, wine, and stock. Bring to a boil and boil until reduced by half. Stir in parsley. To serve, slice meat and spoon about 1 tablespoon sauce over each serving. Makes 10 to 12 servings.

Each 3 ounce serving with sauce contains about:

> 188 calories; 55 mg sodium; 76 mg
> cholesterol; 8 g fat; 2 g carbohydrate;
> 26 g protein; tr fiber. 39% calories
> from fat.
> Exchanges: 3 meat

VIENNA DIP

French Bread (p. 46)
Au jus sauce from Roast Beef au Jus (preceding recipe), heated
Thinly sliced roast beef

Slice French Bread and dip slices into sauce. Arrange beef slices on dipped slices of bread. Top each with dipped bread slice. Ladle more juice over sandwich, if desired.

Each sandwich (2 ounces meat, 2 slices bread) contains about:

271 calories; 78 mg sodium; 46 mg cholesterol;
9 g fat; 26 g carbohydrate; 19 g protein;
1 g fiber. 30% calories from fat.
Exchanges: 2 meat, 2 bread

STEAK DIANE

6 (4-ounce) [115 g] sirloin steaks or filets mignons
2 tablespoons low-calorie margarine
4 shallots, minced
1 clove garlic, minced
6 tablespoons Dijon Mustard (p. 182)
1 teaspoon chopped chives
2 tablespoons dry Sherry
¼ cup [59 ml] Cognac

Place the steaks between sheets of wax paper and pound with a mallet until very thin. Heat margarine in a large skillet. Add shallots and garlic and sauté until shallots are tender. Remove shallots and garlic and discard. Spread 1 tablespoon Dijon Mustard over each steak and place in skillet. Cook 3 minutes on each side. Combine chives, Sherry, and Cognac. Pour over meat and cook 1 minute longer. Makes 6 servings.

Each serving contains about:

233 calories; 101 mg sodium; 66 mg
cholesterol; 9 g fat; 9 g carbohydrate;
23 g protein; tr fiber. 38% calories
from fat.
Exchanges: 3 meat

STEAK DIJON

¼ cup [60 g] Dijon Mustard (p. 182)
½ cup [119 ml] dry red wine
6 (4-ounce) [115 g] top sirloin or New York steaks, trimmed
  of fat
  Freshly ground pepper to taste

Blend together mustard and wine in a small pan. Dip steaks in wine mixture and marinate, refrigerated, 1 to 2 hours. Remove steaks from marinade and broil to desired doneness, turning once. Season with pepper to taste. Makes 6 servings.

NOTE: Boneless chicken breasts may be used in place of beef.

Each serving contains about:

> 175 calories; 52 mg sodium; 66 mg
> cholesterol; 7 g fat; 2 g carbohydrate;
> 23 g protein; 0 fiber. 30% calories
> from fat.
> Exchanges: 3 meat

STEAK OSCAR

> 6 (4-ounce) [115 g] filets mignons
> 12 asparagus spears, cooked (p. 127)
> 6 Alaskan king crab legs, 3 inches [8 cm] each, cooked and
>   shelled
> ½ cup [119 ml] Blender Béarnaise (p. 169)
>   Watercress sprigs

Broil meat to desired doneness. Place 2 asparagus spears and 1 crab leg on top of each cooked filet. Pour a generous tablespoon Béarnaise Sauce over each. Garnish with watercress. Makes 6 servings.

Each serving contains about:

> 215 calories; 92 mg sodium (content unavailable
> for fresh crab); 70 mg cholesterol;
> 10 g fat; 3 g carbohydrate; 21 g protein;
> 1 g fiber. 43% calories from fat.
> Exchanges: 3 meat

TOURNEDOS ROSSINI

> 6 (4-ounce) [115 g] top sirloin or tenderloin steaks
>   Garlic powder, lemon juice, and pepper to taste
>   Madeira Sauce (p. 175)

Season steaks with garlic powder, lemon juice, and pepper. Broil to desired doneness. Serve with Madeira Sauce. Makes 6 servings.

Each serving without sauce contains about:

> 172 calories; 71 mg sodium; 66 mg
> cholesterol; 7 g fat; 2 g carbohydrate;
> 22 g protein; tr fiber. 30% calories
> from fat.
> Exchanges: 3 meat

———————— LAMB ————————

IRISH STEW

1½ pounds [675 g] meat from leg of lamb, cut in 1-inch
  [2½ cm] cubes
1 onion, coarsely chopped
1 small turnip, cut in 1-inch [2½ cm] cubes
2 stalks celery with some leaves, sliced
4 carrots, sliced
3 cups [710 ml] low-sodium Beef Stock (p. 37), or water
¼ teaspoon pepper
  Bouquet Garni (p. 181)
1½ cups [180 g] peeled and cubed potatoes (about 2 potatoes)
1 tablespoon cornstarch or arrowroot
1 tablespoon water
2 teaspoons Worcestershire sauce
1 tablespoon minced parsley

In a large saucepan, cook lamb cubes, onion, turnip, celery, and carrots over low heat until lamb cubes are browned. Add stock, pepper, and Bouquet Garni. Bring to a boil, reduce heat, cover, and simmer for 1 hour. Add potatoes, cover, and cook 30 minutes longer, or until potatoes are tender. Dissolve cornstarch in water and stir into stew liquid. Simmer until broth is translucent. Stir in Worcestershire sauce. Sprinkle with parsley. Makes 6 servings.

Each ½ cup serving contains about:

> 209 calories; 119 mg sodium; 78 mg
> cholesterol; 8 g fat; 23 g carbohydrate;
> 21 g protein; 2 g fiber. 27% calories
> from fat.
> Exchanges: 3 meat, 1 B vegetable, ¼ bread

ROAST LEG OF LAMB WITH PINEAPPLE SAUCE

1 (3-pound) [1⅓ kg] leg of lamb
4 shallots, slivered
4 cloves garlic, slivered
  Juice of 1 lemon
  Herb Blend (p. 184) and pepper to taste
  Pineapple Sauce (p. 177)
  Fresh mint sprigs

With a sharp, pointed knife blade, make incisions in several places in meat and insert slivers of shallots and garlic into openings. Squeeze lemon juice over lamb and sprinkle with Herb Blend and pepper. Roast at 325°F [163°C] for 1½ to 2 hours, or until meat thermometer registers 160°F [71°C]. Slice lamb and serve with Pineapple Sauce. Garnish with mint sprigs. Makes 6 servings.

Each serving without sauce contains about:

195 calories; 59 mg sodium; 69 mg
cholesterol; 7 g fat; 4 g carbohydrate;
21 g protein; tr fiber. 33% calories
from fat.
Exchanges: 3 meat

———————————— VEAL ————————————

VEAL ABEL

6 (4-ounce) [115 g] veal scallops (about 1½ pounds)
  [675 g]
2 tablespoons low-calorie margarine
½ pound [225 g] mushrooms, sliced
¼ cup [119 ml] dry white wine
  Juice of 1 lemon
  Sauce Abel (p. 176)
8 asparagus spears, cooked and kept warm (p. 127)

Place veal scallops between sheets of wax paper and pound lightly with a mallet until very thin. Melt margarine in a large skillet and sauté veal about 2 minutes on each side, or until golden brown. Remove veal and arrange on a heated platter. Add mushrooms, wine, and lemon juice to skillet and cook until mushrooms are tender, about 3 minutes. Top veal with Sauce Abel and garnish with asparagus spears and mushrooms. Makes 6 servings.

Each serving without sauce contains about:

> 171 calories; 125 mg sodium; 107 mg cholesterol;
> 6 g fat; 4 g carbohydrate; 22 g protein;
> 1 g fiber. 31% calories from fat.
> Exchanges: 3 meat

VEAL BOURGUIGNONNE

2 tablespoons olive oil
2 pounds [900 g] veal rump roast, cut in 1-inch [2½ cm]
  cubes
1 pound [450 g] mushrooms, sliced
1 pound [450 g] pearl onions, chopped
1 cup [237 ml] Burgundy wine
2 cups [473 ml] low-sodium Veal Stock (p. 37)
1 tablespoon dried basil
1 bay leaf
2 tablespoons arrowroot
¼ cup [59 ml] water

Heat olive oil in a large kettle. Add veal and brown on all sides. Add mushrooms and onions and sauté until glazed. Add wine, veal stock, basil, and bay leaf. Cook over medium heat 10 minutes. Dissolve arrowroot in water, then stir into kettle. Reduce heat to a very low simmer, cover, and simmer 45 minutes, stirring often. Remove bay leaf. Makes 8 servings.

NOTE: Lean lamb or beef may be substituted for the veal.

Each ½ cup serving contains about:

> 233 calories; 156 mg sodium; 128 mg
> cholesterol; 8 g fat; 11 g carbohydrate;
> 29 g protein; 1 g fiber. 30% calories
> from fat.
> Exchanges: 3 meat

VEAL PARMIGIANA

6 (4-ounce) [115 g] veal scallops (about 1½ pounds) [675 g]
1 tablespoon olive oil
2 cups [473 ml] Marinara Sauce (p. 174)
3 ounces [90 g] mozzarella cheese, grated
2 tablespoons grated Parmesan cheese

Place veal scallops between sheets of wax paper and pound with a mallet until very thin. Heat olive oil in a large skillet and sauté veal about 2 minutes on each side, or until golden brown. Place veal in an 11-by-14-inch [28-by-36 cm] baking dish and top with Marinara Sauce. Sprinkle mozzarella and Parmesan cheese over sauce. Bake at 375°F [190°C] for 20 minutes, or until cheese is bubbly and golden. Makes 6 servings.

Each serving contains about:

244 calories; 160 mg sodium; 93 mg cholesterol;
12 g fat; 4 g carbohydrate; 27 g protein;
1 g fiber. 40% calories from fat.
Exchanges: 1 vegetable, 3 meat

VENETIAN VEAL

6 (4-ounce) [115 g] veal scallops (about 1½ pounds)
   [675 g]
12 sage leaves, or 1 tablespoon dried sage
1 tablespoon olive oil
½ cup [119 ml] dry white wine
1 teaspoon arrowroot
1 teaspoon water
   Pepper to taste
2 lemons, thinly sliced

Place veal scallops between sheets of wax paper and pound with a mallet until very thin. Place a sage leaf on each side of each veal scallop. (If using dried sage, sprinkle on both sides of each scallop.) Heat oil in a large skillet and sauté veal 2 minutes on each side, or until golden brown. Remove veal with slotted spoon and arrange, the slices overlapping, on a heated platter. Add wine to liquid remaining in the skillet. Dissolve arrowroot in water and add to pan. Cook and stir until slightly thickened and smooth. Season with pepper. Pour sauce in a ribbon over veal and garnish with lemon slices. Makes 6 servings.

Each serving contains about:

> 156 calories; 68 mg sodium; 107 mg cholesterol;
> 6 g fat; 2 g carbohydrate; 22 g protein;
> tr fiber. 32% calories from fat.
> Exchanges: 3 meat

PORK

APPLE-STUFFED PORK CHOPS

6 (4-ounce) [115 g] lean rib pork chops (about 1½ pounds)
[675 g]
1 tablespoon low-calorie margarine
1 tablespoon arrowroot or cornstarch
½ teaspoon maple extract
1 cup [237 ml] unsweetened apple juice concentrate
3 small tart green apples, peeled, cored, and sliced

Have your butcher cut a pocket for stuffing in each pork chop. Melt margarine in a large skillet and brown pork chops about 3 minutes on each side. Remove and set aside. Add arrowroot, maple extract, and apple juice concentrate to saucepan. Cook over medium heat until well blended and smooth. Remove from heat and stir in apples. Cool filling slightly and stuff chops, reserving some for garnish. Secure chops with wood picks. Place chops in a baking dish, cover, and bake at 350°F [177°C] for 1 hour, or until well done. Reheat any remaining filling in a small saucepan and spoon over chops to serve. Makes 6 servings.

Each chop with stuffing contains about:

> 148 calories; 52 mg sodium; 38 mg
> cholesterol; 7 g fat; 10 g carbohydrate;
> 12 g protein; 2 g fiber. 43% calories
> from fat.
> Exchanges: 3 meat, ¼ fruit

CHINESE STIR-FRY PORK

1 pound [450 g] pork tenderloin
1 small onion
6 mushrooms
6 stalks celery
6 asparagus spears
1 tablespoon safflower oil
¼ cup [30 g] chopped green onions
¼ teaspoon dry mustard
¼ teaspoon ground ginger
2 tablespoons low-sodium Soy Sauce (p. 187)

Cut pork, onion, mushrooms, celery, and asparagus in thin julienne-style diagonal strips. Heat oil in a skillet or wok until it smokes. Add pork and stir-fry about 10 to 15 minutes. Add onion, mushrooms, celery, asparagus, green onions, mustard, and ginger, and stir-fry until vegetables are tender, about 2 to 3 minutes. Sprinkle with Soy Sauce. Makes 6 servings.

Each serving contains about:

> 108 calories; 103 mg sodium; 56 mg
> cholesterol; 3 g fat; 5 g carbohydrate;
> 19 g protein; 1 g fiber. 25% calories
> from fat.
> Exchanges: 3 meat, 1 vegetable

MEXICAN PORK STEW

You'll find the fresh tomatillos and cilantro at any Mexican market. If fresh tomatillos are not available, use small green or red tomatoes. Substitute Italian parsley for cilantro, if necessary. Try the tomatillo sauce with chicken or swordfish, too, for a low-calorie version.

1 tablespoon vegetable oil
1½ pounds [675 g] lean pork, cut in 1-inch [2½ cm] cubes
3 cloves garlic, minced
1½ pounds [675 g] tomatillos, husks removed
1 fresh jalapeño chili pepper, seeded and chopped
1 small onion, chopped
4 or 5 sprigs cilantro (fresh coriander), chopped

Heat oil in a kettle. Add pork and garlic and sauté over medium-high heat until browned. Remove meat from pan and set aside. Place tomatillos in a saucepan with water to cover, bring to a boil, reduce heat to medium and cook, uncovered, about 5 minutes. Drain, reserving about ½ cup [119 ml] of the liquid. In a blender container, combine cooked tomatillos, chili pepper, and onion, and blend until pureed. Pour tomatillo sauce into kettle used for browning meat and simmer for 5 minutes. Add reserved meat, cover, and simmer 45 minutes to 1 hour, or until meat is tender. Add some reserved liquid if sauce becomes too thick. Sprinkle with cilantro. Makes 8 servings.

Each ½ cup serving contains about:

> 195 calories; 56 mg sodium; 57 mg
> cholesterol; 11 g fat; 6 g carbohydrate;
> 18 g protein; tr fiber. 51% calories from fat.
> Exchanges: 3 meat, 1 vegetable

PORK WITH SAGE

1 (4- to 5-pound) [1¾ to 2¼ kg] pork loin
2 cloves garlic, slivered
2 tablespoons fresh lemon juice
1 tablespoon ground sage
  Pepper to taste
  Pineapple Sauce (p. 177, optional)

With a sharp, pointed knife blade, make incisions in several places in pork loin and insert slivers of garlic into the openings. Mix together lemon juice, sage, and pepper and rub mixture over pork. Place pork in a roasting pan and roast at 350°F [177°C] for 35 to 45 minutes per pound, or until meat thermometer registers 185°F [85°C] (about 2½ hours in all). Slice and top with Pineapple Sauce, if desired. Makes 12 servings.

Each 3 ounce serving without sauce contains about:

> 220 calories; 64 mg sodium; 81 mg cholesterol;
> 11 g fat; tr carbohydrate; 24 g protein;
> 0 fiber. 45% calories from fat.
> Exchanges: 3 meat

PASTA AND GRAINS

Grains, like vegetables, are complex carbohydrates that load the body with essential nutrients, as well as fiber. That's why it is vitally important to include whole-wheat breads, cereals, and grain-based foods in your diet every day. The USDA recommends six or more servings from the grain group per day.

The calories from this food group are low (4 calories per gram compared with 9 calories per gram for fat), so you can afford to be inventive with pastas and rice dishes.

Light Style recipes show you how to keep the calories low and still enjoy sauces and toppings, thanks to nonfat or low-fat products and fat-reducing cooking methods. For instance, there is no need to put salt or oil in the water used to cook pasta.

Another trick to lowering calories in rice and pasta dishes is to reduce the portion size. You'll be surprised at the suggested serving size (a half cup) of rice and pasta recommended in the USDA Daily Food Guide. It is small enough to make you enjoy every bite.

KATHY'S CANNELLONI

This recipe gets its name from Kathy DeKarr, a fine cook who has helped us test the recipes in this book.

> 1 tablespoon olive oil
> ½ cup [181 g] minced onion
> 1 teaspoon minced garlic
> 1 (10-ounce) [285 g] package frozen chopped spinach,
>   thawed and drained
> ½ pound [225 g] ground lean beef
> 3 tablespoons grated Parmesan cheese
> 1 tablespoon evaporated nonfat milk
> 3 tablespoons egg substitute, or 1 egg white
> 1¼ teaspoons dried oregano
>   Pepper to taste
> 18 Cannelloni Noodles (following recipe)
> 1 cup [237 ml] Marinara Sauce (p. 174)
> ¾ cup [178 ml] Béchamel Sauce (p. 169)

Heat oil in a nonstick skillet and add onion and garlic. Sauté over medium-high heat until onion is golden and tender. Stir in spinach. Cook, stirring, 3 to 4 minutes, or until all moisture has evaporated. Transfer spinach mixture to large bowl. In same skillet add beef and cook until lightly browned. Add beef mixture to spinach mixture. Add 2 tablespoons Parmesan cheese, milk, egg substitute or egg white, oregano, and pepper and mix well. Place 1 tablespoon of filling on each Cannelloni Noodle. Fold sides over filling until they overlap, and tuck in ends. Repeat until all noodles are filled and folded. Pour thin layer of Marinara Sauce in shallow 14-by-10-inch [36-by-25 cm] baking pan. Arrange cannelloni in a single layer over sauce. Pour Béchamel Sauce over cannelloni and spoon remaining Marinara Sauce on top. Sprinkle with remaining cheese and bake, uncovered, at 375°F [190°C] for 20 minutes. Place under broiler 30 seconds to brown top. Makes 18 cannelloni.

CANNELLONI NOODLES

Make these low-calorie, low-fat crêpes ahead and stack between sheets of wax paper in the refrigerator or freezer to use with fillings and toppings of your choice.

½ cup [70 g] unbleached flour
½ cup [119 ml] water
¾ cup [180 g] egg substitute, or 2 egg whites
2 teaspoons low-calorie margarine

Combine flour, water, and egg substitute or egg whites and beat with a rotary beater or wire whisk until well blended. Chill batter. Heat a 5-inch skillet or crêpe pan until very hot and brush lightly with some of the margarine. Remove from heat and pour in about 1 tablespoon batter. Lift and tilt pan to evenly spread batter over pan bottom. Return to heat and cook until crêpe is lightly browned on underside. Turn and cook about 5 seconds, then remove to wax paper. (Crêpe should *not* brown; it should remain pale.) Repeat until all batter is used, lightly greasing the pan occasionally. Makes 18.

Each cannelloni contains about:

> 84 calories; 78 mg sodium; 8 mg cholesterol; 4 g fat; 6 g carbohydrate; 6 g protein; 1 g fiber. 4% calories from fat. Exchanges: ½ meat, ½ bread

FETTUCCINI ALFREDO

8 ounces [225 g] dry fettuccini noodles
2 quarts [2 L] low-sodium Chicken Stock (p. 38)
½ cup [115 g] low-calorie sour cream
½ cup [115 g] low-fat plain yogurt
2 tablespoons low-calorie margarine
2 cloves garlic, minced
3 tablespoons chopped parsley
1 tablespoon poppy seeds
2 tablespoons grated Parmesan cheese (optional)

Cook noodles in boiling stock until tender but firm to the bite, about 12 minutes. Drain and set aside. In a small bowl, mix together sour cream and yogurt until smooth; set aside. Melt margarine in a large skillet and sauté garlic 1 minute. Reduce heat to low and add yogurt mixture, blending well. Add noodles and toss gently until sauce is evenly distributed. Sprinkle with parsley, poppy seeds, and Parmesan cheese, if desired. Makes 8 servings.

Each ½-cup serving with cheese contains about:

> 159 calories; 78 mg sodium; 8 mg cholesterol;
> 5 g fat; 24 g carbohydrate; 6 g protein;
> 1 g fiber. 26% calories from fat.
> Exchanges: 1 bread, 1 fat

LASAGNA

This lasagna goes light on fats and starch to help lower the calories.

> *8 ounces [225 g] lasagna noodles*
> *1 pound [450 g] ricotta cheese (made from partially*
>   *skimmed milk)*
> *6 tablespoons egg substitute, or 2 egg whites*
> *⅛ teaspoon ground nutmeg*
> *2 tablespoons minced parsley*
> *3 cups [711 ml] Italian Meat Sauce (p. 172)*
> *1 pound [450 g] mozzarella cheese, shredded*
> *½ cup [60 g] grated Parmesan cheese (optional)*

Cook lasagna until just tender. Drain, rinse, and let stand in cold water. Beat ricotta cheese with egg substitute or egg whites. Stir in nutmeg and parsley. Cover the bottom of a 9-by-13-inch [23-by-33 cm] nonstick baking pan with a ¼-inch [½ cm] layer of Italian Meat Sauce. Top with a layer of half the noodles and add half of the remaining meat sauce. Spread half of the ricotta cheese mixture over meat sauce and sprinkle with half of the mozzarella cheese. Repeat layers, ending with mozzarella cheese. Sprinkle evenly with Parmesan cheese if desired, and bake at 375°F [190°C] for 35 minutes, or until cheese melts and is golden. Makes 16 servings.

Each 2-by-3-inch piece with Parmesan cheese contains about:

> 225 calories; 207 mg sodium; 35 mg cholesterol;
> 10 g fat; 16 g carbohydrate; 14 g protein;
> 1 g fiber. 40% calories from fat.
> Exchanges: 1 vegetable, 3 meat, ½ bread

NOODLES SIMPLICE

2 quarts [2 L] low-sodium Chicken Stock (p. 38)
8 ounces [225 g] dry noodles
2 tablespoons olive oil
2 cloves garlic, minced
2 tablespoons chopped parsley
1 tablespoon grated Parmesan cheese

Bring stock to a boil in a large pot. Add noodles and cook until tender but firm to the bite, about 8 minutes. Drain and place on a heated platter. Heat olive oil in a small saucepan and stir in garlic and parsley. Heat gently. Pour parsley mixture over noodles and toss to coat well. Sprinkle with Parmesan cheese. Makes 8 servings.

Each ½ cup serving contains about:

> 139 calories; 13 mg sodium; 0 cholesterol;
> 4 g fat; 22 g carbohydrate; 4 g protein;
> 1 g fiber. 25% calories from fat.
> Exchanges: 1 bread

SPAGHETTI WITH ITALIAN MEAT SAUCE

1 quart [1 L] each water and low-sodium Chicken Stock
(p. 38)
8 ounces [225 g] spaghetti
1½ cups [355 ml] Italian Meat Sauce (p. 172), heated
2 tablespoons grated Parmesan cheese (optional)

Place water and chicken stock in a large pot and bring to a boil. Add spaghetti and cook until tender but firm to the bite, about 10 minutes; drain. Place spaghetti in a heated serving platter or bowl. Spoon Italian Meat Sauce over spaghetti and toss quickly until well coated. Sprinkle with cheese if desired. Makes 6 to 8 servings.

Each ½ cup serving with cheese contains about:

> 151 calories; 33 mg sodium; 8 mg cholesterol;
> 3 g fat; 25 g carbohydrate; 7 g protein;
> 1 g fiber. 17% calories from fat.
> Exchanges: 1 bread, 1 meat

CHICKEN PASTA AL PESTO

½ cup [50 g] basil or spinach, chopped
1 tablespoon pine nuts or hazelnuts
4 cloves garlic, minced
1 tablespoon low-calorie margarine
2 tablespoons freshly grated Parmesan cheese
1 tablespoon olive oil
4 small zucchini, thinly sliced
4 small carrots, peeled, thinly sliced
½ pound [225 g] snow peas, optional
½ cup [225 g] green peas
½ red pepper, cut in julienne strips, optional
8 ounces [225 g] dry pasta noodles
2 quarts [2 L] low-sodium chicken stock or water
2 cups [302 g] cooked chicken or turkey cut into bite-size pieces
Freshly ground pepper to taste

Puree basil, pine nuts, garlic, margarine, and Parmesan cheese in a food processor or blender. Place oil, zucchini, carrots, peas, and red pepper in a skillet or wok. Stir continuously over medium-high heat, until tender. Cook pasta in boiling stock or water until tender but firm to the bite, about 10 minutes. Drain. In a large bowl, toss together vegetables, noodles, chicken-basil mixture, and pepper to taste. Serves 6.

Each serving contains about:

> 320 calories; 125 mg sodium; 41 mg cholesterol;
> 7 g fat; 41 g carbohydrate; 23 g protein;
> 4 g fiber. 25% calories from fat.
> Exchanges: 3 meat, 1 bread

RICE

CONFETTI RICE

2 cups [473 ml] low-sodium Beef Stock (p. 37), or Chicken
Stock (p. 38)
1 cup [225 g] long-grain rice
2 tablespoons low-calorie margarine
10 mushrooms, sliced
½ cup [225 g] frozen petite peas, thawed, or fresh shelled
peas
2 tablespoons chopped parsley

Bring stock to a boil in a saucepan. Add rice and 1 tablespoon of the margarine and bring again to a boil. Stir, cover, reduce heat to low, and cook for 25 minutes or until rice is tender and moisture is absorbed.

Just before rice is cooked, melt remaining 1 tablespoon margarine in a skillet. Add mushrooms and sauté over high heat until almost tender and liquid has evaporated, stirring frequently. Add peas and toss with mushrooms until peas are hot. Add mushroom mixture and parsley to cooked rice. Toss lightly to mix. Makes 6 servings.

Each ½ cup serving contains about:

> 125 calories; 50 mg sodium; 0 cholesterol;
> 2 g fat; 20 g carbohydrate; 2 g protein;
> 1 g fiber. 13% calories from fat.
> Exchanges: 1 bread

RICE PILAF

2½ cups [592 ml] low-sodium chicken stock
1½ cups [355 ml] unsweetened apple juice
¼ cup [60 g] wild rice
1 cup [225 g] long-grain rice
1 tablespoon low-calorie margarine

Bring stock and apple juice to a boil in a saucepan. Add wild rice and bring again to a boil. Reduce heat to low, cover, and cook for 15 minutes. Add long-grain rice, cover, and continue to cook for 30 minutes, or until rice is tender and moisture is absorbed. Turn into a serving bowl and fluff with a fork. Add margarine to rice and toss lightly. Makes 6 servings.

Each ½ cup serving contains about:

> 173 calories; 27 mg sodium; 0 cholesterol;
> 1 g fat; 37 g carbohydrate; 3 g protein;
> 1 g fiber. 6% calories from fat.
> Exchanges: 1 bread

SAFFRON RICE

1 teaspoon low-calorie margarine
½ medium onion, finely chopped
1 clove garlic, minced
2 cups [473 ml] low-sodium Chicken Stock (p. 38)
1 cup [225 g] long-grain rice
* Pinch saffron threads*

In a saucepan, melt margarine and add onion and garlic. Sauté until onion is tender and golden. Add stock, bring to a boil, and add rice and saffron. Bring again to a boil, stir, cover, reduce heat to low, and cook 25 minutes or until rice is tender and moisture is absorbed. Makes 6 servings.

Each ½ cup serving contains about:

> 119 calories; 10 mg sodium; 0 cholesterol;
> tr fat; 26 g carbohydrate; 1 g protein;
> tr fiber. 4% calories from fat.
> Exchanges: 1 bread

SPANISH RICE

2 cups [473 ml] low-sodium Chicken Stock (p. 38)
½ cup [115 g] low-sodium tomato puree*
1 tablespoon vegetable oil
1 small onion, chopped
1 small green pepper, minced
1 cup [225 g] long-grain rice

Combine stock, tomato puree, and oil in a saucepan. Bring to a boil and stir in onion, green pepper, and rice. Bring again to a boil, reduce heat, cover, and cook 25 minutes or until rice is tender and moisture is absorbed. Makes 8 servings.

* To make your own low-sodium tomato puree, place fresh peeled tomatoes or low-sodium canned tomatoes in a blender container and blend until smooth.

Each ½ cup serving contains about:

> 112 calories; 5 mg sodium; 0 cholesterol;
> 2 g fat; 22 g carbohydrate; 2 g protein;
> 1 g fiber. 15% calories from fat.
> Exchanges: 1 bread

STEAMED RICE

2 cups [473 ml] low-sodium Chicken Stock (p. 38)
1 cup [225 g] long-grain rice
1 tablespoon low-calorie margarine

Bring stock to a boil in a saucepan. Add rice and bring again to a boil. Reduce heat to low, cover, and cook 25 minutes, or until rice is tender and moisture is absorbed. Turn into a serving bowl and fluff with a fork. Add margarine and toss lightly. Makes 6 servings.

Each ½ cup serving contains about:

> 120 calories; 25 mg sodium; 0 cholesterol;
> 1 g fat; 25 g carbohydrate; 2 g protein;
> tr fiber. 8% calories from fat.
> Exchanges: 1 bread

WILD RICE SKILLET

Wild rice is loaded with nutrients. It is expensive because it is difficult to harvest. You can stretch pennies and taste by combining cooked wild rice with white or brown rice. Just remember that 1 cup of uncooked wild rice will yield about 3 cups cooked.

4 cups [1 L] low-sodium Chicken Stock (p. 38); or amount
specified in wild rice package directions
1 cup [225g] wild rice
1½ tablespoons low-calorie margarine
1 clove garlic, pressed
¼ pound [115 g] mushrooms, thinly sliced
6 water chestnuts, sliced
2 tablespoons slivered almonds
Minced parsley

Bring stock to a boil in a saucepan. Add rice, reduce heat to low, cover, and cook about 60 minutes, or until rice is tender and moisture is absorbed.

Melt margarine in a large skillet and add garlic and mushrooms. Sauté until mushrooms are almost tender, about 3 minutes. Add water chestnuts and almonds and sauté 1 minute longer, or until mushrooms are tender. Add rice and toss lightly. Sprinkle with parsley. Makes 6 servings.

Each ½ cup serving contains about:

> 138 calories; 39 mg sodium; 0 cholesterol;
> 3 g fat; 24 g carbohydrate; 5 g protein;
> 2 g fiber. 19% calories from fat.
> Exchanges: 1 bread, ¼ fat

VEGETABLES

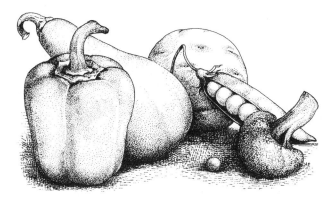

There has been a growing awareness in the last decade of the importance of a diet high in complex carbohydrates. The *Dietary Guidelines for Americans* recommends that 60 percent of the total daily intake of food be made up of complex carbohydrates, which include not only grains usually associated with carbohydrates but also vegetables and fruits.

Vegetables are high in many important vitamins, especially vitamins C and A, found in dark green leafy vegetables. Carotene, an orange plant pigment, is found in carrots, sweet potatoes, and other red and dark green vegetables, which should be included in the diet three or four times a week.

Teenagers can get the extra riboflavin and calcium they need for their growing bones and body tissues from broccoli and other dark green leafy vegetables.

Vegetables also contain fiber, which the USDA urges us to increase in our diets.

Cruciferous vegetables, such as broccoli, cauliflower, and cabbage, have been singled out as especially beneficial in reducing the risk of certain cancers.

The *Light Style* approach to vegetables stresses low calories and high nutrient density. We use nonfat dairy products for sauces; low-fat margarine eliminates cholesterol and reduces calories; and plenty of herbs complement the naturally strong flavors of vegetables.

We favor steaming over cooking in water. To steam vegetables, place in a steamer rack or colander that sits in a deep pot. Place rack in pot and add enough water to fill bottom without touching steamer rack, about 1½ inches. Cover and cook at medium-high heat until vegetables reach a high color and are tender but crisp. Cooking time will depend on variety and size of vegetable. Remove vegetables to serving bowl or platter and season as desired. Reserve steaming liquid for use in sauces, soups, and stocks.

Vegetables that stand too long deteriorate in vitamin and mineral content.

Microwave cooking is an even better way to preserve the nutrients, color, and texture of vegetables. If you do cook vegetables in water, reserve the water for use in sauces, soups, and stocks.

Stir-frying preserves nutrients and enhances the flavor of all foods, especially vegetables. It's the quick cooking over high heat that does the trick. Water, wine, or broth can be used to keep vegetables from scorching when stir-frying, but vegetables themselves also contain liquid. Avoid overcooking: overexposure to high heat will destroy anything, including vegetables.

Choose vegetables that look healthy and have good color. If they are shriveled or bruised, don't buy them. Fresh vegetables keep well in the refrigerator for up to a week. Root vegetables can be stored for several weeks in a cool, dry place away from light.

STEAMED ASPARAGUS

1½ pounds [675 g] asparagus spears
1 tablespoon low-calorie margarine
1 teaspoon dried marjoram

Trim woody ends of asparagus spears. Steam asparagus according to preceding directions for about 5 to 7 minutes. Drain. Melt margarine in a small saucepan and stir in marjoram. Pour over asparagus. Makes 6 servings.

NOTE: For a more elaborate dish, add 1 tablespoon sesame seeds to the margarine-marjoram mixture and sauté until golden. Then add 2 tablespoons fresh lemon juice and heat through. Nutrient Analysis: 33 calories; 26 mg sodium; 2 g fat.

Each serving (4 spears) contains about:

> 20 calories; 26 mg sodium; 0 cholesterol;
> 1 g fat; 4 g carbohydrate; tr protein;
> 1 g fiber. 21% calories from fat.
> Exchanges: 1 vegetable

ASPARAGUS PICANTE

Prepare Steamed Asparagus as in preceding recipe. Add to margarine-marjoram mixture 2 tablespoons fresh lemon juice and 1 tablespoon each mild sesame oil and white wine vinegar. Sprinkle with chopped cilantro (fresh coriander).

Each serving (4 spears) contains about:

> 40 calories; 26 mg sodium; 0 cholesterol;
> 3 g fat; 5 g carbohydrate; tr protein;
> 1 g fiber. 40% calories from fat.
> Exchanges: 1 vegetable

BROCCOLI ALLA ROMANA

1 tablespoon safflower oil or olive oil
1 teaspoon finely chopped garlic
3 cups [900 g] broccoli flowerets (about 2 pounds broccoli)
    Pepper to taste
    Juice of 1 lemon
6 tablespoons Mock Hollandaise (p. 180, optional)

Heat oil in a skillet or wok. Add garlic and cook for 30 seconds. Add broccoli flowerets and toss until tender but crisp (about 7 minutes). With a slotted spoon, transfer flowerets to a heated bowl and sprinkle with pepper and lemon juice. If desired, top each serving with 1 tablespoon Mock Hollandaise. Makes 6 servings.

Each ½ cup serving without sauce contains about:

> 35 calories; 12 mg sodium; 0 cholesterol;
> 2 g fat; 3 g carbohydrate; tr protein;
> 1 g fiber. 50% calories from fat.
> Exchanges: 1 vegetable, ¼ fat

CARROTS À L'ORANGE

1½ pounds [675 g] carrots, peeled and thinly sliced
4½ teaspoons low-calorie orange marmalade
1 teaspoon low-calorie margarine
    Dash ground nutmeg

Cook carrots according to directions for steaming vegetables (p. 126). When almost tender (about 7 to 10 minutes), drain carrots and place in a skillet. Add marmalade, margarine, and nutmeg to skillet and cook, stirring occasionally, until carrots are glazed. Makes 6 servings.

Each ½ cup serving contains about:

> 35 calories; 48 mg sodium; 0 cholesterol;
> tr fat; 12 g carbohydrate; tr protein;
> 3 g fiber. 8% calories from fat.
> Exchanges: 1 vegetable

CAULIFLOWER IN LEMON SAUCE

1 medium head cauliflower
1 tablespoon low-calorie margarine
2 cloves garlic, minced
2 tablespoons chopped parsley
2 teaspoons fresh lemon juice

Cut off tough end of cauliflower stem and remove any leaves. Cook cauliflower according to directions on steaming vegetables and cook until stalk is just tender, about 10 minutes. Drain and place cauliflower in serving dish. Melt butter in small saucepan and stir in garlic, parsley, and lemon juice. Pour over cauliflower. Makes 6 servings.

Each ½ cup serving contains about:

> 27 calories; 52 mg sodium; 0 cholesterol;
> 2 g fat; 2 g carbohydrate; tr protein;
> 1 g fiber. 33% calories from fat.
> Exchanges: 1 vegetable, ¼ fat

CHINESE STIR-FRY VEGETABLES

½ cup [119 ml] low-sodium Beef Stock (p. 37)
2 tablespoons minced ginger root
¼ head cauliflower, broken into flowerets
¼ pound [115 g] broccoli, broken into flowerets
½ cup [76 g] julienne-cut celery
¼ pound [115 g] pea pods (snow peas)
¼ head Napa cabbage, shredded
10 mushrooms, diced
¼ pound [115 g] bamboo shoots, diced
1 tablespoon low-sodium Soy Sauce (p. 187)
½ cup [115 g] water chestnuts, thinly sliced
1 medium onion, thinly sliced
¼ pound [115 g] bean sprouts

Heat stock in a heated wok or skillet. Add ginger root, cauliflowerets, broccoli, celery, and pea pods. Stir-fry 2 minutes over high heat. Add cabbage, mushrooms, and bamboo shoots. Stir-fry 1 minute. Stir in Soy Sauce and simmer over low heat 1 minute. Add water chestnuts, onion, and bean sprouts and stir-fry 1 minute over high heat. Do not overcook; vegetables should be tender but crisp. Makes 10 servings.

Each ½ cup serving contains about:

> 39 calories; 25 mg sodium; 0 cholesterol;
> tr fat; 9 g carbohydrate; tr protein; 2 g fiber.
> 6% calories from fat.
> Exchanges: 1 vegetable

CREAMED SPINACH

½ cup [119 ml] water
2 pounds [900 g] fresh spinach, trimmed, or 2 (10-ounce)
  [285 g] packages frozen chopped spinach
1 tablespoon low-calorie margarine
1½ tablespoons flour
¼ cup [59 ml] nonfat milk
¼ cup [59 ml] evaporated skim milk
¼ teaspoon ground nutmeg
  Dash onion powder

Heat water in a large skillet, add spinach, cover, and cook over high heat until steam appears. Reduce heat and simmer until tender, about 5 minutes. Drain and chop spinach; set aside. (If using frozen spinach, cook according to package directions, omitting salt; drain well.)

In a small saucepan, melt margarine, add flour, and stir until smooth. Slowly add milks, stirring continuously to make a smooth sauce. Bring to a boil, reduce heat, and simmer for 1 minute, stirring constantly. Sauce will be very thick. Remove from heat and season with nutmeg and onion powder. Mix the sauce with the spinach until evenly blended. Makes 6 servings.

Each ½ cup serving contains about:

> 61 calories; 24 mg sodium; 1 mg cholesterol;
> 1 g fat; 8 g carbohydrate; 2 g protein;
> 2 g fiber. 19% calories from fat.
> Exchanges: ½ bread

GREEN BEANS AMANDINE

1½ pounds [675 g] green beans, trimmed
½ cup [119 ml] low-sodium Chicken Stock (p. 38)
1 tablespoon low-calorie margarine
2 cloves garlic, minced
1 tablespoon slivered almonds
1 tablespoon chopped shallots, or 1 small onion, chopped

Sliver (French cut) beans or leave them whole. Place in a skillet with stock, bring to a boil, reduce heat, cover, and cook until beans are tender, about 5 to 7 minutes for French cut or about 10 to 15 minutes for whole beans. Drain beans and place on a heated platter. Melt margarine in skillet and add garlic, almonds, and shallots. Sauté until shallots are glazed and golden; do not brown. Add to beans and toss to coat well. Makes 6 servings.

Each ½ cup serving contains about:

> 40 calories; 31 mg sodium; 0 cholesterol;
> 1 g fat; 10 g carbohydrate; tr protein;
> 2 g fiber. 21% calories from fat.
> Exchanges: 1 vegetable

HERBED CROOKNECK SQUASH

6 small crookneck squash (about 1 pound) [450 g], trimmed
1 teaspoon dried basil
¼ teaspoon each onion powder and garlic powder
    Pepper to taste
    Low-sodium Chicken Stock (p. 38)

Cut squash in half lengthwise. Place squash, basil, onion and garlic powders, and pepper in a skillet with 1 inch [2½ cm] of stock. Cover and cook 7 to 8 minutes, or until squash is crisp but tender. Remove with a slotted spoon to a heated serving platter. Makes 6 servings.

Each ½ cup serving contains about:

> 16 calories; 2 mg sodium; 0 cholesterol;
> tr fat; 3 g carbohydrate; tr protein;
> 2 g fiber. 10% calories from fat.
> Exchanges: 1 vegetable

LEMON SPINACH

1 teaspoon olive oil
2 cloves garlic, minced
¼ cup [59 ml] water (if using fresh spinach)
2 pounds [900 g] fresh spinach, trimmed, or 2 (10-ounce)
  [285 g] packages frozen chopped spinach
  Juice of 1 large lemon
  Lemon wedges

Heat oil in a skillet, add garlic, and sauté 1 minute. Add water and spinach, cover, and simmer 2 to 3 minutes, or until spinach is tender. Drain off excess liquid. (If using frozen spinach, cook according to package directions, omitting salt. Add, without water, to sautéed garlic and heat through.) Turn spinach onto serving plate. Sprinkle with lemon juice and garnish with lemon wedges. Makes 6 servings.

Each ½ cup serving contains about:

> 35 calories: 27 mg sodium; 0 cholesterol;
> 1 g fat; 7 g carbohydrate; tr protein; 3 g fiber.
> 30% calories from fat.
> Exchanges: 1 vegetable

MINTED BABY CARROTS

1½ pounds [675 g] small carrots, peeled
1 tablespoon low-calorie margarine
1 tablespoon brown sugar
2 tablespoons chopped fresh mint

Cook carrots according to directions for steaming vegetables (p. 126). Drain. Melt margarine in a small saucepan and stir in brown sugar. Add carrots and toss to coat well. Place on a serving platter and sprinkle with mint. Makes 6 servings.

Each ½ cup serving contains about:

> 44 calories; 64 mg sodium; 0 cholesterol; 1 g fat; 10 g
> carbohydrate; tr protein; 1 g fiber. 14% calories from fat.
> Exchanges: 1 vegetable

MUSHROOM SAUTÉ

An excellent flavor complement for beef, veal, or chicken.

> *1 tablespoon low-calorie margarine*
> *1 pound [450 g] mushrooms, sliced*
> *2 tablespoons chopped shallots*
> *3 tablespoons dry red wine*
> *2 tablespoons minced parsley*

Melt margarine in a large skillet and add mushrooms and shallots. Sauté until shallots are glazed and mushrooms are tender. Add wine and cook until juices reduce slightly, about 2 to 3 minutes. Stir in parsley. Makes 6 servings.

Each ½ cup serving contains about:

> 30 calories; 28 mg sodium; 0 cholesterol;
> 1 g fat; 4 g carbohydrate; tr protein;
> 1 g fiber. 31% calories from fat.
> Exchanges: 1 vegetable

PEAS AND PODS

High in calories and nutrients, too.

> *Romaine lettuce leaves*
> *1½ pounds [675 g] fresh peas, shelled, or 2 (10-ounce) [285 g] packages frozen peas*
> *1 pound [450 g] fresh pea pods (snow peas), or 1 (10-ounce) [285 g] package frozen pea pods*
> *4 green onions, thinly sliced*
> *2 tablespoons minced celery leaves*
> *½ teaspoon dried rosemary*
> *Pepper to taste*

Line a heavy skillet with 3 large lettuce leaves. Place peas and pea pods on lettuce leaves. Sprinkle with green onions, celery leaves, rosemary, and pepper. Top with another layer of lettuce leaves. Tightly cover and cook over medium heat 10 to 12 minutes, or until tender. Do not overcook or peas will stick to pan bottom. Cut up cooked lettuce leaves and serve with peas, if desired. Makes 8 servings.

NOTE: Those on an extremely low sodium-restricted diet should use fresh peas and pea pods.

Each ½ cup serving contains about:

> 60 calories; 8 mg sodium; 0 cholesterol;
> tr fat; 18 g carbohydrate; 2 g protein; 2 g fiber.
> 3% calories from fat.
> Exchanges: 1 B vegetable

RATATOUILLE

An excellent low-fat, no-cholesterol accompaniment to meats.

> 1 tablespoon olive oil or safflower oil
> 6 green onions, chopped
> 6 small zucchini, thinly sliced
> 4 cloves garlic, minced
>   Pepper to taste
> 1 medium eggplant, diced
> 1 small green bell pepper, chopped
> 3 tomatoes, peeled and chopped
> 2 teaspoons dried basil, or 2 tablespoons chopped fresh basil
> 1 teaspoon dried oregano, or 1 tablespoon chopped fresh
>   oregano
> 2 tablespoons chopped parsley

Using a Dutch oven or flameproof casserole, heat oil and add onions, zucchini, garlic, and pepper. Sauté for 2 minutes, stirring constantly. Add eggplant, green pepper, tomatoes, basil, and oregano. Cover and simmer 10 minutes. Remove cover and simmer until juices are reduced and thickened. Sprinkle with parsley. Serve hot or cold. Makes 6 servings.

Each ½ cup serving contains about:

> 25 calories; 9 mg sodium; 0 cholesterol;
> tr fat; 11 g carbohydrate; tr protein;
> 1 g fiber. 28% calories from fat.
> Exchanges: 1 vegetable

SAVORY GREEN BEANS

1¼ pounds [560 g] green beans, trimmed
½ cup [119 ml] low-sodium Chicken Stock (p. 38)
1 tablespoon low-calorie margarine
½ teaspoon dill weed or 1 fresh sprig dill, minced
¾ teaspoon dried marjoram or summer savory
  Lemon wedges

Cut beans on the diagonal into 1½-inch [4 cm] slices. Cook green beans in stock until tender. Drain and arrange on a heated platter. In a saucepan, melt margarine and add dill and marjoram. Spoon herb-margarine mixture over green beans and toss gently. Garnish with lemon wedges. Makes 6 servings.

Each ½ cup serving contains about:

> 25 calories; 29 mg sodium; 0 cholesterol;
> 1 g fat; 7 g carbohydrate; tr protein;
> 2 g fiber. 21% calories from fat.
> Exchanges: 1 vegetable

SHREDDED ZUCCHINI

2 pounds [900 g] zucchini or pattypan squash, trimmed
¼ cup [4 tablespoons] chopped parsley
3 cloves garlic, minced
1 tablespoon low-calorie margarine
6 green onions, chopped
  Pepper to taste
2 tablespoons grated Parmesan cheese (optional)

Shred the squash. In a skillet, combine the squash, parsley, garlic, margarine, onions, and pepper. Sauté over medium-high heat 2 minutes. To serve, sprinkle with cheese, if desired. Makes 6 servings.

Each ½ cup serving without cheese contains about:

> 21 calories; 19 mg sodium; 0 cholesterol;
> 6 g carbohydrate; tr protein; 1 g fiber.
> 8% calories from fat.
> Exchanges: 1 vegetable

WHIPPED BUTTERNUT SQUASH

1 (1½-pound) [675 g] butternut squash
2 tablespoons low-calorie margarine
1 tablespoon brown sugar
¼ teaspoon ground cinnamon
    Dash ground allspice
¼ cup [59 ml] unsweetened orange juice concentrate

Place squash on oven rack. Bake at 375°F [190°C] until it can be pierced easily with wood pick, about 1 hour. Cut in half and remove and discard seeds. Scoop out flesh and mash. Add margarine, brown sugar, cinnamon, allspice, and orange juice, and beat until smooth. Makes 6 servings.

Each ½ cup serving contains about:

> 87 calories: 52 mg sodium; 0 cholesterol;
> 2 g fat; 19 g carbohydrate; tr protein;
> 2 g fiber. 2% calories from fat.
> Exchanges: 1 vegetable, ¼ fat

ZUCCHINI OREGANO

1½ pounds [675 g] zucchini, sliced
1 large tomato, chopped
2 tablespoons minced shallots or green onions (white part only)
1 tablespoon fresh lemon juice
1½ teaspoons chopped fresh oregano, or ½ teaspoon dried oregano
1 tablespoon chopped parsley
    Pepper to taste

Place zucchini, tomato, and shallots in a skillet. Cover and cook over low heat until zucchini is crisp but tender. Place in a heated serving dish. In a small bowl, combine lemon juice, oregano, parsley, and pepper. Pour over zucchini mixture and mix gently. Makes 6 servings.

Each ½ cup serving contains about:

> 27 calories; 7 mg sodium; 0 cholesterol;
> tr fat; 6 g carbohydrate; tr protein;
> 1 g fiber. 8% calories from fat.
> Exchanges: 1 vegetable

———————— POTATOES ————————

CANDIED SWEETS

An excellent source of vitamin A and fiber.

> *3 medium sweet potatoes*
> *1½ tablespoons low-calorie margarine*
> *1½ teaspoons cornstarch*
> *⅛ teaspoon maple extract*
> *½ cup [119 ml] unsweetened pineapple juice concentrate*

Cook sweet potatoes in boiling water to cover until almost tender, about 20 minutes. Peel and cut lengthwise in ½-inch [1 cm] slices. Put the slices in a baking dish and set aside. Dissolve cornstarch and maple extract in pineapple juice concentrate in a small saucepan. Cook and stir until smooth and thickened. Spoon glaze over potatoes. Bake at 375°F [190°C] for about 20 minutes. Makes 6 servings.

Each ½ cup serving contains about:

> 81 calories; 41 mg sodium; 0 cholesterol;
> 2 g fat; 25 g carbohydrate; tr protein;
> 1 g fiber. 11% calories from fat.
> Exchanges: 1 bread

CHANTILLY POTATOES

> *3½ cups [829 ml] boiling water*
> *1 small onion, or 1 clove garlic, split*
> *1 bay leaf*
> *Celery leaves from 1 stalk celery*
> *3 medium potatoes (about 1½ pounds) [675 g], peeled and*
> *quartered*
> *¼ cup [59 ml] low-fat milk*
> *¼ cup [59 ml] low-calorie sour cream*
> *1 tablespoon low-calorie margarine*
> *1 tablespoon minced chives*
> *⅛ teaspoon each onion powder and garlic powder*
> *Pepper to taste*
> *⅛ teaspoon paprika*

Combine water, onion, bay leaf, and celery leaves in a large kettle. Bring to a boil, add potatoes, and cook, covered, until potatoes are tender, about 25 to 35 minutes. Remove and mash potatoes. Add milk, sour cream, and margarine to potatoes and beat until creamy. Blend in chives, onion powder, garlic powder, and pepper. Sprinkle with paprika. Makes 6 servings.

Each ½ cup serving contains about:

> 84 calories; 59 mg sodium; 5 mg cholesterol;
> 2 g fat; 15 g carbohydrate; 1 g protein;
> tr fiber. 21% calories from fat.
> Exchanges: ½ bread, 1 fat

OVEN-FRIED POTATOES

You'll preserve nutrients and fiber if you don't peel.

> *3 medium potatoes, peeled or unpeeled*
> *2 tablespoons low-calorie margarine, melted*
> *1½ teaspoons olive oil*
> *Paprika*

Cut potatoes lengthwise into strips about 4-by-½-by-¼ inches [10-by-1½-by-½ cm]. Arrange in a single layer on a baking sheet. Pour margarine and olive oil over potatoes, and toss to coat well. Sprinkle with paprika. Bake at 450°F [232°C] for 30 to 40 minutes, tossing several times during baking. Drain on paper toweling. Makes 6 servings.

Each serving (½ potato) contains about:

> 83 calories; 55 mg sodium; 0 cholesterol;
> 3 g fat; 21 g carbohydrate; tr protein;
> 1 g fiber. 25% calories from fat.
> Exchanges: ½ bread, ½ fat

POMMES PARISIENNE

> *24 small new red potatoes*
> *1 tablespoon low-calorie margarine*
> *1 tablespoon olive oil*
> *3 tablespoons chopped parsley, dill, chives, or rosemary*
> *leaves*

Peel a thin strip of skin from around the center of each potato. Place potatoes in 1 inch [2½ cm] of water in a saucepan. Bring to a boil, cover, reduce heat, and simmer until tender, about 25 minutes. Drain. Melt margarine with olive oil in a saucepan over low heat and add potatoes. Shake pan gently until potatoes are well coated. Sprinkle with parsley. Makes 6 servings.

Each serving (4 potatoes) contains about:

> 100 calories; 30 mg sodium; 0 cholesterol;
> 3 g fat; 23 g carbohydrate; tr protein;
> 1 g fiber. 18% calories from fat.
> Exchanges: 1 bread, ½ fat

Potatoes are loaded with vitamin C, supply fiber and iron, and are practically free of salt and fat. Stick to our low-calorie fillings and your baked potato is easy and quick to prepare—the perfect one-dish meal.

POTATOES VEGETARIAN

4 (7-ounce) [200 g] baking potatoes
1 cup [115 g] broccoli flowerets, steamed until tender
4 ounces [115 g] low-fat Cheddar cheese, shredded
Freshly ground pepper, to taste.

Place potatoes on a rack in oven and bake at 425°F [218°C] (or microwave according to manufacturer's directions) until tender when pierced with a fork, about 1 hour. Remove from oven, split open and fill each potato with ¼ cup [29 g] broccoli, chopped, 1 ounce [28 g] cheese, and pepper to taste.

Each potato contains about:

> 298 calories; 117 mg sodium; 0 cholesterol;
> 4 g fat; 54 mg carbohydrate; 12 g protein;
> 4 g fiber. 13% calories from fat.
> Exchanges: 1 bread, 1 milk, 1 fat

POTATOES NICOISE

4 (7-ounce) [200 g] baking potatoes
4 leaves lettuce, shredded
4 ounces [115 g] tuna, water-packed, loosened
2 small tomatoes, chopped
2 whites of hard-boiled egg, chopped
1 teaspoon caper, minced, optional
¼ cup [59 ml] low-calorie Italian salad dressing, or
*   2 tablespoons olive oil and 2 tablespoons wine*
*   vinegar, mixed*
*   Freshly ground pepper to taste*

Place potatoes in oven on a rack. Bake at 425°F [218°C] (or microwave according to manufacturer's directions) until tender when pierced with a fork, about 1 hour. Remove from oven, split open, and fill each potato with one-fourth of the lettuce, 1 ounce tuna, ½ tomato, ½ white of a hard-boiled egg, and ¼ teaspoon capers, and sprinkle on dressing mixture and pepper to taste.

Each potato contains about:

> 322 calories; 358 mg sodium; 18 mg cholesterol;
> 5 g fat; 54 mg carbohydrate; 15 mg protein;
> 5 g fiber. 16% calories from fat.
> Exchanges: 2 bread, 1 meat

SALADS

You don't have to do much to make salads conform to *Light Style* eating, because they are naturally light.

But we trim calories, fats, and cholesterol even further by using low-fat dressings and sauces with the help of low-fat yogurt, low-fat sour cream, evaporated nonfat milk, and unsweetened fruit juices. No salt is added, but we do employ herbs and use low-fat and low-cholesterol cheeses where appropriate.

Salads require some care to make them as crisp and appealing as possible. Wash greens and shake out any excess moisture to keep them crisp. Wrap well-drained greens in a clean towel or plastic bag and use them within a day. It's better to replenish the vegetable bin than risk deterioration of nutrients and looks by storing them too long. Keep salads chilled (but not ice cold) until ready to serve.

Add the dressing at the last moment to prevent wilting, unless the recipe specifies earlier use of the dressing.

You'll find a *Light Style* salad for every occasion. There are main-dish salads, side-dish salads, and sparkling buffet fruit salads. And all of them are as low in calories, fats, cholesterol, and salt as we could make them.

———————— VEGETABLE SALADS ————————

AVOCADO SALAD

¼ cup [59 ml] low-sodium Soy Sauce (p. 187)
¼ cup [59 ml] dry white wine
3 avocados
　Lettuce leaves
　Lemon wedges

Combine Soy Sauce and wine and chill. When ready to serve, cut avocados in half lengthwise and remove pits, but do not peel. Arrange avocado halves on a bed of lettuce leaves on a platter or on individual plates. Pour about 1½ tablespoons of the chilled soy mixture into each avocado cavity. Garnish with lemon wedges. Makes 6 servings.

Each serving contains about:

168 calories; 62 mg sodium; 0 cholesterol;
15 g fat; 8 g carbohydrate; 2 g protein;
2 g fiber. 78% calories from fat.
Exchanges: 4 fat

CALIFORNIA TOSTADA

This handsome meal-in-a-dish, do-it-yourself salad-sandwich borrowed from the Mexican cuisine makes wonderful party food. Stack the toasted tortillas, place the fillings in separate bowls, and allow guests to make their own highrise salads. Just double, triple, or quadruple the recipe according to the size of the crowd.

6 corn tortillas
1¼ cups [190 g] shredded cooked chicken, pork, or beef
1¼ cups [81 g] shredded iceberg lettuce
1¼ cups [252 g] chopped tomatoes
6 tablespoons grated low fat Cheddar cheese
¾ cup Spanish Sauce (p. 174)
6 tablespoons Guacamole (p. 15, optional)
3 tablespoons low-calorie sour cream
2 tablespoons minced green onion
Cilantro sprigs (fresh coriander)

Place tortillas on an oven rack and bake at 450°F [232°C] until toasted and crisp. Place each tortilla on a dinner plate. Top each tortilla with about 3 tablespoons *each* chicken, lettuce, tomato, 1 tablespoon Cheddar cheese, 2 tablespoons Spanish Sauce, and 1 tablespoon Guacamole. Top each tostada with ½ tablespoon sour cream. Sprinkle with green onion and garnish with cilantro sprigs. Makes 6 servings.

Each tostada with Guacamole contains about:

211 calories; 214 mg sodium; 14 mg cholesterol;
7 g fat; 21 g carbohydrate; 16 g protein;
3 g fiber. 29% calories from fat.
Exchanges: 1 bread, 1 meat, 1 vegetable, 1 fat

CHINESE CHICKEN SALAD

3 chicken breasts (about 1½ pounds [675 g] boned weight),
* skinned, boned, and split*
½ cup [119 ml] low-sodium Chicken Stock (p. 38)
1 head iceberg lettuce, shredded
4 green onions, sliced
¼ cup [4 tablespoons] chopped cilantro (fresh coriander)
1 (4-ounce) [115 g] can water chestnuts, thinly sliced
1 stalk celery, thinly sliced
3 radishes, thinly sliced
2 tablespoons sesame seeds, toasted*
* Rice Vinegar Dressing (p. 165)*

Place chicken breasts in a skillet with stock, cover, and cook over low heat for 10 to 15 minutes. Remove from stock and let cool. Dice chicken meat and combine with lettuce, onions, cilantro, water chestnuts, celery, radishes, and sesame seeds. Drizzle with Rice Vinegar Dressing and toss to mix well. Makes 6 servings.

*To toast sesame seeds, place in a dry pan over medium heat and heat, stirring, until golden.

Each serving with dressing contains about:

227 calories; 81 mg sodium; 60 mg cholesterol;
8 g fat; 6 g carbohydrate; 28 g protein;
1 g fiber. 33% calories from fat.
Exchanges: 3 meat, 1 vegetable

COLESLAW DE LUXE

¾ cup [180 g] low-fat plain yogurt
½ cup [115 g] low-fat vanilla yogurt
2 tablespoons low-calorie mayonnaise
1 tablespoon fresh lemon juice
½ teaspoon celery seeds
1 tablespoon chopped chives
⅛ teaspoon pepper
1 head cabbage, shredded
1 small carrot, grated
1 (4-ounce) [115 g] can unsweetened crushed pineapple,
    well drained

Mix together yogurts and mayonnaise until smooth. Add lemon juice, celery seeds, chives, and pepper and mix well. Fold in cabbage, carrots, and pineapple until evenly coated. Chill. Makes 12 servings.

Each ½ cup serving contains about:

> 49 calories; 44 mg sodium; 2 mg cholesterol;
> 1 g fat; 8 g carbohydrate; 2 g protein;
> 1 g fiber. 17% calories from fat.
> Exchanges: 1 vegetable, ¼ fat

CUCUMBERS IN YOGURT

2 large cucumbers, peeled
1 cup [225 g] low-fat plain yogurt
1 tablespoon fresh lemon juice
3 cloves garlic, minced
¼ teaspoon pepper
1 tablespoon each chopped parsley and chives or green
    onion tops
¼ teaspoon Worcestershire sauce (optional)
    Butter lettuce leaves

Cut cucumbers in halves lengthwise and scrape out seeds with spoon. Thinly slice cucumbers and place in bowl. Combine yogurt, lemon juice, garlic, pepper, parsley, chives, and Worcestershire sauce. Add to cucumber slices and toss to coat well. Chill 1 hour. Serve on bed of lettuce leaves. Makes 8 servings.

Each ½ cup serving contains about:

> 33 calories; 27 mg sodium; 2 mg cholesterol; tr fat;
> 5 g carbohydrate; tr protein; tr fiber. Tr calories from fat.
> Exchanges: 1 vegetable

ENDIVE-WATERCRESS SALAD

1 large or 2 small Belgian endives
1 bunch watercress
⅓ cup [79 ml] Lemon Dressing (p. 163)
1 tablespoon chopped pecans
1 tomato, cut in wedges

Cut large endive into eighths and small ones into quarters lengthwise. Immerse in cold water and let soak for 10 minutes. Drain and dry well. Chill 1 hour before using. (Endive should be crisp when ready to use.) Wash, drain, and dry watercress. Wrap in a clean dry cloth and refrigerate until ready to use. Just before serving, combine endive and watercress in a bowl. Add dressing and toss. Sprinkle with pecans and garnish with tomato wedges. Makes 6 servings.

Each 1 cup serving contains about:

> 42 calories; 13 mg sodium; 0 cholesterol;
> 3 g fat; 3 g carbohydrate; tr protein;
> 1 g fiber. 35% calories from fat.
> Exchanges: ½ fat

FABULOUS SALAD

1 bunch spinach
1 small head butter lettuce
1 small head red leaf lettuce
¼ head romaine lettuce
2 tablespoons chopped chives
2 tablespoons chopped parsley
1 teaspoon dried tarragon
2 teaspoons Dijon Mustard (p. 182)
3 tablespoons egg substitute, or 1 egg white
  Juice of 1 lemon
3 tablespoons vegetable oil
½ cup [115 g] low-calorie sour cream or low-fat plain
  yogurt
  Dash hot pepper sauce
1 cup [151 g] cooked tiny bay shrimp or small shrimp,
  deveined, optional
  Pepper to taste

Tear spinach and lettuces in bite-size pieces and combine with chives and parsley. Chill. In a small bowl, combine tarragon, mustard, egg substitute or egg white, and lemon juice and stir briskly to blend well. Slowly add oil, beating constantly until thickened. Stir in sour cream and hot pepper sauce. Add to greens with shrimp and toss to coat well. Sprinkle generously with pepper. Makes 12 servings.

NOTE: If on a low-cholesterol diet, substitute Alaskan king crab for shrimp.

Each 1 cup serving contains about:

> 71 calories; 56 mg sodium; 27 mg cholesterol;
> 5 g fat; 3 g carbohydrate; 4 g protein;
> 1 g fiber. 63% calories from fat.
> Exchanges: 1 B vegetable, 1 fat

GINGHAM SALAD

1 cup [225 g] low-fat cottage cheese
¼ teaspoon celery seeds
3 tablespoons chopped chives
1½ cups [150 g] coarsely chopped spinach leaves
2 cups [202 g] shredded red cabbage
6 large lettuce leaves
6 tablespoons Buttermilk-Cucumber Dressing (p. 161)

Combine cottage cheese, celery seeds, and chives in a bowl and mix well. Add spinach and cabbage and toss to coat well. For each serving, place a ½-cup serving on a lettuce leaf and top with 1 tablespoon dressing. Makes 6 servings.

Each ½ cup serving contains about:

56 calories; 187 mg sodium; 3 mg cholesterol;
tr fat; 5 g carbohydrate; 6 g protein;
1 g fiber. 16% calories from fat.
Exchanges: ½ meat

MARINATED MUSHROOMS

1 pound [450 g] large mushrooms, sliced
2 tablespoons chopped parsley
1 teaspoon dried tarragon
¼ cup [59 ml] Lemon Dressing (p. 163)

Combine mushroom slices, parsley, and tarragon in a bowl. Pour dressing over mushroom mixture and toss to coat well. Chill at least 1 hour before serving. Makes 6 servings.

Each ½ cup serving contains about:

31 calories; 4 mg sodium; 0 cholesterol;
2 g fat; 5 g carbohydrate; tr protein;
1 g fiber. 55% calories from fat.
Exchanges: 1 vegetable, ¼ fat

MEDITERRANEAN SALAD

1 cucumber, sliced
1 bunch radishes, trimmed
1 red bell pepper, cut in strips
1 green bell pepper, cut in strips
3 tomatoes, cut in wedges
½ bunch chicory or curly endive lettuce, shredded
6 green onions, sliced
¼ cup [59 ml] Oregano Dressing (p. 164)
2 tablespoons crumbled feta cheese or low-sodium cheese

Combine cucumber, radishes, peppers, tomatoes, chicory, and onions in a bowl. Drizzle with Oregano Dressing and toss. Sprinkle with feta cheese. Makes 6 servings.

NOTE: Use low-sodium cheese if on a sodium-restricted diet.

Each ½ cup serving with dressing and cheese contains about:

> 45 calories; 52 mg sodium; 2 mg cholesterol;
> 3 g fat; 9 g carbohydrate; 2 g protein;
> 1 g fiber. 40% calories from fat.
> Exchanges: 1 vegetable, 1 fat

ORANGE-CAULIFLOWER SALAD

3 oranges, peeled and sectioned, or 2 (10½-ounce) [298 g]
*   cans unsweetened mandarin orange segments, drained*
1 medium head cauliflower, separated in flowerets
½ cup [115 g] chopped green bell pepper
2 cups [202 g] chopped spinach leaves
¼ cup [59 ml] Orange Blossom Dressing (p. 164)
*   Lettuce leaves*
2 tablespoons slivered almonds

Combine orange segments, cauliflowerets, green pepper, spinach, and Orange Blossom Dressing in a bowl. Toss and place 1 cup salad on lettuce leaf for each serving. Sprinkle with almonds. Makes 6 servings.

Each 1 cup serving contains about:

> 55 calories; 27 mg sodium; 0 cholesterol;
> 1 g fat; 14 g carbohydrate; tr protein;
> 3 g fiber. 20% calories from fat.
> Exchanges: 1 fruit

SCANDINAVIAN CUCUMBERS

2 medium cucumbers, thinly sliced
1 small onion, thinly sliced
½ cup [119 ml] rice or tarragon vinegar
½ cup [119 ml] water
2 sprigs fresh dill, chopped, or 1 teaspoon dill weed

Combine cucumber and onion slices in a bowl. Combine vinegar and water and pour over cucumber mixture. Cover and chill at least 2 hours. Drain, then sprinkle with dill to serve. Makes 6 servings.

Each ½ cup serving contains about:

19 calories; 5 mg sodium; 0 cholesterol;
tr fat; 5 g carbohydrate; tr protein;
tr fiber. 4% calories from fat.
Exchanges: 1 vegetable

TOMATO-CAULIFLOWER SALAD

1 medium head cauliflower, separated into flowerets
2 tomatoes, cut in wedges
1 onion, thinly sliced
3 tablespoons chopped parsley
¼ cup [59 ml] Herb Dressing (p. 163)

Cook flowerets in 1 inch [2½ cm] boiling water until tender, about 15 minutes; drain. Combine flowerets, tomatoes, onion, parsley, and dressing and marinate 1 hour. Serve at room temperature. Makes 6 servings.

NOTE: If using red onion, do not add it until after the salad has marinated, as the red color will leach out and discolor salad. Add and toss just before serving.

Each ½ cup serving contains about:

45 calories; 23 mg sodium; 0 cholesterol;
3 g fat; 6 g carbohydrate; tr protein;
1 g fiber. 30% calories from fat.
Exchanges: 1 vegetable, ½ fat

TOMATO-MUSHROOM SALAD

½ pound [225 g] mushrooms, sliced
2 medium tomatoes, sliced ¼ inch [½ cm] thick
½ cup [60 g] thinly sliced green onions
2 tablespoons chopped parsley or cilantro (fresh coriander)
¼ cup [59 ml] Basil Dressing (p. 161)

Combine mushrooms, tomatoes, onions, and parsley in a bowl. Add Basil Dressing and toss to coat well. Chill at least 1 hour. Makes 6 servings.

Each ½ cup serving with dressing contains about:

> 46 calories; 6 mg sodium; 0 cholesterol;
> 3 g fat; 5 g carbohydrate; tr protein;
> 1 g fiber. 30% calories from fat.
> Exchanges: 1 vegetable, ½ fat

FRUIT SALADS

AVOCADO-ORANGE SALAD

¼ head romaine lettuce
¼ head iceberg lettuce
1 head butter lettuce
2 navel oranges, peeled and sectioned, or 2 (10½-ounce cans) [298 g] unsweetened mandarin orange segments, drained
½ medium red onion, thinly sliced
½ small avocado, peeled, pitted, and cut into chunks
Orange Juice Vinaigrette (following recipe)

Wash, dry, and tear lettuces into bite-size pieces. Arrange lettuce on individual salad plates, and top with orange segments, onions, and avocado chunks. Pour dressing evenly over each plate. Serves 12.

ORANGE JUICE VINAIGRETTE

¼ cup [59 ml] rice vinegar
¼ cup [59 ml] orange juice
1 teaspoon grated orange peel
Juice of 1 lemon
1 tablespoon sugar
¼ teaspoon dry mustard
2 tablespoons vegetable oil

In a small bowl combine vinegar, orange juice, orange peel, lemon juice, sugar, dry mustard, and oil. Mix until well combined.

Each serving of salad with vinaigrette contains about:

60 calories; 3 mg sodium; 0 cholesterol;
4 g fat; 6 g carbohydrate; 0 g protein;
1 g fiber. 58% calories from fat.
Exchanges: 1 fruit, 1½ fat

CALIFORNIA SALAD

2 grapefruits, peeled and sectioned
2 oranges, peeled and sectioned, or 1 (10½-ounce) [298 g]
   can unsweetened mandarin orange segments, drained
   Butter lettuce leaves
⅓ cup [79 ml] Buttermilk-Cucumber Dressing (p. 161)
*2 tablespoons slivered almonds, toasted**

For each serving, arrange 3 grapefruit sections and 4 orange segments on a leaf of lettuce. Drizzle with 1 tablespoon Buttermilk-Cucumber Dressing. Garnish with toasted almonds. Makes 6 servings.

* To toast almonds, place in a dry pan over medium heat and heat, stirring, until golden.

Each 1 cup serving without dressing contains about:

55 calories; 16 mg sodium; 0 cholesterol;
2 g fat; 14 g carbohydrate; tr protein;
2 g fiber. 20% calories from fat.
Exchanges: 1 fruit

CANTALOUPE CRAB BOATS

3 small cantaloupes
  Romaine lettuce leaves
1 cup [225 g] diced celery
1 pound [450 g] Alaskan king crab meat, shredded (fresh or
  frozen), or 2 (6½-ounce) [184 g] cans water-packed,
  unsalted tuna, drained
6 tablespoons Green Goddess Yogurt Dressing (p. 162)

Cut cantaloupes in half crosswise. Scoop out and discard seeds. Using a serrated flexible knife, cut out flesh, leaving shells intact. Dice cantaloupe flesh. Line each cantaloupe shell with lettuce leaves. Combine diced cantaloupe, celery, and crab meat and pile into melon shells. Cover and chill at least 20 minutes. Place each shell on a bed of lettuce leaves on a plate. Top each salad with 1 tablespoon Green Goddess Yogurt Dressing. Makes 6 servings.

NOTE: Canned crab has a high salt content. We suggest that those watching their salt intake use only fresh or frozen Alaskan king crab meat.

Each serving with dressing contains about:

> 161 calories; 42 mg sodium; 41 mg cholesterol;
> 2 g fat; 19 g carbohydrate; 17 g protein;
> 2 g fiber. 13% calories from fat.
> Exchanges: 2½ meat, 1 fruit

CHICKEN-STUFFED PAPAYA

3 chicken breasts (about 1½ pounds [675 g] boned weight)
1 cup [237 ml] low-sodium Chicken Stock (p. 38)
⅓ cup [76 g] low-sodium, low-calorie mayonnaise
⅓ cup [76 g] low-fat plain yogurt
½ teaspoon Dijon mustard
1 tablespoon fresh lime juice
½ cup [115 g] chopped celery
2 tablespoons chopped green onion
2 tablespoons chopped chives
½ teaspoon ground ginger or curry powder
  Pepper to taste
3 papayas
  Lettuce leaves
*2 tablespoons slivered almonds, toasted**
  Watercress or parsley sprigs or lime slices (optional)

Skin, bone, and split chicken breasts. Place chicken in a skillet and add stock. Cover and simmer 10 to 15 minutes, or until chicken is tender. Drain, cool, and cube chicken. Combine mayonnaise, yogurt, mustard, lime juice, celery, onion, chives, ginger, and pepper and blend well. Add cubed chicken and toss to coat well. Chill.

Peel and halve papayas. Scoop out and discard seeds. Arrange each papaya half on a serving plate lined with lettuce leaves. Pile chicken salad in papaya cavities and sprinkle with almonds. Garnish with watercress sprigs, if desired. Makes 6 servings.

* To toast almonds, place in a dry pan over medium heat and heat, stirring, until golden.

Each serving contains about:

> 189 calories, 147 mg sodium, 46 mg
> cholesterol; 8 g fat; 14 g carbohydrate;
> 17 g protein; 2 g fiber. 36% calories
> from fat.
> Exchanges: 3 meat, 1 fruit

BLOSSOM PEACH SALAD

⅓ cup [76 g] Cream Cheese (p. 185)
2 tablespoons chopped pecans
6 ripe peaches
  Fresh lemon juice
  Watercress sprigs
2 tablespoons Orange Blossom Dressing (p. 164)
  Mint leaves

Divide cheese into 6 equal portions. Form each portion into a ball, then roll in chopped nuts. Peel and pit peaches and cut in half if using fresh peaches. Place a ball of cheese between 2 peach halves and press back into shape of peach. Brush with lemon juice to prevent discoloration. (Omit this step if using canned peaches.) Chill in a covered container until ready to use. Place each stuffed peach on a bed of watercress. Drizzle each peach with 1 teaspoon Orange Blossom Dressing and garnish with mint leaves. Makes 6 servings.

NOTE: Any fresh fruit or fruit canned in water may be substituted for the peaches.

Each serving without dressing contains about:

> 90 calories; 29 mg sodium; 3 mg cholesterol;
> 3 g fat; 15 g carbohydrate; 2 g protein;
> 2 g fiber. 23% calories from fat.
> Exchanges: 1 fruit, ½ fat

WALDORF SALAD

A low-caloried twist to a favorite classic salad.

> *Juice of 1 lemon*
> *3 red Delicious apples, diced*
> *1 cup [225 g] diced celery*
> *¼ cup [41 g] raisins*
> *⅓ cup [50 g] pecans or walnuts, chopped*
> *¾ cup [340 g] low-fat vanilla yogurt*
> *Lettuce leaves*

Sprinkle lemon juice over diced apples to prevent discoloration. Combine apples, celery, raisins, pecans, and yogurt in a bowl. Toss to coat well. Arrange on a bed of lettuce. Makes 12 servings.

Each ½ cup serving contains about:

> 63 calories; 19 mg sodium; 1 mg
> cholesterol; 3 g fat; 10 g carbohydrate;
> 1 g protein; 2 g fiber. 34% calories
> from fat.
> Exchanges: ½ fat, 1 fruit

———————— GELATIN SALADS ————————

AUTUMN SALAD

> *2 (⅜-ounce) [18 g] packages regular or low-calorie lime-*
>   *flavored gelatin*
> *2 cups [473 ml] boiling water*
> *1 (8-ounce) [225 g] can unsweetened crushed pineapple*
> *1 cup [150 g] grated carrots*
> *¼ cup [38 g] chopped walnuts*
> *¼ cup [115 g] low-calorie mayonnaise*

Dissolve gelatin in boiling water. Drain pineapple, reserving juice. Combine reserved juice and enough cold water to make 1 cup [237 ml]. Stir into gelatin mixture and chill until syrupy. Fold in drained pineapple, carrrots, and walnuts and turn into an 8-inch [20 cm] square pan. Chill until firm. Cut into squares to serve. Top each serving with 1 teaspoon mayonnaise. Makes 12 servings.

Each serving regular flavored gelatin (2⅔-by-2⅔ inches) contains about:

> 55 calories; 44 mg sodium; 2 mg cholesterol;
> 3 g fat; 5 g carbohydrate; 3 g protein.
> 48% calories from fat.
> Exchanges: 1 bread, ½ fruit, ½ fat (½ fruit, ½ fat if using low-calorie gelatin)

SUNSHINE SALAD

2 (⅝-ounce) [18 g] packages regular or low-calorie lemon-flavored gelatin
2 cups [473 ml] boiling water
1 (8-ounce) [225 g] can unsweetened mandarin orange sections
1 (8-ounce) [225 g] can unsweetened crushed pineapple
1 (4-ounce) [115 g] can unsweetened grapefruit sections
½ cup [91 g] Heavenly Whipped Topping (p. 184)
2 tablespoons toasted unsweetened shredded coconut, optional

Dissolve gelatin in boiling water. Drain juice from cans of orange, pineapple, and grapefruit, reserving 2 cups [473 ml] juice. Stir reserved juice into gelatin mixture. Chill until syrupy. Fold in well-drained fruit. Turn into an 8-inch [20 cm] square pan and chill until firm. Spread Heavenly Whipped Topping over gelatin. Sprinkle with toasted coconut. Cut into squares to serve. Makes 9 servings.

Each serving (2⅔-by-2⅔ inches) without coconut contains about:

> 42 calories; 18 mg sodium; 0 cholesterol;
> tr fat; 8 g carbohydrate; tr protein;
> 1 g fiber. Tr calories from fat.
> Exchanges: 1 bread, 1 fruit (1 fruit if using low-calorie gelatin)

HOLIDAY SALAD

2 (⅝-ounce) [18 g] packages regular or low-calorie
   strawberry-flavored gelatin
1 quart [1 L] boiling water
1 basket [450 g] strawberries, hulled and sliced, or 1 (10-
   ounce) [285 g] package frozen, unsweetened strawberries,
   thawed
1 (20-ounce) [560 g] can unsweetened pineapple chunks,
   drained
1 cup [225 g] low-calorie Cream Cheese (p. 185)
1 cup [225 g] low-fat strawberry or vanilla yogurt
1 cup [181 g] Heavenly Whipped Topping (p. 184)

Dissolve gelatin in boiling water. Chill until syrupy. Fold in strawberries
and pineapple. Pour half the mixture into a 1½-quart [1½ L] mold and chill
until just firm. Spread Cream Cheese evenly over set gelatin, then spread
strawberry yogurt over Cream Cheese. Pour remaining gelatin mixture
over yogurt. Chill at least 24 hours. Unmold onto serving plate. Serve with
Heavenly Whipped Topping. Makes 12 servings.

Each ½ cup serving of regular flavored gelatin with topping contains
about:

> 84 calories; 64 mg sodium; 5 mg cholesterol;
> 1 g fat; 13 g carbohydrate; 5 g protein;
> 1 g fiber. 15% calories from fat.
> Exchanges: 1 bread, 1 fruit, ¼ milk (1 fruit, ¼ milk if using
> low-calorie gelatin)

WALNUT-FIG-SPINACH SALAD

1 *small red onion, thinly sliced*

2 *tablespoons tarragon wine vinegar*

2 *tablespoons lemon juice*

1 *teaspoon Dijon mustard*

1 *tablespoon walnut oil or salad oil*

1 *tablespoon olive oil*

¼ *teaspoon freshly ground pepper*

½ *teaspoon dried tarragon, or 2 tablespoons fresh, chopped tarragon*

2 *bunches fresh spinach, washed, dried and cut into bite-size pieces*

3 *dried or fresh figs, sliced crosswise*

¾ *cup [85 g] julienned jicama*

1 *small red pepper, cut in ⅛-inch [½ cm] strips*

6 *radishes, sliced*

⅓ *cup [50 g] coarsely chopped walnuts, toasted, or sliced water chestnuts*

Place red onion in a strainer. Pour on boiling water to wilt. Drain. Place in a small bowl. Combine vinegar, lemon juice, mustard, oils, pepper, and tarragon and stir until well blended. Add the red onion to the dressing and toss. In a large bowl, combine spinach, figs, jicama, red pepper, and radishes. Add marinated onions and walnuts or water chestnuts and toss. Makes 6 servings.

Each serving contains about:

> 133 calories; 61 mg sodium; 0 cholesterol;
> 9 g fat; 13 g carbohydrate; 3 g protein;
> 4 g fiber. 17% calories from fat.
> Exchanges: 1 fruit, 1½ fat

SALAD DRESSINGS

If convenience is a priority, by all means use the commercial brand salad dressings. The grocery aisles are filled with far more types, flavors, and sizes today than when we first printed our recipes in 1979.

However, if you insist on quality, quantity, and cost control, or if you wish to cut salt, these homemade dressings are for you.

The dressings in this chapter contain no added salt and are low in cholesterol and fat. They have no preservatives and they cost a fraction of their commercial counterparts.

There is a bonus, too: by using these recipes you learn how to modify your own dressing concoctions. To lower serum blood cholesterol, we suggest using olive oil, a monounsaturated oil with beneficial fatty acids, but you can check the fat comparison chart on p. 276 to determine which oil is best suited to your needs. You may, for instance, want to use canola oil (called Puritan oil in markets), which is even lower in saturated fat and higher in monounsaturated fat than any other vegetable oil.

Our cream dressings make use of low-fat or nonfat dairy products. We compensate the lack of salt in the dressings by using herbs, fruit juices, and flavored vinegars. Fresh herbs are more subtle flavor enhancers than dried ones; use the type best suited to your taste and the recipe.

If you use vinaigrette-type dressings, we encourage you to use balsamic, tarragon, and champagne vinegars for flavor enhancement. If you use vinaigrette dressings often, you might want to prepare them in quantity and store them in jars with tight-fitting lids for up to a month. Creamy dressings should be stored in the refrigerator for no longer than a week. To cut calories and fat, use a spray bottle to spray on dressing evenly but lightly over a salad.

And remember, in this chapter you will find the percentages of calories from fat in the high range, but the total fat content of salad dressings is relatively low. The percentage of calories from fat will be relatively high, though the actual amount of calories is small. Remember when you add the dressing to vegetables or pasta dishes, the percentage of fat is reduced.

BASIL DRESSING

¼ cup [59 ml] safflower oil
3 tablespoons wine vinegar or rice vinegar, or fresh lemon
    juice
¼ cup [59 ml] water
2 tablespoons minced fresh basil, or 1½ teaspoons dried
    basil
1 teaspoon finely chopped garlic
Pepper to taste

Combine oil, vinegar, water, basil, garlic, and pepper to taste in blender container. Blend until smooth. Makes ¾ cup.

Each 1 tablespoon serving contains about:

42 calories; 0 sodium; 0 cholesterol;
4 g fat; tr carbohydrate; 0 protein;
0 fiber. 96% calories from fat.
Exchanges: 1 fat

BUTTERMILK-CUCUMBER DRESSING

¼ cup [59 ml] buttermilk
2¼ tablespoons low-fat cottage cheese
1½ tablespoons fresh lemon juice
1 teaspoon dill weed, or
    1 tablespoon chopped fresh dill
1 clove garlic, minced
Pepper to taste
½ cucumber, peeled and diced
⅓ cup [60 g] diced red bell pepper or sliced radishes
    (optional)

Mix together buttermilk, cottage cheese, lemon juice, garlic, and pepper. Stir in cucumber and red pepper. Chill. Makes about ¾ cup [178 ml].

Each 2 tablespoon serving contains about:

> 16 calories; 34 mg sodium; 1 mg cholesterol;
> tr fat; 3 g carbohydrate; 1 g protein;
> tr fiber. 16% calories from fat.
> Exchanges: negligible

CREAMY GARLIC DRESSING

1¼ [285 g] low-fat plain yogurt
½ cup [119 ml] nonfat milk or evaporated nonfat milk
4 cloves garlic, minced
1 teaspoon dried basil, or 1 tablespoon chopped fresh basil
1 teaspoon dried oregano, or 1 tablespoon chopped fresh oregano
1 teaspoon dried rosemary, or 1 tablespoon chopped fresh rosemary
1 teaspoon dried sage, or 1 tablespoon chopped fresh sage
1 teaspoon dill weed, or 1 tablespoon chopped fresh dill

Combine yogurt, milk, garlic, basil, oregano, rosemary, sage, and dill in blender container and blend until smooth. Makes about 1¾ cups [414 ml].

Each 2 tablespoon serving contains about:

> 18 calories; 19 mg sodium; 1 mg cholesterol;
> tr fat; 2 g carbohydrate; 1 g protein;
> tr fiber. 19% calories from fat.
> Exchanges: negligible

GREEN GODDESS YOGURT DRESSING

2 tablespoons white wine vinegar or rice vinegar
¾ teaspoon dried tarragon, or 1 tablespoon chopped fresh tarragon
1½ tablespoons chopped green onion or chives
3 tablespoons minced parsley
¾ cup [180 g] low-fat plain yogurt
¼ cup [60 g] low-calorie mayonnaise

Combine vinegar, tarragon, onion, parsley, yogurt, and mayonnaise in a blender container. Blend until smooth and very green, 2 to 3 minutes. Makes about 1½ cups [355 ml].

Each 1 tablespoon serving contains about:

>11 calories; 18 mg sodium; 1 mg cholesterol;
>tr fat; 1 g carbohydrate; tr protein;
>0 fiber. 4% calories from fat.
>Exchanges: negligible

HERB DRESSING

3 tablespoons safflower oil
2 teaspoons chopped parsley
2 teaspoons chopped chives
2 teaspoons dried chervil, or 2 tablespoons chopped fresh chervil
  Pepper to taste
½ cup [119 ml] rice vinegar
2 tablespoons water
3 cloves garlic, minced
2 teaspoons dry mustard

Combine oil, parsley, chives, chervil, pepper, vinegar, water, garlic, and dry mustard in a blender container. Blend well. Makes 1 cup [237 ml].

Each 1 tablespoon serving contains about:

>23 calories; 0 mg sodium; 0 cholesterol;
>3 g fat; 1 g carbohydrate; tr protein;
>0 fiber. 89% calories from fat.
>Exchanges: 1 fat

LEMON DRESSING

¼ cup [59 ml] fresh lemon juice
2 tablespoons water
1 teaspoon Dijon Mustard (p. 182)
  Pinch cayenne pepper
2 tablespoons olive oil or vegetable oil
½ teaspoon dried chervil, or 1½ teaspoons chopped fresh chervil
½ teaspoon dried tarragon, or 1½ teaspoons chopped fresh tarragon
2 tablespoons chopped pecans (optional)

Combine lemon juice, water, mustard, and pepper in a blender container and blend well. Add oil, chervil, and tarragon and blend to a smooth sauce. Mix in nuts, if desired. Makes ½ cup [119 ml].

Each 1 tablespoon serving without pecans contains about:

> 15 calories; 8 mg sodium; 0 cholesterol;
> tr fat; 3 g carbohydrate; tr protein;
> 0 fiber. 6% calories from fat.
> Exchanges: ½ fat

ORANGE BLOSSOM DRESSING

1 cup [225 g] low-fat plain yogurt
½ cup [119 ml] evaporated nonfat milk
1 (6-ounce) [180 g] can frozen unsweetened orange juice concentrate, thawed

Combine yogurt, milk, and orange juice in a blender container and blend well. Makes 2½ cups [592 ml].

Each 1 tablespoon serving contains about:

> 15 calories; 8 mg sodium; 0 cholesterol;
> tr fat; 3 g carbohydrate; tr protein;
> 0 fiber. 6% calories from fat.
> Exchanges: ½ fruit

OREGANO DRESSING

3 tablespoons red wine vinegar or rice vinegar
1 tablespoon water
1 tablespoon fresh lemon juice
3 tablespoons olive oil
2 tablespoons minced parsley
¾ teaspoon dried oregano, or 1 tablespoon chopped fresh oregano
Pepper to taste

Combine vinegar, water, lemon juice, oil, parsley, oregano, and pepper in a blender container and blend thoroughly. Let stand at least 1 hour before using to allow flavors to blend. Makes ½ cup [119 ml].

Each 1 tablespoon serving contains about:

> 47 calories; 0 sodium; 0 cholesterol;
> 5 g fat; tr carbohydrate; 0 protein;
> 0 fiber. 94% calories from fat.
> Exchanges: 1 fat

RICE VINEGAR DRESSING

The rice vinegar provides a sweet, delicate flavor.

> *2 tablespoons corn or olive oil*
> *3 tablespoons rice vinegar*
> *1 tablespoon water*
> *Pepper to taste*

Combine oil, vinegar, water, and pepper in a small jar and shake until well blended. Makes ½ cup [119 ml].

Each 1 tablespoon serving contains about:

> 30 calories; 0 sodium; 0 cholesterol;
> 3 g fat; tr carbohydrate; 0 protein;
> 0 fiber. 90% calories from fat.
> Exchanges: 1 fat

VINAIGRETTE

> *2 tablespoons safflower or olive oil*
> *3 tablespoons plus 1 teaspoon fresh lemon juice*
> *2 tablespoons water*
> *1 teaspoon Dijon Mustard (p. 182)*
> *Pepper to taste*
> *¼ teaspoon capers, minced**
> *⅛ teaspoon dill weed, or ½ teaspoon chopped fresh dill*
> *½ teaspoon dried chervil, or 1½ teaspoons chopped fresh chervil (optional)*
> *1 teaspoon each chopped parsley and chives*

In a small bowl, combine safflower oil, olive oil, lemon juice, water, mustard, pepper, capers, dill, chervil, parsley, and chives. Blend with a wire whisk until well blended. Chill. Makes about ½ cup [119 ml].

* One teaspoon of capers contains 100 milligrams sodium.

Each 1 tablespoon serving contains about:

> 32 calories; 7 mg sodium; 0 cholesterol;
> 3 g fat; tr carbohydrate; tr protein;
> 0 fiber. 96% calories from fat.
> Exchanges: 1 fat

LOW-CALORIE RUSSIAN DRESSING

2 teaspoons unflavored gelatin
¼ cup [59 ml] rice vinegar
¼ cup [59 ml] boiling water
½ cup [115 g] Catsup (p. 182)
1½ teaspoons Worcestershire sauce
2 tablespoons finely minced onion
  Pepper to taste
2 tablespoons safflower oil

Soften gelatin in 2 tablespoons of the rice vinegar. Dissolve gelatin mixture in boiling water. Cool. Stir in remaining rice vinegar, Catsup, Worcestershire sauce, onion, pepper, and oil. Beat well with a wire whisk. Chill. Before serving, shake well or beat with wire whisk. Makes about 1¼ cups [296 ml].

Each 1 tablespoon serving contains about:

> 19 calories; 7 mg sodium; 0 cholesterol;
> 1 g fat; 1 g carbohydrate; tr protein;
> 0 fiber. 64% calories from fat.
> Exchanges: negligible

Sauces, Condiments, and Specialty Recipes

Commercial brand diet condiments and sauces are filling aisles in grocery stores throughout America. And that's fine. But if you are concerned about the salt and preservative contents, the quality, and the cost of the increasingly pricey condiments and sauces in the markets today, you might consider making your own.

We provide plenty of recipes for condiments and specialty items necessary for cooking the *Light Style* way: recipes for light mayonnaise, catsup, mustard, low-calorie margarine, soy sauce, and numerous sauces, including Italian tomato sauce, mornay sauce, Madeira sauce, and velouté sauce for fish dishes.

The sauces in this chapter make use of low-calorie margarine and low-fat stocks to reduce both calories and cholesterol.

For the sake of convenience, we give the option of substituting low-sodium canned tomatoes for fresh ones.

Wine is a reliable flavor enhancer, especially in sauces. Our recipes also use low-fat and low-cholesterol brand cheeses and unsweetened fruit juices and fruit.

Condiments such as catsup, mustard, and soy sauce can be stored up to a month with no worry of spoilage, provided you observe rules of food safety. Store them in the refrigerator in containers with tight-fitting lids. Sauces should be stored for no longer than a week in the refrigerator.

Condiments and unusual sauces make charming gifts when packed in pretty jars with labels. You might even add a recipe or two for an appreciative friend.

SAUCES, HOT

BÉCHAMEL SAUCE
WHITE SAUCE

2 tablespoons low-calorie margarine
2 tablespoons flour
½ cup [119 ml] nonfat milk
½ cup [119 ml] evaporated nonfat milk
Pinch white pepper

Melt margarine in a saucepan. Stir in flour until smooth. Gradually stir in milks. Continue to cook and stir until sauce comes to a boil. Reduce heat and simmer 2 to 3 minutes, stirring constantly, until sauce is thickened and smooth. Season with pepper. Makes about 1¼ cups [296 ml].

Each 1 tablespoon serving contains about:

> 15 calories; 24 mg sodium; 0 cholesterol;
> tr fat; 2 g carbohydrate; tr protein;
> 0 fiber. 36% calories from fat.
> Exchanges: negligible

BLENDER BÉARNAISE

Light Style Béarnaise has half the calories and fat of the classic version.

2 tablespoons each white wine vinegar and dry white wine
1½ teaspoons minced shallots or green onion
¼ teaspoon dried tarragon, or ¾ teaspoon chopped fresh
tarragon
Dash paprika
Dash cayenne pepper
6 tablespoons egg substitute
2 tablespoons low-calorie margarine, melted
1 tablespoon fresh lemon juice

Combine vinegar, wine, shallots, tarragon, paprika, and cayenne pepper in a small saucepan and bring to a boil. Boil until liquid has reduced to about 1 tablespoon. Pour into a blender container and let cool. Add egg substitute to blender container and blend until smooth. With the blender motor running at low speed, add the melted margarine in a fine steady stream. Pour sauce into top of a double boiler placed over simmering water. Cook and stir until sauce thickens, about 1 minute. Remove from heat. Makes ½ cup [119 ml].

NOTE: To reheat Béarnaise, place it in the top pan of a double boiler placed over hot water and stir just until sauce is warm and reconstituted.

Each 2 tablespoon serving contains about:

> 48 calories; 112 mg sodium; 0 cholesterol;
> 4 g fat; 1 g carbohydrate; 3 g protein;
> 0 fiber. 66% calories from fat.
> Exchanges: 1 fat

CHICKEN OR TURKEY GRAVY

3 tablespoons low-calorie margarine
1 clove garlic, minced
2 tablespoons arrowroot
1½ cups [355 ml] low-sodium Chicken or Turkey Stock
   (p. 38), heated
1 bay leaf
¼ cup [59 ml] white wine

Melt margarine in a saucepan. Add garlic and cook about 30 seconds. Stir in arrowroot until smooth. Add stock, bay leaf, and wine and cook and stir until sauce thickens, about 5 minutes. Remove bay leaf. Serve with meat or poultry. Makes about 2 cups [473 ml].

Each 3 tablespoon serving contains about:

> 26 calories; 38 mg sodium; 0 cholesterol;
> 2 g fat; 2 g carbohydrate; tr protein; tr fiber.
> 54% calories from fat.
> Exchanges: ¼ fat

DRAWN MARGARINE

Margarine does not contain milk solids, so it's unnecessary to melt down milky residue as you would for butter.

6 tablespoons low-calorie margarine
4½ teaspoons fresh lemon juice or white vinegar
1 teaspoon chopped capers
1 tablespoon finely chopped parsley
2 teaspoons finely chopped shallots

Melt margarine in a small saucepan over low heat. Stir in lemon juice, capers, parsley, and shallots all at once. Makes about ½ cup [119 ml].

Each 1 tablespoon serving contains about:

> 39 calories; 133 mg sodium; 0 cholesterol;
> 4 g fat; tr carbohydrate; tr protein; 0 fiber.
> 94% calories from fat.
> Exchanges: 1 fat

FRENCH PROVINCIAL SAUCE
BROWN SAUCE

This is the *Light Style* version of the French classic brown sauce used as a base for many sauces added to meat, fish, or fowl.

> *2 teaspoons low-sodium tomato puree*
> *⅛ teaspoon maple extract*
> *2 cups [473 ml] low-sodium Beef Stock (p. 37)*
> *½ cup [119 ml] plus 1 tablespoon dry red wine*
>   *Bouquet Garni (p. 181)*
> *¼ cup chopped onion*
> *1½ tablespoons arrowroot*

Combine tomato puree, maple extract, beef stock, ½ cup of the wine, Bouquet Garni, and onion in a saucepan. Simmer, covered, for 45 minutes. Strain broth through a fine sieve or cheesecloth to measure about 1½ cups [355 ml]. Return broth to the saucepan. Dissolve arrowroot in remaining 1 tablespoon wine. Mix arrowroot mixture into broth with a wire whisk. Place over low heat and simmer, stirring until sauce thickens, about 5 minutes.

Use as much sauce as is needed for one meal and refrigerate remainder in a tightly covered jar for up to 2 days, or freeze in a plastic container leaving 1-inch [2½ cm] head space for expansion during freezing for up to 1 month. Makes about 1½ cups [355 ml].

Each 1 tablespoon serving contains about:

> 10 calories; 2 mg sodium; 0 cholesterol;
> 0 fat; 2 g carbohydrate; 0 protein;
> tr fiber. Tr calories from fat.
> Exchanges: negligible

MORNAY SAUCE

1½ tablespoons low-calorie margarine
1 tablespoon arrowroot
1 cup [237 ml] evaporated nonfat milk
  Dash ground nutmeg
  Dash white pepper
1 tablespoon dry sherry
⅓ cup [37 g] grated low-fat Gouda or Cheddar cheese

Melt margarine in a saucepan. Blend in arrowroot until smooth. Add milk all at once. Cook and stir until thickened and bubbly. Add nutmeg and pepper and stir in sherry. Mix in cheese and heat, stirring, until cheese is melted. Makes about 1¼ cups [296 ml].

Each 2 tablespoon serving contains about:

> 49 calories; 81 mg sodium; 5 mg cholesterol;
> 2 g fat; 4 g carbohydrate; 3 g protein;
> tr fiber. 35% calories from fat.
> Exchanges: ¼ milk

ITALIAN MEAT SAUCE

Use Italian plum tomatoes when in season for best flavor and texture.

½ pound [300 g] ground beef sirloin
2 large onions, chopped
3 cloves garlic, minced
10 Italian plum tomatoes, peeled and diced, or 1 (20-ounce) [560 g] can low-sodium tomatoes, diced
1 (16-ounce) [450 g] can low-sodium tomato juice
1 tablespoon dried oregano, or 3 tablespoons chopped fresh oregano
1 teaspoon dried thyme, or 1 tablespoon chopped fresh thyme
½ teaspoon dried marjoram, or 1½ teaspoons chopped fresh marjoram
2 teaspoons fennel seeds
1 teaspoon dried basil, or 1 tablespoon chopped fresh basil
1 bay leaf
¾ cup [64 g] chopped parsley
½ teaspoon pepper
½ cup [119 ml] dry red wine (preferably Chianti)

Combine meat, onions, and half the garlic in a large saucepan. Sauté until onions are tender and meat is crumbly. Add tomatoes, tomato juice, remaining garlic, oregano, thyme, marjoram, fennel, basil, bay leaf, parsley, and pepper. Bring to a boil, reduce heat, partially cover, and simmer 2 hours, stirring occasionally. Add wine and simmer 30 minutes longer, stirring occasionally. Remove bay leaf. Makes about 6½ cups [1½ L].

NOTE: It is necessary to peel the tomatoes to make a thick sauce.

Each ¼ cup serving contains about:

> 44 calories; 12 mg sodium; 4 mg cholesterol;
> 1 g fat; 5 g carbohydrate; 2 g protein;
> tr fiber. 41% calories from fat.
> Exchanges: 1 B vegetable

ITALIAN TOMATO SAUCE

> 10 ripe Italian plum tomatoes, peeled and diced, or 1 (20-ounce) [560 g] can low-sodium tomatoes with their juice
>
> 2 tablespoons chopped fresh oregano, or 2 teaspoons dried oregano
>
> ½ teaspoon dried thyme, or 1½ tablespoons chopped fresh thyme
>
> ½ teaspoon dried marjoram, or 1½ teaspoons chopped fresh marjoram
>
> 1 teaspoon fennel seeds
>
> 1 bay leaf
>
> ½ large onion, minced
>
> 4 cloves garlic, minced
>
> ½ teaspoon white pepper
>
> ½ cup [115 g] dry red wine (preferably Chianti)
>
> ¼ cup [4 tablespoons] chopped parsley

In a large saucepan, combine tomatoes, oregano, thyme, marjoram, fennel seeds, bay leaf, onion, garlic, and pepper. Bring to a boil, reduce heat, and simmer, uncovered, for 1 hour, stirring occasionally. Add wine and parsley and simmer 30 minutes. Remove bay leaf. Makes about 5 cups [1½ L].

Each ¼ cup serving contains about:

> 16 calories; 3 mg sodium; 0 cholesterol;
> tr fat; 4 g carbohydrate; tr protein;
> tr fiber. 9% calories from fat.
> Exchanges: ½ vegetable

MARINARA SAUCE

1 teaspoon olive oil
½ cup [90 g] finely chopped onion
1½ cups [194 g] peeled and coarsely chopped fresh tomatoes
1 cup [225 g] low-sodium canned tomatoes with their liquid
2 teaspoons dried basil, or 2 tablespoons chopped fresh basil
Pepper to taste

Heat oil in a saucepan and add onion. Sauté until golden and tender, about 1 minute. Add fresh and canned tomatoes, basil, and pepper. Simmer, partially covered, over very low heat for 40 minutes, stirring occasionally. Place cooked tomato mixture in a blender container and puree. Reheat to serve. Makes 2 cups [473 ml].

Each ¼ cup serving contains about:

34 calories; 7 mg sodium; 0 cholesterol;
tr fat; 4 g carbohydrate; tr protein;
tr fiber. Tr calories from fat.
Exchanges: 1 vegetable

SPANISH SAUCE

½ teaspoon olive oil
1 teaspoon minced garlic
1½ green bell peppers, sliced
1½ medium onions, sliced lengthwise, then slices halved crosswise
3 large tomatoes, diced
¼ cup [59 ml] tomato juice
*1½ cups [355 ml] low-sodium tomato puree**
1 teaspoon dried oregano, or 1 tablespoon chopped fresh oregano
2 dashes ground cumin

Heat oil in a skillet and add garlic, green peppers, and onions. Sauté until tender, about 5 to 6 minutes. Add tomatoes, tomato juice, tomato puree, oregano, and cumin to the onion mixture. Simmer, uncovered, for 30 minutes, stirring occasionally. Serve as topping for omelets, fish, chicken, or tacos. Makes 3 cups [710 ml].

*To make your own low-sodium tomato puree, place fresh peeled tomatoes or low-sodium canned tomatoes in a blender container and blend until smooth.

Each ¼ cup serving contains about:

> 35 calories; 130 mg sodium; 0 cholesterol;
> tr fat; 8 g carbohydrate; 1 g protein;
> 1 g fiber. 18% calories from fat.
> Exchanges: 1 vegetable

MADEIRA SAUCE

Truffles add an authentic touch to this classic meat sauce, but mushrooms will do, too.

> 4½ teaspoons low-calorie margarine
> 2 tablespoons minced shallots, or 2 tablespoons minced
>   onion
> 2 cloves garlic, minced
> ½ cup [115 g] sliced mushrooms, or 2 tablespoons chopped
>   truffles
> 1 cup [237 ml] low-sodium Beef Stock (p. 37)
> ¼ cup [59 ml] Madeira or dry sherry
> 1 tablespoon chopped fresh basil, or 1 teaspoon dried basil
> 1 bay leaf
> 2½ teaspoons arrowroot
> 1 teaspoon water
>   Pepper to taste

Melt margarine in a skillet. Add shallots, garlic, and mushrooms and sauté until mushrooms are tender but not brown. Add stock, wine, basil, and bay leaf. Dissolve arrowroot in water and stir into wine mixture with a wire whisk. Cook, stirring, until sauce thickens, about 15 minutes. Remove bay leaf. Season to taste with pepper. Makes about 1¼ cups [296 ml].

Each 2 tablespoon serving contains about:

> 32 calories; 41 mg sodium; 0 mg cholesterol;
> 1 g fat; 4 g carbohydrate; tr protein;
> tr fiber. 30% calories from fat.
> Exchanges: negligible

SAUCE ABEL

2 tablespoons low-calorie margarine
2 cloves garlic, minced
2 tablespoons arrowroot
1 tablespoon water
1 cup [237 ml] low-sodium Chicken Stock (p. 38) or Beef
Stock (p. 37), heated
1 cup [225 g] nonfat milk, heated
1 bay leaf
2 tablespoons dry sherry (optional)

Melt margarine in a saucepan. Add garlic and cook 15 seconds. Dissolve arrowroot in water and stir into margarine until smooth with a wire whisk. Gradually add stock, milk, and bay leaf and cook and stir until sauce thickens. Remove bay leaf and stir in sherry, if desired. Makes 2½ cups [592 ml].

Each ¼ cup serving contains about:

33 calories; 38 mg sodium; 0 cholesterol;
1 g fat; 5 g carbohydrate; 1 g protein;
tr fiber. 28% calories from fat.
Exchanges: negligible

SAUCE VELOUTÉ

This "neo" classic sauce goes well with fish or shellfish.

2 tablespoons low-calorie margarine
4 shallots, minced
2 tablespoons arrowroot
½ cup [119 ml] plus 1 tablespoon evaporated nonfat milk
1 cup [237 ml] Fish Stock (p. 38)
Pinch each white pepper and cayenne pepper

Melt margarine in a saucepan. Add shallots and sauté until tender. Blend together arrowroot and 1 tablespoon of the milk and stir into margarine mixture until smooth. Gradually add stock, the remaining milk, and the white and cayenne peppers. Cook and stir until sauce is smooth and thickened. Makes about 1½ cups [355 ml].

Each 2 tablespoon serving contains about:

> 33 calories; 38 mg sodium; 1 g fat;
> 5 g carbohydrate; 1 g protein; tr fiber.
> 28% calories from fat.
> Exchanges: negligible

PINEAPPLE SAUCE

A versatile sauce for both meat and dessert.

> *2 teaspoons arrowroot*
> *¾ cup [178 ml] unsweetened pineapple juice*
> *1 cup [225 g] canned water-packed, drained pineapple
> chunks*

Dissolve arrowroot in 1 tablespoon of the pineapple juice mixture and return to pan. Place over medium heat and cook and stir until thickened. Stir in pineapple chunks. Serve with lamb, ham, or ice cream. Makes 1½ cups [355 ml].

Each 2 tablespoon serving contains about:

> 14 calories; 0 mg sodium; 0 cholesterol;
> 0 fat; 3 g carbohydrate; tr protein;
> tr fiber. 0 calories from fat.
> Exchanges: ½ fruit

TARRAGON SAUCE

> *1 tablespoon low-calorie margarine*
> *1 tablespoon arrowroot*
> *1 tablespoon water*
> *½ cup [119 ml] low-sodium Chicken Stock (p. 38)*
> *½ cup [119 ml] evaporated nonfat milk*
> *¼ cup [59 ml] dry white wine*
> *½ teaspoon dried tarragon, or 2 sprigs fresh tarragon,
> minced*
> *1 clove garlic, minced*
> *Pepper to taste*

Melt margarine in a saucepan over medium heat. Dissolve arrowroot in water and stir into margarine until smooth. Gradually add stock, stirring constantly. Continue to cook and stir until smooth and thickened, about 4 minutes. Add milk, wine, tarragon, garlic, and pepper to saucepan and mix well. Continue to cook and stir until smooth. Serve with chicken or other poultry. Makes about 1¼ cups [296 ml].

Each ¼ cup serving contains about:

> 51 calories; 58 mg sodium; 1 mg cholesterol;
> 1 g fat; 6 g carbohydrate; 2 g protein;
> tr fiber. 21% calories from fat.
> Exchanges: ½ bread

———————— SAUCES, COLD ————————

APPLESAUCE

8 tart green apples, cored, peeled, and sliced
4 Rome Beauty or Jonathan cored, peeled, and sliced
1½ cups [355 ml] unsweetened apple juice concentrate
½ cup [119 ml] water
2 teaspoons ground cinnamon
¼ teaspoon ground nutmeg
1 teaspoon lemon juice

Combine apples, apple juice, water, cinnamon, nutmeg, and lemon juice in a large saucepan. Bring to a boil, reduce heat, cover, and simmer until apples are very soft, about 45 minutes. Drain off liquid and discard. Mash apples with a fork and return to saucepan. Cook, covered, over very low heat until excess moisture is absorbed and applesauce is light. Let cool and chill. Applesauce may be stored in a covered plastic container in the refrigerator for up to 2 weeks. Makes 1½ quarts.

Each ½ cup serving contains about:

> 70 calories; 9 mg sodium; 0 cholesterol;
> tr fat; 17 g carbohydrate; tr protein;
> 1 g fiber. 3% calories from fat.
> Exchanges: 1 fruit

CRANBERRY SAUCE

1 cup [181 g] peeled and chopped apples
1 pound [450 g] fresh cranberries (4 cups), or 1 (10-ounce)
*   [285 g] package frozen cranberries, thawed*
1 cup [237 ml] hot water
¼ teaspoon baking soda
1½ teaspoons low-calorie cherry-flavored gelatin

Place apples and cranberries in a 2-quart [2 L] saucepan. Add water, bring to a boil, and cook until berries pop. Reduce heat and stir in baking soda. Remove from heat. Skim foam from berries and drain, reserving liquid. Dissolve gelatin into hot berry liquid. Chill until syrupy. Fold in berries and spoon into jars with tight-fitting lids. Chill. For the best flavor, prepare the sauce a few days before serving. Makes about 3 cups [710 ml].

Each 2 tablespoon serving contains about:

> 13 calories; 10 mg sodium; 0 cholesterol;
> tr fat; 3 g carbohydrate; tr protein;
> 1 g fiber. 6% calories from fat.
> Exchanges: ½ fruit

MAYONNAISE

¼ cup [59 ml] egg substitute
1 egg white
1⅛ teaspoons dry mustard
*   Dash cayenne pepper*
2 tablespoons fresh lemon juice
1 tablespoon white vinegar or rice vinegar
⅔ cup [172 ml] plus 1 tablespoon corn oil

Combine egg substitute, egg white, mustard, cayenne pepper, lemon juice, vinegar, and ⅓ cup [79 ml] of the oil in a blender container and blend at high speed until smooth. With blender motor running, gradually add remaining oil in a fine, steady stream, blending until mixture emulsifies and thickens. Chill 1 hour before using. Store in tightly covered jar in the refrigerator for up to 1 week. Makes 1⅓ cups.

Each 1 tablespoon serving contains about:

> 71 calories; 8 mg sodium; 0 cholesterol;
> 8 g fat; tr carbohydrate; tr protein;
> 0 fiber. 96% calories from fat.
> Exchanges: 1 ¾ fat

CURRY MAYONNAISE

¾ cup [180 g] low-calorie Mayonnaise (p. 180)
1 teaspoon curry powder
1 teaspoon fresh lemon juice
2 tablespoons grated onion
Pepper to taste

Mix together mayonnaise, curry powder, lemon juice, onion, and pepper, and blend well. Chill. Makes about ¾ cup.

Each 1 tablespoon serving contains about:

> 73 calories; 8 mg sodium; 0 cholesterol;
> 8 g fat; tr carbohydrate; tr protein;
> 0 fiber. 94% calories from fat.
> Exchanges: 1¾ fat

MOCK HOLLANDAISE

You'll love this mock version of hollandaise when you're rushed for time—or even when you're not.

½ cup [115 g] low-calorie Mayonnaise (p. 180)
3 tablespoons Dijon Mustard (p. 182)
2 teaspoons fresh lemon juice

Combine mayonnaise, mustard, and lemon juice in a small bowl. Blend with a wire whisk until smooth and creamy. Makes about 1 cup.

Each 1 tablespoon serving contains about:

> 41 calories; 4 mg sodium; 0 cholesterol;
> 4 g fat; tr carbohydrate; tr protein; 0 fiber.
> 91% calories from fat.
> Exchanges: 1 fat

STRAWBERRY SAUCE

1½ baskets [675 g] strawberries, hulled
1 tablespoon fresh lemon juice

Combine strawberries and lemon juice in a blender container and puree until smooth. Chill. Use as a topping for pies, cakes, ice cream, or puddings. Makes 1½ cups.

Each 2 tablespoon serving contains about:

> 8 calories; 0 sodium; 0 cholesterol;
> tr fat; 2 g carbohydrate; tr protein.
> 0 calories from fat.
> Exchanges: ¼ fruit

CONDIMENTS AND SPECIALTY PRODUCTS

BOUQUET GARNI

Seasonal garden herbs can heighten the flavor of a saltless stock, soup, or sauce.

> *1 fresh sprig each parsley, thyme, basil, and marjoram*
> *1 bay leaf*
> *Celery leaves from 1 stalk*
> *1 leaf tarragon*
> *2 cloves garlic, split*

Place parsley, thyme, basil, marjoram, bay leaf, celery tops, tarragon, and garlic in a cheesecloth square. Fold to form a bag and tie with string. Use as seasoning for sauces and soups.

NOTE: If using dried herbs, combine a pinch each of the suggested herbs in dried form. Place in cheesecloth square, fold, and tie.

Calories and sodium negligible; 0 mg cholesterol and fat

CATSUP

¾ cup [178 ml] low-sodium tomato juice
3 cups [675 g] low-sodium tomato paste
¼ cup [59 ml] wine vinegar
2 cloves garlic, minced

Combine tomato juice, paste, vinegar, and garlic in a mixing bowl and blend well. Refrigerate to blend flavors. Store in jars with tight-fitting lids up to 1 month in the refrigerator. Makes 1 quart.

Each 1 tablespoon serving contains about:

11 calories; 8 mg sodium; 0 cholesterol;
0 fat; 3 g carbohydrate; tr protein;
tr fiber. 0 calories from fat.
Exchanges: negligible

DIJON MUSTARD

An excellent seasoning for broccoli, Brussels sprouts, cabbage, cauliflower, or greens. Try it as a marinade for beef or lamb, too.

1 cup [237 ml] white vinegar or rice vinegar
1 cup [237 ml] dry white wine
2 cups [473 ml] dry vermouth
1 cup [181 g] finely chopped onion
2 cloves garlic, minced
1 (4-ounce) [115 g] can dry mustard
2 tablespoons honey
1 tablespoon vegetable oil
¼ teaspoon aromatic bitters

Combine vinegar, wine, vermouth, onion, and garlic in a saucepan and heat to boiling. Reduce heat and simmer 5 minutes. Remove from heat and cool. Strain wine mixture through a fine sieve. Put dry mustard in a saucepan and pour one-fourth of the wine mixture into it, beating constantly with a wire whisk or electric mixer until smooth. Beat in remaining wine mixture, then blend in honey, oil, and bitters. Heat slowly, stirring constantly, until mixture thickens, about 10 minutes. Do not boil. Remove from heat and let cool. Pour into a glass or plastic (nonmetal) container. Cover and refrigerate at least 2 days to allow flavors to blend. Store in the refrigerator up to 3 months. Makes about 1 quart.

Each 1 tablespoon serving contains about:

> 27 calories; 2 mg sodium; 0 cholesterol;
> tr fat; 2 g carbohydrate; tr protein;
> 0 fiber. Tr calories from fat.
> Exchanges: negligible

CHOLESTEROL-FREE EGG SUBSTITUTE

¼ cup [59 ml] nonfat milk
1 tablespoon nonfat milk powder
1 teaspoon vegetable oil
3 egg whites

Combine milk, nonfat milk powder, and vegetable oil. Beat egg whites lightly with a fork. Add milk mixture to egg whites and beat until well blended. Cover and store in the refrigerator up to 3 days. Stir well before using. Makes 6 tablespoons.

NOTE: A dash of egg yolk can be added for yellow color.

A 3 tablespoon serving contains about:

> 26 calories; 36 mg sodium; 2 mg cholesterol;
> 1 g fat; 1 g carbohydrate; 2 g protein;
> 0 fiber. 40% calories from fat.
> Exchanges: 1 meat

FRESH CRANBERRY RELISH

1 large orange
¼ cup [50 g] sugar
1 tablespoon grated orange peel
1 pound [450 g] fresh cranberries (4 cups)

Peel orange and cut into pieces, removing seeds and connecting membranes. Put orange pieces in a blender container with sugar and grated orange peel and blend well. Add cranberries, a few at a time, until all berries have been blended into a fairly coarse relish. Refrigerate in a covered jar several days to ripen. Serve the relish with meat or fowl, or spread on bread. Makes 4 cups.

Each 2 tablespoon serving contains about:

> 20 calories; 1 mg sodium; 0 cholesterol;
> tr fat; 5 g carbohydrate; tr protein;
> tr fiber. Tr calories from fat.
> Exchanges: ½ fruit

HEAVENLY WHIPPED TOPPING

1 teaspoon unflavored gelatin
¼ cup [59 ml] cold water
1 tablespoon sugar
1 teaspoon pure vanilla extract
3 tablespoons whipping cream
4 egg whites, at room temperature
½ teaspoon cream of tartar, or 1 teaspoon white vinegar

In a small saucepan, soften gelatin in water for 1 minute. Add sugar and place over medium heat, stirring, until gelatin dissolves. Remove from heat and transfer to small bowl. Stir in vanilla and cream. Refrigerate until set, about 1 hour. Beat egg whites at low speed until foamy. Add cream of tartar and beat at high speed until stiff, glossy peaks form. With electric beater, beat gelatin mixture until creamy, then fold into egg whites. Refrigerate until ready to use. For best results, use within 1 hour. Makes 2½ cups.

Each 1 tablespoon serving contains about:

> 6 calories; 5 mg sodium; 1 mg cholesterol; 0 fat;
> 1 g carbohydrate; 0 protein; 0 fiber. 0 calories from fat.
> Exchanges: negligible

HERB BLEND

1 teaspoon each dried basil, marjoram, thyme, oregano,
parsley, summer savory, ground cloves, mace, and black
pepper
¼ teaspoon each ground nutmeg and cayenne pepper

Combine basil, marjoram, thyme, oregano, parsley, summer savory, cloves, mace, black pepper, nutmeg, and cayenne pepper in a jar with a tight-fitting lid. Store in a cool place up to 6 months. Use as seasoning for meats and vegetables. Makes about ¼ cup.

Each ¼ cup contains about:

> 0 calories; 12 mg sodium; 0 cholesterol;
> 0 fat; tr carbohydrate; tr protein;
> tr fiber. 0 calories from fat.
> Exchanges: negligible

LOW-CALORIE MARGARINE

Low-calorie margarine is margarine whipped with water. To save money, make your own. It is necessary to use at least three cups of margarine to incorporate the water completely.

> *3 cups [675 g] regular or unsalted margarine, chilled*
> *3 tablespoons nonfat milk powder*
> *1½ cups [355 ml] ice water*

Place the margarine, milk powder, and water in a food processor or blender container and whip until water is well incorporated and margarine is light and fluffy. (You will need to turn the blender on and off, scraping mixture into blades when off.) Store in a covered plastic container for 2 to 3 weeks, or freeze for up to 3 months. Use as you would regular margarine. Makes about 6 cups.

NOTE: For each additional cup of margarine you wish to whip, add ½ cup water.

Each tablespoon of low-calorie margarine contains about:

> 52 calories; 68 mg sodium; 0 cholesterol;
> 6 g fat; tr carbohydrate; tr protein;
> tr fiber. 98% calories from fat.
> Exchanges: 1 fat

CREAM CHEESE

Now you can make your own with about half the calories of regular cream cheese.

> *1 cup [225 g] ricotta cheese (made from partially skimmed milk)*
> *½ cup [115 g] low-fat cottage cheese*
> *¼ cup [60 g] low-fat plain yogurt*
> *1 tablespoon buttermilk, or as needed*

Combine ricotta cheese, cottage cheese, and yogurt in a blender container or food processor and blend well. Add buttermilk as needed for cream cheese consistency. Store refrigerated up to 1 week. Makes 1¾ cups.

Each tablespoon contains about:

> 17 calories; 29 mg sodium; 3 mg cholesterol;
> tr fat; tr carbohydrate; 2 g protein;
> 0 fiber. 30% calories from fat.
> Exchanges: ¼ milk

SEAFOOD COCKTAIL SAUCE

¾ cup [180 g] Catsup (p. 182), or 1 (12½-ounce) [354 g]
  bottle low-sodium catsup
¼ cup [59 ml] fresh lemon juice, or juice of 1 large lemon
¼ cup [45 g] minced onion
½ cup [115 g] minced celery
¼ cup [4 tablespoons] minced cilantro (fresh coriander) or
  parsley
4 drops hot pepper sauce
2 drops Worcestershire sauce
2 teaspoons dry horseradish
1 (16-ounce) [450 g] can tomato puree*

Combine Catsup, lemon juice, onion, celery, cilantro, hot pepper sauce, Worcestershire sauce, horseradish and tomato puree. Chill. Store refrigerated up to 1 week. Makes 3 cups.

* To make your own low-sodium tomato puree, place fresh peeled tomatoes or canned low-sodium tomatoes in a blender container and blend until smooth.

Each ¼ cup serving contains about:

> 20 calories; 13 mg sodium; 0 cholesterol;
> tr fat; 4 g carbohydrate; tr protein;
> tr fiber. Tr calories from fat.
> Exchanges: negligible

SOY SAUCE

Soy sauce diluted with broth reduces sodium content, but not flavor.

3 tablespoons mild soy sauce
1½ cups [355 ml] low-sodium Beef Stock (p. 37)
¼ cup [59 ml] water, or 3 tablespoons strained fresh lemon
*   juice*
1 teaspoon grated lemon peel (optional)

Combine soy sauce, beef broth, water, and lemon peel. To store, refrigerate in a jar with a tight-fitting lid up to 2 weeks. Makes about 2 cups [473 ml].

Each tablespoon contains about:

> 1 calorie; 78 mg sodium; 0 cholesterol;
> 0 fat; tr carbohydrate; tr protein;
> 0 fiber. 0 calories from fat.
> Exchanges: negligible

TARTAR SAUCE

1 cup [225 g] low-calorie mayonnaise
1 tablespoon fresh lemon juice
2 tablespoons chopped fresh dill, or 1 teaspoon dill weed
1½ teaspoons minced parsley
1 tablespoon minced onion
2 dashes hot pepper sauce

In a small bowl, combine mayonnaise, lemon juice, dill, parsley, onion, and hot pepper sauce. Blend together until smooth. Chill at least 1 hour before serving. Makes 1½ cups [355 g].

Each 1 tablespoon serving contains about:

> 24 calories; 51 mg sodium; 2 mg cholesterol;
> 2 g fat; 2 g carbohydrate; tr protein;
> 0 fiber. 70% calories from fat.
> Exchanges: ½ fat

DILL SAUCE

½ cup [115 g] low-fat plain yogurt
1 tablespoon Dijon Mustard (p. 182)
2 tablespoons fresh dill, minced, or 2 teaspoons dry dill
1½ tablespoons fresh lemon juice
1 tablespoon caper,* optional

In a bowl, combine yogurt, mustard, dill, lemon juice, and capers. Mix well. Refrigerate for at least 30 minutes to allow flavors to blend. Makes ½ cup [119 g].

* Capers are very high in salt, so use in moderation.

Each tablespoon contains about:

> 12 calories; 103 mg sodium; 1 mg cholesterol;
> tr fat; 2 g carbohydrate; tr protein;
> 0 fiber. 22% calories from fat.
> Exchange: negligible

DESSERTS

Here comes the pièce de résistance: the dessert chapter, filled with *Light Style* desserts that show you can have your cake and eat it, too.

It's all here: the glamor, the flavor, the low, low (as low as we could get them) calories. A chocolate mousse pie with only 184 calories per serving? A comparable piece of pie bought in the store has three times as many calories. A soufflé with negligible cholesterol? Of course. That's because we've developed one without egg yolks. We use sugar in minimal amounts.

We seldom add any fat and never any salt. You can make pies, cakes, even a low-calorie baklava and cheesecake that you won't believe are true—but they are.

However, we have put the emphasis on desserts using fruit, nature's naturally sweet, low-calorie, highly nutritious dessert. How does a 139-calorie per serving French apple tart sound? Or a 43-calorie peach Melba?

Perhaps more important than our recipes are the future recipes you will be able to reduce in calories, fat, cholesterol, sugar, and salt once you've worked with ours.

Don't be alarmed if the fat content of some of the desserts seems high. It's the daily total fat intake over several days that counts. The nutrient analyses will help you fit desserts appropriately into your daily food plan. Remember, when you want a dessert higher in fat, serve it with a low-fat meal.

Once you learn the basic principles of calorie, fat, sugar, and sodium reduction, the rest is easy.

PIES, CAKES, AND COOKIES

BAKLAVA

No one believes that the calories of this exquisitely light but rich-tasting baklava could possibly be as low as they are. But they are, thanks to *Light Style* reductions of fats, sugar, and nuts. The baklava is made with half the amount of sugar and a fraction of the margarine you would normally use. The results will fool anyone.

We thank Chef Mo Ezzani of Yemen for developing this treasured recipe for us.

> *½ pound [225 g] shelled pistachio nuts, ground*
> *1 tablespoon sugar*
> *¾ teaspoon ground cinnamon*
> *1½ tablespoons rosewater*
> *½ pound [225 g] filo dough*
> *½ cup [115 g] low-calorie margarine, melted*
> *Rosewater Syrup (following recipe)*
> *Whole cloves (optional)*

Combine pistachio nuts, sugar, cinnamon, and rosewater in a small bowl. Using half the filo sheets (cover remaining sheets with plastic wrap to prevent them from drying out), place 3 sheets in bottom of a lightly greased 13-by-9-inch [33-by-23 cm] baking sheet. Brush with some of the margarine. Sprinkle evenly with nuts. Lay remaining filo sheets over nut filling, brushing after every third sheet and after the top sheet. Cut baklava at 1½-inch [4 cm] intervals diagonally to form a pattern of about 35 diamond shapes. Bake at 400°F [204°C] for 25 minutes or until golden. Place on a wire rack to cool. Drizzle Rosewater Syrup evenly over the top and allow to soak several hours. Stud each diamond shape with a whole clove. Makes 35 servings.

NOTE: Filo dough and rosewater are available in the freezer section of many markets, Middle Eastern grocery stores, and gourmet food shops.

ROSEWATER SYRUP

> *1 cup [237 ml] water*
> *½ cup [100 g] sugar*
> *1½ tablespoons fresh lemon juice*
> *1 teaspoon rosewater or rum extract*

Combine water and sugar in a small saucepan. Bring to a boil and boil about 30 minutes. Stir in lemon juice and rosewater. Cool completely.

Each piece of baklava contains about:

> 85 calories; 32 mg sodium; 0 cholesterol;
> 5 g fat; 9 g carbohydrate; 2 g protein;
> tr fiber. 40% calories from fat.
> Exchanges: ½ bread, 1 fat

CALIFORNIA CHEESECAKE

1 (16-ounce) [450 g] package ricotta cheese (made from
partially skimmed milk) or low-fat cottage cheese
4 tablespoons egg substitute, or 2 egg whites
¼ cup [50 g] sugar
¼ cup [60 g] low-fat vanilla yogurt
1¼ teaspoons grated lemon peel
1 teaspoon fresh lemon juice
2 teaspoons vanilla extract
3 egg whites
¼ teaspoon cream of tartar, or 1 teaspoon white vinegar
Graham Cracker Crumb Crust (following recipe)
Lemon Topping (p. 193)

Combine cheese, egg substitute or egg whites, sugar, vanilla yogurt, lemon peel and juice, and vanilla extract in a mixing bowl. Beat at low speed with an electric mixer until blended, then increase speed and blend until smooth. In a small bowl, beat egg whites with cream of tartar until stiff but not dry. Gently fold egg white mixture into cheese mixture. Turn into the Graham Cracker Crumb Crust and bake at 325°F [163°C] for 35 minutes, or until set. Remove from the oven and cool on a wire rack. Spread Lemon Topping over pie. Chill at least 12 hours or overnight before serving. Makes 12 servings.

GRAHAM CRACKER CRUMB CRUST

1 cup [73 g] fine graham cracker crumbs (about 10 graham
crackers), or fine zwieback crumbs (about 5 zwieback)
¼ teaspoon ground cinnamon
Dash ground nutmeg (optional)
2 tablespoons low-calorie margarine, melted

Combine crumbs, cinnamon, and nutmeg in a bowl. Work in melted margarine until evenly distributed. With your fingertips, press crumb mixture evenly over the bottom and sides of a nonstick 9-inch [23 cm] spring-form pan. (Grease pan with low-calorie margarine, if desired.) Bake at 425°F [218°C] for 5 to 7 minutes, or until crumb mixture browns slightly around edges.

LEMON TOPPING

2 tablespoons sugar

1½ teaspoons cornstarch

⅓ cup [79 ml] water

2 tablespoons fresh lemon juice

1 tablespoon egg substitute, or 1 drop of egg yolk

In a small saucepan, combine sugar, cornstarch, water, and lemon juice. Cook and stir over low heat until thickened. Remove from heat and let cool. Stir in egg substitute or egg yolk for color. Use as topping for cheesecake or other cakes.

Each serving (one-twelfth of cake) contains about:

> 130 calories; 149 mg sodium; 12 mg cholesterol;
> 5 g fat; 15 g carbohydrate; 7 g protein; tr
> fiber. 34% calories from fat.
> Exchanges: ½ milk, ½ bread, ½ fat

CHOCOLATE MOUSSE PIE

1½ cups [285 g] semisweet chocolate pieces

4 tablespoons brewed coffee

1½ teaspoons orange-flavored liqueur (optional)

1½ cups [355 ml] egg substitute, or 8 egg whites

1 teaspoon vanilla extract

3 egg whites

¼ teaspoon cream of tartar

Chocolate Crumb Crust (following recipe)

¾ cup [68 g] Heavenly Whipped Topping (p. 184)

Melt the chocolate in the top pan of a double boiler placed over simmering water and blend in coffee and liqueur. Add egg substitute, a little at a time, blending well after each addition. Stir in vanilla and let cool slightly. In a small bowl, beat egg whites with cream of tartar until soft peaks form.

Gently fold egg white mixture into chocolate mixture, blending well but lightly. Turn into Chocolate Crumb Crust. Freeze until firm. Remove from freezer 10 minutes before serving and garnish with Heavenly Whipped Topping, allowing 1 tablespoon per serving. Sprinkle with chocolate shavings or sprinkles, if desired. Makes 12 servings.

NOTE: Chocolate leaves may be added as a decorative touch.

CHOCOLATE CRUMB CRUST

20 Nabisco Famous Chocolate Wafers, finely crushed
1 tablespoon plus 2 teaspoons low-calorie margarine

Work together crumbs and margarine until crumbs are moistened. With your fingertips, press crumb mixture evenly over the bottom and sides of a greased 9-inch [23 cm] spring-form pan. Bake at 325°F [163°C] for 10 minutes. Let cool before filling.

Each serving (one-twelfth of pie) without topping contains about:

> 184 calories; 131 mg sodium; 0 cholesterol;
> 6 g fat; 19 g carbohydrate; 6 g protein;
> tr fiber. 40% calories from fat.
> Exchanges: 2 bread, 1 fat.

COLD PUMPKIN SOUFFLÉ

½ teaspoon low-calorie margarine (p. 185)

¼ cup [119 ml] ginger-flavored brandy (optional)

1 envelope (1 tablespoon) unflavored gelatin

½ cup egg substitute (p. 183), or 4 egg whites

¼ cup [50 g] sugar

1 (16-ounce) [450 g] can unsweetened pumpkin

1 teaspoon freshly grated orange zest

1 teaspoon ground cinnamon

½ teaspoon ground ginger

¼ teaspoon ground mace

¼ teaspoon ground cloves

4 egg whites, at room temperature

1 teaspoon white vinegar

1 cup Heavenly Whipped Topping (p. 184) or commercial low-calorie whipped topping

¼ cup [38 g] chopped toasted walnuts, pecans, or almonds for garnish (optional)

2 tablespoons unsweetened frozen orange juice concentrate, thawed (optional)

Cut a 7-inch [18 cm]-wide band of wax paper that is long enough to encircle a 1-quart [1 L] soufflé dish with a 2-inch [5 cm] overlap. Lightly grease the wax paper and secure it to the dish with tape, greased side in, so that it forms a 2-inch [5 cm]-wide collar above the rim of the dish. (Or prepare six 3-inch [8 cm]-wide bands of wax paper around 6 individual soufflé dishes.) Pour the brandy into the top pan of a double boiler placed over simmering water and sprinkle in the gelatin. Stir constantly until the gelatin completely dissolves.

Combine the egg substitute or egg whites and 2 tablespoons of the sugar in a medium bowl and beat until thick. Blend in the pumpkin, orange zest, cinnamon, ginger, mace, and cloves, then mix in the dissolved gelatin. Beat the egg whites at low speed until foamy. Add the vinegar and beat at medium speed until soft peaks form. Gradually adding the remaining sugar, beat at high speed until stiff, glossy peaks form. Stir one-fourth of the egg whites into the pumpkin mixture to lighten it, then gently fold in the remaining whites. Fold the whipped topping into the pumpkin mixture and spoon into the soufflé dish or dishes. Chill until set, at least 8 hours.

Carefully remove the collar(s). Decorate the soufflé(s) with a border of nuts. If desired, blend the orange juice concentrate with the ice cream and pass separately as a sauce. Makes 6 servings.

NOTE: The sodium content can be reduced by approximately 80 mg per serving by using fresh pumpkin, or canned pumpkin without added salt.

Each ½ cup serving contains about:

> 121 calories; 231 mg sodium; 1 mg
> cholesterol; tr fat; 17 g carbohydrate;
> 6 g protein; 1 g fiber. Tr calories
> from fat.
> Exchanges: 1 B vegetable, 1 meat

FRENCH APPLE TART

½ cup [119 ml] unsweetened apple juice concentrate
¼ teaspoon maple extract
¼ teaspoon ground cinnamon
½ teaspoon cornstarch
3 medium tart green apples, peeled, cored, and thinly sliced
Pie Crust (following recipe)

In a saucepan, combine apple juice, maple extract, cinnamon, and cornstarch. Stir until blended. Cook and stir over low heat until thickened and smooth. Remove from heat, add sliced apples, and stir to coat apple slices well. Turn into pie crust, arranging apple slices pinwheel fashion. Bake at 425°F [218°C] for 20 to 30 minutes, or until apples are tender and crust is browned. Makes 8 servings.

PIE CRUST

¾ cup [105 g] unbleached flour
¼ teaspoon each grated lemon peel and orange peel
3 tablespoons vegetable oil
1½ tablespoons nonfat milk

Combine flour and lemon and orange peels in a small mixing bowl. Combine oil and milk in a measuring cup, but do not stir. Add all at once to flour mixture. Mix quickly with a fork until flour mixture begins to form a ball. Roll out between sheets of wax paper to a very thin 12-inch [30 cm] circle. Fit over an 8- or 9-inch [20- or 23 cm] pie plate or French tart pan, trimming edges. (To make individual tarts, divide the dough into 8 portions. Roll out each ball into a 5-inch [13 cm] circle and fit over individual 3-inch [8 cm] tart pans or muffin cups.) Dough may be chilled at this point. Pierce dough with a fork in several places to allow steam to escape during baking. Bake at 450°F [232°C] for 5 minutes or until golden. Cool before filling.

Each serving (one-eighth of pie) contains about:

> 125 calories; 2 mg sodium; 0 cholesterol;
> 5 g fat; 19 g carbohydrate; 1 g protein; 2 g
> fiber. 38% calories from fat.
> Exchanges: ½ fruit, 1 bread, 1 fat

NO-BAKE FRUIT CAKE

This delicious, easy do-ahead cake will help meet your daily fiber needs.

> *½ pound [225 g] each raisins, pitted dates, and dry figs*
> *½ cup [76 g] walnuts, shelled*
> *½ teaspoon vanilla*
> *⅛ teaspoon dark rum (optional)*

Combine raisins, dates, figs, walnuts, vanilla, and rum in a food processor. Blend until coarsley chopped. *Caution*: do not over-blend. Spoon and press mixture into a loaf pan. Cover with plastic wrap, and place a heavy object on top to weigh it down. Put in refrigerator for two or three days to blend flavors. Unmold, and serve thinly sliced. Serves 12.

Each slice contains about:

> 162 calories; 4 mg sodium; 0 cholesterol;
> 3 g fat; 34 g carbohydrate; 1 g protein;
> 7 g fiber. 12% calories from fat.
> Exchanges: 2 fruit, ½ fat

MEXICAN BREAD PUDDING

> *3 to 5 cups [180 to 285 g] toasted French Bread cubes, or*
>   *3½ cups [200 g] stale French Bread cubes (p. 47)*
> *¼ cup [165 g] raisins, plumped in hot water*
> *2 cups [473 ml] nonfat milk*
> *2 tablespoons low-calorie margarine*
> *1 cup [237 ml] unsweetened apple juice*
> *6 tablespoons egg substitute, or 2 egg whites*
> *2 tablespoons sugar*
> *1 teaspoon vanilla extract*
> *1 teaspoon ground cinnamon*
> *½ teaspoon ground nutmeg*
>   *Grated peel and juice of ½ lemon*

Combine bread cubes and raisins in a 13-by-9-inch [33-by-23 cm] nonstick baking dish. In a saucepan, scald milk and add margarine. Stir until margarine melts. Add apple juice, egg substitute or egg whites, sugar, vanilla extract, cinnamon, nutmeg, and lemon peel and juice and mix well. Pour over bread cubes in pan and mix well. Bake at 350°F [177°C] for 30 minutes, or until knife inserted in center of pudding comes out clean. Makes 8 servings.

Each ½ cup serving contains about:

> 150 calories; 98 mg sodium; 1 mg cholesterol;
> 3 g fat; 26 g carbohydrate; 6 g protein;
> 1 g fiber. 21% calories from fat.
> Exchanges: 1 bread, ¼ milk

SNOWDROP COOKIES

3 egg whites, at room temperature
¼ teaspoon cream of tartar, or 1 teaspoon white vinegar
1 teaspoon vanilla extract
*¾ cup [50 g] sugar**
¼ cup [145 g] semisweet chocolate chips (tiny size)

Beat egg whites until soft peaks form. Add cream of tartar, and vanilla extract and beat until stiff peaks form. Add sugar, 2 tablespoons at a time, beating after each addition. Fold in chocolate chips. Drop by heaping teaspoonfuls onto an ungreased foil-lined cookie sheet and bake at 250°F [121°C] for 20 to 25 minutes, or until pale cream in color. Outside of cookie will be hard; inside will be slightly soft. Makes 36 cookies.

* Sugar substitute cannot be substituted for sugar in this recipe.

Each cookie contains about:

> 24 calories; 6 mg sodium; 0 cholesterol;
> tr fat; 5 g carbohydrate; tr protein;
> 0 fiber. Tr calories from fat.
> Exchanges: ½ bread

PEANUT BUTTER COOKIES

⅓ *cup [76 g] margarine*

¼ *cup plus 2 tablespoons sugar*

3 *tablespoons egg substitute, or 1 egg white*

1 *cup [260 g] low-sodium, cream-style peanut butter*

½ *teaspoon baking soda*

¼ *teaspoon ground cinnamon*

1 *teaspoon vanilla extract*

1 *cup [140 g] sifted unbleached flour*

Cream together margarine and sugar until well blended. Beat in egg substitute or egg white, peanut butter, baking soda, cinnamon, and vanilla extract until smooth. Add flour and beat until well blended. Roll dough into balls about ¾ inch [2 cm] in diameter and place on ungreased cookie sheets. Score in crisscross fashion with fork tines to flatten. Bake at 375°F [190°C] for 10 to 12 minutes or until browned. Remove cookies from sheets and cool on wire racks. Makes 80 cookies.

Each cookie contains about:

> 35 calories; 31 mg sodium; 0 cholesterol;
> 2 g fat; 3 g carbohydrate; 1 g protein;
> tr fiber; 59% calories from fat.
> Exchanges: ½ bread

OATMEAL COOKIES

¼ *cup [59 ml] apple juice concentrate or brown sugar,*
packed

⅓ *cup [5 tablespoons] plus 2 tablespoons fig paste (ground*
figs), packed

¾ *cup margarine*

6 *tablespoons egg substitute, or 2 egg whites*

½ *teaspoon vanilla*

1 *teaspoon baking soda*

½ *tablespoon cinnamon*

¼ *teaspoon ground nutmeg*

1½ *cups [215 g] unbleached flour*

1⅓ *cups [113 g] quick rolled oats*

In a mixing bowl, cream together apple juice concentrate, fig paste, margarine, egg substitute, and vanilla. In a separate bowl, mix together baking soda, cinnamon, flour, and oatmeal. Add to fig paste mixture and blend until well incorporated. Spoon onto ungreased baking sheet, allowing room to spread. Bake at 350°F [177°C] for 10 to 15 minutes. Remove from baking sheet and cool. Makes 3 dozen cookies.

Each cookie contains about:

> 76 calories; 73 mg sodium; 0 cholesterol;
> 4 g fat; 9 g carbohydrate; 1 g protein;
> 1 g fiber. 49% calories from fat.
> Exchanges: 1 bread, 1 fat

FRUIT

BERRY BOWL

3 cups [675 g] strawberries, hulled and halved lengthwise
1 cup [225 g] fresh or frozen unsweetened raspberries,
*   thawed, or any berries*
1 tablespoon Framboise or Kirsch, optional

Combine strawberries and raspberries in a bowl. Drizzle with Framboise. Toss and serve. Makes 8 servings.

Each ½ cup serving contains about:

> 32 calories; 1 mg sodium; 0 cholesterol;
> tr fat; 7 g carbohydrate; tr protein;
> 2 g fiber. 11% calories from fat.
> Exchanges: 1 fruit

CITRUS COMPOTE

3 oranges
1 grapefruit
½ cup [119 ml] water
½ teaspoon vanilla extract
⅛ teaspoon ground cloves
2 tablespoons raisins
*   Fresh mint sprigs*

Grate peels of oranges and grapefruit into a saucepan. Be careful to use only color part of peels. Peel, seed, and dice oranges and grapefruit over the saucepan so no juice is lost. Add diced fruit, water, vanilla extract, cloves, and raisins to pan, bring to a boil, and simmer, uncovered, 10 minutes. Cool and chill. Spoon into stemmed glasses and garnish with mint sprigs, if desired. Makes 6 servings.

Each ½ cup serving contains about:

> 64 calories; 0 sodium; 0 cholesterol;
> tr fat; 16 g carbohydrate; tr protein;
> 2 g fiber. Tr calories from fat.
> Exchanges: 1 fruit

PAPAYA WITH LIME

> *3 papayas*
> *Juice of 2 limes*
> *6 lime wedges*
> *Fresh mint sprigs*

Peel and halve papayas. Remove seeds and discard. Place each papaya half, cut side down, on a serving plate. Slice horizontally ¼ inch [½ cm] thick and fan out slices slightly on plate. Sprinkle slices with lime juice and garnish with lime wedges and mint sprigs. Makes 6 servings.

Each serving contains about:

> 46 calories; 3 mg sodium; 0 cholesterol;
> tr fat; 12 g carbohydrate; tr protein;
> 1 g fiber. Tr calories from fat.
> Exchanges: 1 fruit

PEACHES GALLIANO

> *3 cups [675 g] peeled and sliced peaches (6 small peaches)*
> *½ cup [115 g] fresh or frozen unsweetened blueberries,*
>   *thawed*
> *1 tablespoon Galliano*

Place peach slices in a bowl. Top with blueberries and sprinkle with Galliano. Toss just before serving. Makes 6 servings.

Each ½ cup serving contains about:

> 53 calories; 0 sodium; 0 cholesterol;
> tr fat; 12 g carbohydrate; tr protein;
> 2 g fiber. Tr calories from fat.
> Exchanges: 1 fruit

PEACH MELBA

3 peaches, peeled, pitted, and halved, or 6 canned
  water-packed peach halves
6 tablespoons pureed raspberries
6 tablespoons low-fat vanilla yogurt

Place a peach half in each of six parfait glasses. Put 1 tablespoon raspberry puree on each peach. Top each with a tablespoon of yogurt. Makes 6 servings.

Each serving contains about:

> 43 calories; 9 mg sodium; 1 mg cholesterol;
> tr fat; 10 g carbohydrate; 1 g protein;
> 1 g fiber. Tr calories from fat
> Exchanges: 1 fruit

PEARS ALEXANDER

This quick-change artist triples as an appetizer, salad, or dessert.

6 small ripe pears, or 12 canned water-packed pear halves
1 tablespoon fresh lemon juice
½ cup [115 g] ricotta cheese (made from partially skimmed
  milk), at room temperature
2 tablespoons low-calorie Cream Cheese (p. 185)
1 tablespoon golden raisins
3 tablespoons crushed pistachio nuts, pecans, or walnuts

If using fresh pears, peel and cut each pear in half lengthwise, leaving stems intact on one pear half. Core centers to form cavities. Brush pears with lemon juice to prevent discoloration. Beat ricotta and cream cheese with a wooden spoon until soft and fluffy. Mix in raisins. Fill each pear cavity with about 1 tablespoon cheese mixture and then put pear halves together to form whole pears. Sprinkle in crushed nuts. Arrange on a serving plate and chill 2 hours before serving. If desired, cut pears horizontally into ½-inch [1½ cm] slices to serve over a bed of lettuce for salad or first-course appetizer. Makes 6 servings.

Each serving contains about:

> 128 calories; 36 mg sodium; 7 mg cholesterol;
> 4 g fat; 22 g carbohydrate; 2 g protein;
> 3 g fiber. 10% calories from fat.
> Exchanges: 1 fruit, 1 fat

PINEAPPLE IN RUM

Freeze the spears and you'll have edible swizzle sticks for tall summery drinks.

> 1 small pineapple, peeled, cored, and cut lengthwise in 12
>   spears
> 2 tablespoons rum extract or 1 teaspoon rum extract
>   Fresh mint sprigs

Marinate pineapple spears in rum, tossing frequently, at least 2 hours or overnight. Allow 2 spears per serving. Place on dessert plates and garnish with mint sprigs. Makes 6 servings.

Each serving contains about:

> 40 calories; 1 mg sodium; 0 cholesterol;
> tr fat; 10 g carbohydrate; tr protein;
> 1 g fiber. Tr calories from fat.
> Exchanges:1 fruit

STRAWBERRIES IN MERINGUE

> 1 basket strawberries [450 g], hulled and halved lengthwise
>   Meringue Shells (following recipe)
> 6 tablespoons low-fat strawberry yogurt or Heavenly
>   Whipped Topping (p. 184)

Arrange sliced strawberries, point up, in Meringue Shells. Top each with 1 tablespoon Heavenly Whipped Topping. Makes 6 servings.

MERINGUE SHELLS

3 egg whites, at room temperature
1 teaspoon cream of tartar
1 teaspoon vanilla extract
¾ cup [145 g] sugar

Beat egg whites until soft peaks form. Add cream of tartar and vanilla and beat until stiff. Add sugar, 2 tablespoons at a time, beating after each addition. For each shell, drop 2 heaping tablespoons of egg white mixture on a foil-lined baking sheet. Make indentations to form shells. Bake at 250°F [121°C] for 30 to 35 minutes, or until pale golden in color. Outside will be hard and inside soft. Cool, then remove from baking sheet. Makes 6 shells.

Each serving contains about:

> 134 calories; 69 mg sodium; 1 mg cholesterol;
> tr fat; 30 g carbohydrate; 2 g protein;
> 1 g fiber. 2% calories from fat.
> Exchanges: 1 fruit

STRAWBERRIES ROMANOFF

1 teaspoon rum extract, or 1 tablespoon rum
1 cup [91 g] low-fat vanilla yogurt or Heavenly Whipped
Topping (p. 184)
2 baskets [900 g] ripe strawberries, hulled and sliced or left
whole

Stir rum into vanilla yogurt. Chill until serving time. Spoon ½ cup berries in each of 6 stemmed sherbet glasses. Top with about 3 tablespoons of the topping. Makes 6 servings.

Each ½ cup strawberries with 3 tablespoons topping contains about:

> 65 calories; 26 mg sodium; 2 mg cholesterol;
> tr fat; 12 g carbohydrate; 2 g protein;
> 2 g fiber. 11% calories from fat.
> Exchanges: 1 fruit

MELON BASKETS

3 small cantaloupes
2 cups [450 g] watermelon balls
2 cups [450 g] honeydew melon balls
2 tablespoons orange-flavored liqueur (optional)
  Fresh mint sprigs

Cut cantaloupes in half. Scoop out seeds and carve balls from flesh, leaving cantaloupe shells intact. Combine cantaloupe balls with watermelon and honeydew in a bowl. Drizzle with liqueur and toss to blend flavors. Place 1 cup melon balls in each of the 6 cantaloupe shells. Garnish with mint sprigs. Makes 6 servings.

Each serving contains about:

> 62 calories; 23 mg sodium; 0 cholesterol;
> tr fat; 15 g carbohydrate; tr protein;
> 2 g fiber. Tr calories from fat.
> Exchanges: 1 fruit

BERRIES ON ICE

24 long-stemmed strawberries
  Crushed ice
2 tablespoons brown sugar
2 tablespoons low-fat plain yogurt

Attractively arrange strawberries on a bed of crushed ice in a bowl. Place brown sugar in one small bowl and the yogurt in another. Dip strawberries first in sugar and then in yogurt to eat. Makes 6 servings.

Each serving (4 strawberries with dips) contains about:

> 32 calories: 5 mg sodium; 0 cholesterol;
> tr fat; 7 g carbohydrate; tr protein;
> 2 g fiber. Tr calories from fat.
> Exchanges: ½ fruit

ICES AND ICE CREAMS

COFFEE ICE

1 envelope (1 tablespoon) unflavored gelatin
¼ cup [59 ml] water
2 cups [473 ml] hot strong coffee
¼ cup [50 g] sugar
   Juice of 2 lemons and 1 orange
1 teaspoon each grated lemon and orange peels

Soften gelatin in water, then dissolve in hot coffee. Add sugar, juices, and peels. Turn into a bowl or freezer tray and freeze until slushy. Beat until evenly blended, return to freezer, and freeze until almost solid. Break up ice and beat until slushy. Return to freezer and freeze solid. Remove from freezer 10 minutes before serving time. Chop with a spoon until mixture is consistency of thick slush. Spoon into serving dishes. Makes 1 quart.

Each ½ cup serving contains about:

     33 calories; 3 mg sodium; 0 cholesterol;
     0 fat; 10 g carbohydrate; tr protein;
     0 fiber. 0 calories from fat.
     Exchanges: ½ bread

STRAWBERRY ICE

1 envelope (1 tablespoon) unflavored gelatin
1 cup [237 ml] water
2 cups [450 g] Strawberry Sauce (p. 181)
1 teaspoon fresh lemon juice

Soften gelatin in ¼ cup [59 ml] of the water. Heat remaining ¾ cup water and add gelatin mixture, stirring until gelatin dissolves. Remove from heat and cool. Stir in Strawberry Sauce and lemon juice. Turn into a bowl or freezer tray and freeze until slushy. Beat until evenly blended, return to freezer, and freeze until almost solid. Break up ice and beat until slushy. Return to freezer and freeze solid. Remove from freezer 10 minutes before serving. Chop with a spoon until mixture is consistency of thick slush. Spoon into serving dishes. Makes about 3 cups.

Each ½ cup serving contains about:

> 32 calories; 2 mg sodium; 0 cholesterol;
> tr fat; 7 g carbohydrate; tr protein;
> 1 g fiber. Tr calories from fat.
> Exchanges: 1 fruit

VANILLA ICE CREAM

This ice cream has half the calories and fat of the commercial ones.

> *3½ cups [829 ml] evaporated nonfat milk*
> *¼ cup [65 g] plus 1 tablespoon sugar*
> *1½ teaspoons vanilla extract*

Combine the evaporated milk, sugar, and vanilla. Put in an ice cream freezer and freeze according to manufacturer's directions. Makes about 5 cups.

Each ½ cup serving contains about:

> 96 calories; 103 mg sodium; 4 mg cholesterol;
> tr fat; 17 g carbohydrate; 6 g protein;
> tr fiber. 0 calories from fat.
> Exchanges: ½ milk, 1 fruit

APRICOT OR PEACH ICE CREAM

Use 4 pounds [1800 g] ripe apricots or peaches. Peel, pit, slice, and puree the fruit. Fold it into Vanilla Ice Cream mixture (preceding recipe) at midpoint of freezing, then finish freezing. Makes about 1½ quarts [1½ L].

STRAWBERRY ICE CREAM

Prepare Strawberry Sauce (p. 181) and fold into Vanilla Ice Cream mixture (preceding recipe) at midpoint of freezing, then finish freezing.

SWEET CRÊPES

APPLE SIZZLE CRÊPES

1 tablespoon low-calorie margarine
2 medium tart green apples or Golden Delicious apples,
*   peeled, cored, and thinly sliced*
½ cup [119 ml] unsweetened apple juice concentrate
2 teaspoons cornstarch
¼ teaspoon each vanilla extract and maple extract
1 teaspoon water
6 Feather Crêpes (p. 63)
¾ cup [80 g] low-fat vanilla yogurt or Heavenly Whipped
*   Topping (p. 184)*
*   Ground cinnamon*
*   Toasted almonds (optional)*

In a skillet, melt margarine over low heat. Add apples and apple juice and mix gently. Cover and cook over low heat until apples are soft, stirring occasionally, about 10 minutes. Mix cornstarch with vanilla and maple extracts, and water. Stir into apple mixture, and cook and stir until apple mixture thickens. Top each crêpe with ¼ cup apple filling. Roll jelly-roll fashion and serve topped with 2 tablespoons vanilla yogurt or Heavenly Whipped Topping. Sprinkle with cinnamon and toasted almonds, if desired. Makes 6 servings.

STRAWBERRY CRÊPES
Fill each Feather Crêpe with ¼ cup [60 g] sliced strawberries. Roll jelly-roll fashion and top with 1 tablespoon low-fat plain yogurt and 2 tablespoons Strawberry Sauce (p. 181).

PEACH CRÊPES
Fill each Feather Crêpe with ¼ cup [60 g] sliced peaches. Roll jelly-roll fashion and top with 2 tablespoons low-fat peach yogurt.

Each apple crêpe contains about:

> 139 calories; 64 mg sodium; 2 mg cholesterol;
> 3 g fat; 24 g carbohydrate; 4 g protein;
> 1 g fiber. 19% calories from fat.
> Exchanges: ½ fruit, ½ bread

FRUIT IN CRÊPE BASKETS

1 medium banana, diagonally sliced
½ teaspoon fresh lemon juice
1 cup [151 g] fresh or unsweetened frozen blueberries or blackberries, thawed
1 cup [225 g] sliced strawberries
½ cup [115 g] melon balls or cubes
6 Feather Crêpe Cups (p. 64)
6 tablespoons low-fat fruit-flavored yogurt of choice
1 kiwi fruit, peeled and sliced (optional)

Place banana slices in a large bowl. Sprinkle with lemon juice to prevent darkening. Add berries and melon balls and toss to blend flavors. Place ½ cup [115 g] of the fruit mixture in each crêpe cup. Top with 1 tablespoon yogurt and garnish with a slice of kiwi fruit, if available, or other cut fruit. Makes 6 servings.

Each crêpe cup with ½ cup fruit contains about:

> 103 calories; 25 mg sodium; 1 mg cholesterol;
> 1 g fat; 21 g carbohydrate; 2 g protein;
> 3 g fiber. 11% calories from fat.
> Exchanges: ½ bread, 1 fruit

———————— SOUFFLÉS ————————

CHOCOLATE SOUFFLÉ

1 tablespoon cornstarch
½ cup [119 ml] nonfat milk
¼ cup [59 ml] evaporated nonfat milk
3 squares (3 ounces) [85 g] semisweet chocolate, broken
1 tablespoon crème de cacao (optional)
½ cup [115 g] egg substitute, or 3 egg whites
3 egg whites

Combine cornstarch and milks in a saucepan. Bring to a boil, reduce heat to low, and cook and stir until thickened and smooth. Add chocolate and crème de cacao. Remove from heat and stir until chocolate melts. Cool slightly. Mix in egg substitute, a tablespoon at a time. Beat egg whites until stiff but not dry. Stir one-fourth of whites into chocolate sauce to lighten it, then gently fold in remaining whites. Spoon into six individual greased ½-cup [115 g] soufflé dishes or a greased 1-quart [1 L] soufflé dish and bake at 350°F [117°C] for 10 to 15 minutes for individual soufflés and 40 minutes for large, or until set and puffy. Do not overcook. Serve at once. Makes 6 servings.

Each ½ cup serving contains about:

> 130 calories; 93 mg sodium; 1 mg cholesterol;
> 6 g fat; 15 g carbohydrate; 6 g protein;
> tr fiber. 38% calories from fat.
> Exchanges: 1 bread, 1¼ fat

LEMON SOUFFLÉ

The staying power of this lemony soufflé is amazing.

> ½ cup [119 ml] evaporated nonfat milk
> ¼ cup [59 ml] water
> 4½ teaspoons cornstarch
> 5 tablespoons fresh lemon juice
> 2 teaspoons grated lemon peel
> ½ cup [115 g] egg substitute, or 4 egg whites
> 2 egg whites
> ¼ teaspoon cream of tartar, or 1 teaspoon vinegar
> ¼ cup [50 g] sugar

Combine milk, water, and cornstarch in small saucepan. Bring to a boil, reduce heat to low, and cook and stir until sauce is thickened and smooth. Remove from heat and stir in lemon juice and peel. Cool slightly. Mix in egg substitute, a tablespoon at a time. Beat egg whites with cream of tartar until stiff but not dry. Beat in sugar. Stir one-fourth of whites into lemon sauce to lighten it, then gently fold in remaining whites. Turn into a greased 1-quart [1 L] soufflé dish or casserole. Bake at 350°F [177°C] for 45 minutes, or until set and puffy. Do not overcook. Serve at once. Makes 6 servings.

Each ½ cup serving contains about:

> 82 calories; 87 mg sodium; 1 mg cholesterol;
> tr fat; 14 g carbohydrate; 5 g protein;
> 0 fiber. Tr calories from fat.
> Exchanges: ½ bread, ½ fruit, 1 fat

STRAWBERRY SOUFFLÉ

1 basket [450 g] strawberries, hulled
2 teaspoons fresh lemon juice
2 tablespoons cornstarch
2 tablespoons water
3 tablespoons sugar
6 tablespoons egg substitute, or 2 egg whites
2 egg whites

Puree strawberries, reserving 4 large whole berries. Mix puree with lemon juice in a saucepan. Finely dice the 4 reserved berries and add to puree. Dissolve cornstarch in water. Add to saucepan with sugar. Bring to a boil, reduce heat to low, and cook and stir until smooth and thickened, about 2 to 3 minutes. Cool slightly. Mix in egg substitute, a tablespoon at a time. Beat egg whites until stiff but not dry. Stir one-fourth of whites into strawberry sauce to lighten it, then gently fold in remaining whites. Turn into a greased 1-quart [1 L] soufflé dish or casserole and bake at 375°F [190°C] 30 minutes, or until set and puffy. Serve at once. Makes 6 servings.

Each ½ cup serving contains about:

> 68 calories; 53 mg sodium; 0 cholesterol;
> tr fat; 12 g carbohydrate; 3 g protein;
> 1 g fiber. Tr calories from fat.
> Exchanges: 1 fruit

BEVERAGES

Beverages are often the culprit in pushing your daily calorie limits over the edge.

A couple of 12-ounce glasses of regular beer consumed each evening can add 300 calories a day to your diet. That's 2,100 calories added each week. An eggnog sipped at a holiday bash can add 350 calories to an already calorie-loaded meal.

We use several tricks to reduce the total calories in these alcoholic and nonalcoholic drinks for every occasion. There are punches for parties, smoothies that wake you up, and nightcaps that bed you down. There are a few beverages that children will enjoy with their cookies and an herb tea you will love to share with friends.

The calories, fat, and cholesterol of a drink made with dairy products go down when nonfat products are used. Relying on the natural sweetness of fruits and fruit juices, instead of adding sugar, will help cut calories, too.

Egg substitute replaces eggs in our eggnog, resulting in 93 calories and very little cholesterol per cup.

Cheers!

BLOODY MARY

1 quart [1 L] low-sodium tomato juice
Dash hot pepper sauce
Pepper to taste
1 teaspoon fresh lemon juice
¼ teaspoon each onion powder and Worcestershire sauce
3 jiggers vodka
Ice cubes
6 celery stalks with leaves

Combine the tomato juice, hot pepper sauce, pepper, lemon juice, onion powder, Worcestershire sauce, and vodka in a pitcher. Stir to blend well.

Pour in individual glasses over ice. Add celery stalk, leaf side up. Makes 6 servings.

Each ¾ cup serving contains about:

> 67 calories; 57 mg sodium; 0 cholesterol;
> tr fat; 7 g carbohydrate; tr protein;
> 1 g fiber. 0 calories from fat.
> Exchanges: 1 B vegetable

VIRGIN MARY

Follow directions for Bloody Mary (preceding recipe) but omit the vodka. Nutrient analysis is the same as for Bloody Mary, except calories are reduced to 32 per serving.

BREAKFAST SHAKE

All you need is some toast to complete this breakfast-in-a-glass.

> *1 cup [225 g] nonfat milk*
> *2 heaping teaspoons sweetened cocoa powder*
> *3 tablespoons egg substitute, or 1 egg white*
> *1 small banana*

Combine milk, cocoa, egg substitute, and banana in a blender container. Blend until frothy and smooth. Makes 1 serving.

Each serving contains about:

> 258 calories; 283 mg sodium; 5 mg cholesterol;
> 3 g fat; 44 g carbohydrate; 16 g protein;
> 3 g fiber. 10% calories from fat.
> Exchanges: 1 milk, 1 meat, 1 fruit, ¼ bread

EGGNOG

> *4 cups [1 L] nonfat milk*
> *1 cup [225 g] egg substitute, or 6 egg whites*
> *2½ tablespoons sugar*
> *2 or 3 teaspoons rum extract*
> *2 egg whites*
>   *About 2 tablespoons Heavenly Whipped Topping (p. 184)*
>   *Ground nutmeg*

Combine milk, egg substitute, 2 tablespoons of the sugar, and rum extract in a bowl. Beat with rotary beater or electric mixer until well blended. Chill thoroughly. Beat egg whites lightly with remaining sugar and fold into milk mixture. Top each serving with 1 teaspoon Heavenly Whipped Topping and sprinkle with nutmeg. Makes 8 servings.

Each 5 ounce serving contains about:

> 93 calories; 131 mg sodium; 3 mg cholesterol;
> 1 g fiber; 10 g carbohydrate; 9 g protein;
> 0 fiber. 12% calories from fat.
> Exchanges: 1 milk

HERB TEA

No calories, cholesterol, or sodium in this tea, so enjoy it as a refreshment any time of the day.

> *Water*
> *Lemon, orange and/or mint leaves*
> *Cinnamon stick (optional)*

Using ¾ cup [178 ml] of water per cup of tea, bring water to a boil. For each serving, add 3 lemon, orange, or mint leaves, or a combination, to the boiling water. Cover, turn off the heat, and steep for 2 to 3 minutes. (The longer the leaves steep, the stronger the tea.) For additional flavor, add ½ cinnamon stick to leaves while brewing.

Sodium is negligible; no calories or cholesterol.

MIMOSA COCKTAIL

> *1 fifth Champagne*
> *4 cups [1 L] unsweetened orange juice*
> *Ice cubes*
> *Orange slices*
> *Fresh mint leaves*

Fill stemmed wine glasses or goblets with half Champagne and half orange juice. Add ice cubes and garnish with orange slices and mint leaves. Makes about 8 servings.

Each 8 ounce serving contains about:

> 127 calories; 5 mg sodium; 0 cholesterol;
> tr fat; 15 g carbohydrate; tr protein;
> tr fiber. 0 calories from fat.
> Exchanges: 1 fruit, ½ bread

PERSIAN REFRESHER

*1 quart [1 L] buttermilk**
1 teaspoon dried mint, or 1 tablespoon chopped fresh mint
Ice cubes
Fresh mint sprigs (optional)

Mix buttermilk with dried or chopped mint. Pour over ice cubes in tall glasses. Garnish with mint sprigs, if desired. Makes 6 servings.

*Note that buttermilk is high in sodium and, if you must watch sodium intake, substitute plain low-fat yogurt.

Each 5 ounce serving contains about:

> 65 calories; 171 mg sodium; 7 mg cholesterol;
> 1 g fat; 8 g carbohydrate; 5 g protein;
> 0 fiber. 19% calories from fat.
> Exchanges: ¾ milk

SPARKLING PUNCH

Unsweetened cranberry juice
Lime-flavored carbonated beverage (sugar-free), or club soda
Ice Ring (following recipe)
Orange slices
Fresh mint sprigs

Combine equal parts cranberry juice and lime beverage in a punch bowl. Add Ice Ring and float orange slices and mint sprigs on top of punch.

ICE RING
Fill ring mold with distilled water to within ¼ inch of rim. Freeze until solid. Dip briefly in hot water to unmold and place in punch bowl.

Each 8 ounce serving contains about:

> 23 calories; 25 mg sodium; 0 cholesterol;
> 0 fat; 6 g carbohydrate; 0 protein; 0 fiber.
> 0 calories from fat.
> Exchanges: ½ fruit

SUNRISE PUNCH

1 quart [1 L] unsweetened cranberry juice
1 quart [1 L] unsweetened orange juice
1 quart unsweetened pineapple juice
  Orange slices
  Fresh mint sprigs

Combine cranberry juice, orange juice, and pineapple juice and stir well to blend. Pour into glasses and garnish each serving with an orange slice and a mint sprig. Makes about 25 servings.

Each 4 ounce serving contains about:

> 48 calories; 2 mg sodium; 0 cholesterol;
> 0 fat; 12 g carbohydrate; 0 protein; tr fiber.
> 0 calories from fat.
> Exchanges: 1 fruit

WINE SPRITZER

1 quart [1 L] club soda
1 quart [1 L] dry white or red wine
  Ice cubes
  Lime or lemon wedges

Put ½ cup [119 ml] club soda and ½ cup [119 ml] wine in each of 8 tall glasses. Add ice cubes and garnish with lime wedges. Makes 8 servings.

Each 8 ounce serving contains about:

> 78 calories; 30 mg sodium; 0 cholesterol;
> 0 fat; 1 g carbohydrate; tr protein;
> 0 fiber. 0 calories from fat.
> Exchanges: 1 bread

Substitute 1 quart [1 L] unsweetened orange juice for the wine in Wine Spritzer. Makes 8 servings.

Each 8 ounce serving contains about:

> 14 calories; 25 mg sodium; 0 cholesterol;
> 0 fat; 3 g carbohydrate; tr protein; 0 fiber.
> 0 calories from fat.
> Exchanges: ½ fruit

YOGURT SMOOTHIE

*½ cup [115 g] frozen or chilled low-fat fruit-flavored or
  plain yogurt
½ cup [119 ml] nonfat milk
½ cup [115 g] fresh or unsweetened canned fruit, drained
3 ice cubes*

Combine ice cubes, yogurt, milk, and fruit. Blend until smooth. Makes 2 servings.

Each 6 ounce serving contains about:

> 98 calories; 62 mg sodium; 3 mg cholesterol;
> tr fat; 19 g carbohydrate; 5 g protein;
> tr fiber. Tr calories from fat.
> Exchanges: ½ milk, ¼ fruit

NOTE: For a nutritionally rich Smoothie, add 2 tablespoons of 1 beaten egg, and blend. Calories will increase to 280, sodium to 188 mg, cholesterol to 228 mg, fat to 3 g. Protein content is 7 g and there are 2% calories from fat.

MENUS

Studies show that most people have difficulty preparing menus. A menu balanced in nutrients, low in calories, fats, cholesterol, salt, and sugar, yet glamorous, quick, and easy to prepare is a tall order. It takes skill and experience and knowledge about nutrients to fill the order.

Our menu suggestions take all the guesswork out of menu planning. Plus the nutrient analysis included with each menu shows you at a glance the amount of sodium, fats, cholesterol, and calories each person is getting as well as the percentages of fat in each meal. This will help you plan meals according to individual or family needs.

That doesn't mean you may not stray from the menu suggestions. We hope they will be used as a guide for further menu planning. If you substitute dishes, you will know the exact nutrient content of each dish because each recipe contains an analysis. These analyses for the complete menu will help you make wise food choices. And that, after all, is the goal of this chapter.

———————— BARBECUE BASH ————————

Pizza Canapé (p. 20)
Grilled Salmon (p. 80)
Corn on the Cob
Marinated Mushrooms (p. 148)
Ice Cream (p. 207)

Nutrient Analysis: 420 calories; 201 mg sodium; 62 mg cholesterol; 10 g fat; 45 g carbohydrate; 38 g protein; 3 g fiber. 22% calories from fat.

FRIED CHICKEN DINNER

Oven-Fried Chicken (p. 91)
Coleslaw De Luxe (p. 145)
Oven-Fried Potatoes (p. 138)
Corn Bread (p. 44)
Melon Baskets (p. 205)

Nutrient Analysis: 494 calories; 391 mg sodium; 75 mg cholesterol; 11 g fat; 67 g carbohydrate; 33 g protein; 5 g fiber. 20% calories from fat.

FRIDAY FISH DINNER

Skinny Dip (p. 16) with assorted raw vegetables
Swordfish Piquant (p. 73)
Steamed Asparagus (p. 127)
Rice Pilaf (p. 120)
Pears Alexander (p. 202)

Nutrient Analysis: 495 calories; 236 mg sodium; 45 mg cholesterol; 15 g fat; 73 g carbohydrate; 25 g protein; 5 g fiber. 27% calories from fat.

SUNDAY LASAGNA DINNER

Chicken Pacifica (p. 18)
Lasagna (p. 117)
Broccoli alla Romana (p. 128)
Marinated Mushrooms (p. 148)
California Cheesecake (p. 192)

Nutrient Analysis: 445 calories; 402 mg sodium; 56 mg cholesterol; 17 g fat; 39 g carbohydrate; 26 g protein; 3 g fiber. 34% calories from fat.

SATURDAY NIGHT SUPPER

Lobster Bisque (p. 32)
Ratatouille Crêpes (p. 62)
Strawberries Romanoff (p. 204)

Nutrient Analysis: 256 calories; 298 mg sodium; 37 mg cholesterol; 4 g fat; 35 g carbohydrate; 18 g protein; 4 g fiber. 14% calories from fat.

CHINESE DINNER

Chinatown Soup (p. 28)
Chicken Oriental (p. 89)
Steamed Rice (p. 122)
Chinese Stir-Fry Vegetables (p. 129)
Melon with Port (p. 19)

Nutrient Analysis: 361 calories; 322 mg sodium; 55 mg cholesterol; 6 g fat; 52 g carbohydrate; 23 g protein; 6 g fiber. 15% calories from fat.

MEXICAN DINNER

Tortilla Salad (p. 24)
Enchiladas Suiza (p. 86)
Spanish Rice (p. 121)
Zucchini Oregano (p. 136)
Pineapple in Rum (p. 203)

Nutrient Analysis: 527 calories; 220 mg sodium; 42 mg cholesterol; 13 g fat; 79 g carbohydrate; 35 g protein; 5 g fiber. 22% calories from fat.

FANCY ITALIAN DINNER

Appetizer Artichokes (p. 17) with Vinaigrette (p. 165)
Kathy's Cannelloni (p. 115)
Tomato-Cauliflower Salad (p. 150)
Peaches Galliano (p. 201)

Nutrient Analysis (based on 2 cannelloni): 357 calories; 216 mg sodium; 16 mg cholesterol; 16 g fat; 40 g carbohydrate; 19 g protein; 7 g fiber. 25% calories from fat.

DINNER for TWO or FOUR

Chilled Crookneck Soup (p. 36)
Steak Diane (p. 103)
Green Beans Amandine (p. 131)
Pommes Parisienne (p. 138)
California Salad (p. 152)
Lemon Soufflé (p. 210)

Nutrient Analysis: 545 calories; 265 mg sodium; 67 mg cholesterol; 17 g fat; 68 g carbohydrate; 28 g protein; 6 g fiber. 28% calories from fat.

FESTIVE HOLIDAY DINNER

Eggnog (p. 215)
Roast Turkey with Royal Glaze (p. 92)
Turkey Gravy (p. 170)
Apple-Onion Stuffing (p. 93)
Peas and Pods (p. 133)
Candied Sweets (p. 137)
Sunshine Salad (p. 156)
Cloud Biscuits (p. 43)
Cold Pumpkin Soufflé (p. 195)

Nutrient Analysis: 703 calories; 677 mg sodium; 76 mg cholesterol; 15 g fat; 106 g carbohydrate; 38 g protein; 6 g fiber. 19% calories from fat.

HOLLYWOOD BOWL PICNIC

Gazpacho Andaluz (p. 36)
Picnic Lobster (p. 78) with Seafood Cocktail Sauce (p. 186)
Mediterranean Salad (p. 149)
Ramona's Rolls (p. 48)
No-Bake Fruit Cake (p. 197)

Nutrient Analysis: 425 calories; 590 mg sodium; 72 mg cholesterol; 8 g fat;
66 g carbohydrate; 24 g protein; 9 g fiber. 17% calories from fat.

SIT-DOWN DINNER

Scallops Dejonghe (p. 20)
Cornish Game Hens with Herb–Corn Bread Stuffing (p. 95)
Green Beans Amandine (p. 131)
Endive-Watercress Salad (p. 146) with Lemon Dressing (p. 163)
Peach Melba (p. 202)

Nutrient Analysis: 447 calories; 297 mg sodium; 78 mg cholesterol; 12 g fat;
41 g carbohydrate; 34 g protein; 6 g fiber. 24% calories from fat.

SPAGHETTI DINNER

Hearty Minestrone (p. 31)
Spaghetti with Italian Meat Sauce (p. 118)
Hearts of Romaine Lettuce with Creamy Garlic Dressing (p. 162)
Lemon Spinach (p. 132)
French Bread (p. 46)
Coffee Ice (p. 206)

Nutrient Analysis: 393 calories; 116 mg sodium; 9 mg cholesterol; 5 g fat;
74 g carbohydrate; 13 g protein; 8 g fiber. 12% calories from fat.

CLUB LUNCHEON

Consommé Madrilène (p. 29)
Chicken-Stuffed Papaya (p. 153)
Bread Sticks (p. 46)
Chocolate Mousse Pie (p. 193)

Nutrient Analysis: 449 calories; 312 mg sodium; 46 mg cholesterol; 14 g fat; 50 g carbohydrate; 25 g protein; 3 g fiber. 28% calories from fat.

SUNDAY FOOTBALL TV LUNCH

Albondigas Soup (p. 27)
California Tostada (p. 143)
Papaya with Lime (p. 201)

Nutrient Analysis: 413 calories; 288 mg sodium; 43 mg cholesterol; 13 g fat; 49 g carbohydrate; 24 g protein; 6 g fiber. 28% calories from fat.

ELEGANT BRUNCH

Bloody Mary (p. 214)
Spinach Soufflé (p. 55)
Waldorf Salad (p. 155)
Ramona's Whole-Wheat Bread, toasted (p. 47)
Ice Cream (p. 207)

Nutrient Analysis: 377 calories; 260 mg sodium; 6 mg cholesterol; 6 g fat; 53 g carbohydrate; 16 g protein; 5 g fiber. 15% calories from fat.

FIRESIDE SUPPER

French Onion Soup (p. 30)
Omelet Supreme (p. 53)
Garlic Bread (p. 45)
French Apple Tart (p. 196)

Nutrient Analysis: 408 calories; 340 mg sodium; 7 mg cholesterol; 14 g fat; 50 g carbohydrate; 20 g protein; 5 g fiber. 30% calories from fat.

MODIFYING RECIPES

Following these tips will help you modify your recipes and menus to reduce calories, fat, cholesterol, sugar, and salt in your diet, while increasing the amount of fiber.

A warning, however: when reducing calories, fats, and cholesterol in the diet, you should be careful not to do so at the expense of essential nutrients, particularly iron, calcium, and zinc, which are especially low among women and teenage girls.

MODIFYING FAT AND CALORIES

When you trim fats you automatically trim calories. Here's how:

- Reduce or eliminate fats wherever appropriate.
- Trim fat from meats as much as possible.
- Use poultry without the skin (this cuts about 60 calories per 3 ounces of light meat).
- Buy lean cuts of meat, such as sirloin, rib roast, top round, filet, lean ground beef (less fatty meat cuts have about 100 fewer calories in every 3 ounces than meat cuts higher in fat content).
- Substitute stocks made with wine and herbs for cream or butter sauces.
- Cut down on oil in dressings by substituting flavored vinegars, such as balsamic, herb, or rice vinegars.
- Use olive oil in salad dressings. Because of its rich flavor, you can use less of this oil than other oils. Olive oil also is thought to help reduce blood cholesterol.
- Use low-calorie margarine, dressings, and sauces (low-calorie margarine has 50 fewer calories per tablespoon than regular margarine).
- Each cube (½ cup) butter or margarine has 800 calories, and each tablespoon oil (all types) has 124 calories—so use sparingly.
- Reduce fat in baked goods.
- Substitute oil or margarine for butter or lard in baked goods.
- Reduce the amount of oil or margarine called for to reduce total fat in baked goods.
- Eliminate high-calorie, high-fat items, such as nuts, coconut, and frosting, when making cakes and cookies.
- Eliminate oil in water when cooking pasta.
- Use egg substitute or egg white to eliminate the need for eggs and egg yolks, which are high in calories, fat, and cholesterol.

- If egg yolks are essential to a recipe, use half the amount called for.
- Season foods with herbs and spices instead of sauces, butter, or margarine.
- Substitute low-fat or nonfat milk products, such as evaporated nonfat milk, for cream or half-and-half.
- Select low-fat cheeses, such as Dorman's, Lite Line, or New Holland (see Specialty Products chapter for a list of low-fat cheeses on p. 293).
- Reduce amount of cheese called for in recipes (for an example, see recipe for Pizza on p. 19).
- In lieu of sour cream, cream cheese, mayonnaise, or margarine, use light versions, such as Fleischman's, Weight Watcher's, Imperial, and Kraft brands (see Specialty Products list on p. 295).
- Make single-crust instead of double-crust pies.
- Make crustless quiches, apple pies, or pumpkin pies.
- Check labels of packaged items for fat content.

MODIFYING SODIUM

- Cut down on salt gradually over a period of time.
- Avoid adding salt when cooking pasta or frozen vegetables.
- To add flavor to pasta or frozen vegetables, cook with chicken or beef stock.
- Avoid adding salt to bread, muffins, or other baked items that contain baking soda, baking powder, butter, or margarine, all of which already contain salt.
- Reduce or eliminate salt in such items as salad dressings, sauces, and soups.
- Use herbs, spices, and flavoring extracts and essences in lieu of salt in recipes (see chart on Herbs and Spices, p. 279, for ideas).
- Use fresh herbs when available.
- Try herb blends made without salt that are available in markets today (see Specialty Products list on p. 296 for sources).
- Check labels of low-calorie dressings and sauces to avoid excess sodium intake.
- Make your own stocks, dressings, sauces, and condiments to control salt content.
- Use lemon juice, wine, herbs, or spices to heighten flavor of salads, vegetables, or soups (for example, see recipe for Chicken Soup on p. 28).

MODIFYING SUGAR

- Rely on the natural sweetness of fruit and fruit juices instead of using sugar.
- Use sugar-free products whenever appropriate.
- Eliminate or reduce sugar and replace liquid with fruit juice concentrates (see French Apple Tart, p. 196).
- Substitute raisins, puree of dates, figs, bananas, or applesauce for sugar in baked recipes (see Oat Bran Muffins, p. 44, and Oatmeal cookies, p. 199).
- Substitute fruit spreads, low-calorie jams, and jellies for sugar in baked recipes.
- Check package labels for sugar content information.

MODIFYING COOKING METHODS

- Steam, poach, bake, broil, grill, and stir-fry meats, fish, and poultry, without added fat.
- Stir-fry in a small amount of oil or nonfat broths, wine, or fruit juices.
- Avoid frying altogether.
- Cook meat on a rack to drain off excess fat.
- Cook with nonstick cooking utensils.
- Use noncaloric vegetable sprays in lieu of oil.
- Scoop off coagulated fat after chilling soups or stocks.
- See Specialty Products list on p. 296 for cooking equipment that eliminates the need for cooking with fat or salt.

INCREASING COMPLEX CARBOHYDRATES AND FIBER

- Eating more fruits, vegetables, and grains on a daily basis will help you reduce your fat and protein intake. (Complex carbohydrates contain only 4 calories per gram; fat contains 9 calories per gram.)
- Substitute fruit for sugary, fatty sweets.
- When adding fiber to the diet, add a good mixture of both soluble and insoluble fiber. You can do this by eating five or more daily servings of fruits and vegetables and six or more servings of breads, cereals, and legumes. Examples of foods with soluble fiber are oat bran, figs, dry beans (kidney, pinto, lima, and navy), black-eyed peas, carrots, green beans, corn, peas, zucchini, broccoli, bananas, apples, oranges, and pears. Examples of foods with insoluble fiber are wheat bran, whole-wheat bread and cereals, and fruits and vegetables. (See the chart on fiber content of common foods on p. 274.)

- Add oat bran to your diet by adding it to baked products, such as pancakes, muffins, or meat loaves.
- Substitute oat flour for all-purpose or bleached flour.
- Add insoluble fiber to your diet in the form of fruits, vegetables, or whole-grain breads by preparing Chinese Stir-Fry Vegetables, p. 129; Fabulous Salad, p. 147; or Chicken Pasta Al Pesto, p. 119.

HOW TO MODIFY YOUR OWN RECIPES

Use the guidelines in the Modifying Recipes chapter to help you make your favorite recipes healthier. The following examples illustrate how easily this can be done.

SPINACH DIP
(original recipe)

1 cup mayonnaise
1 cup sour cream
½ teaspoon salt
4 green onions
3 tablespoons fresh lemon juice
2 cloves garlic, minced
1 (10-ounce) package frozen chopped spinach, thawed, drained, and squeezed dry

Serve with chips

SPINACH DIP
(*Light Style* version)

½ cup low-calorie mayonnaise
1½ cups low-fat plain yogurt
Omit salt
4 green onions
3 tablespoons lemon juice
2 cloves minced garlic
1 (10-ounce) package frozen chopped spinach

Serve with your favorite cut raw vegetables
(directions on p. 16)

CHOCOLATE SOUFFLÉ
(original recipe)

2 tablespoons butter
1 tablespoon flour
1 cup whole milk
3 ounces semisweet chocolate chips
¼ cup sugar
3 egg yolks
1 teaspoon vanilla
3 egg whites
Whipped cream

CHOCOLATE SOUFFLÉ
(*Light Style* version)

Omit butter
1 tablespoon cornstarch
½ cup nonfat milk and ¼ cup nonfat evaporated milk
3 ounces semisweet chocolate
Omit sugar
½ cup egg substitute
1 teaspoon vanilla
3 egg whites
Low-calorie whipped topping
(directions on p. 209)

Melt the butter and stir in the flour until well blended. In a separate saucepan, heat but do not boil milk, chocolate, and sugar. Add the hot milk mixture to the flour mixture, stirring constantly, until well blended. Beat egg yolks. Beat part of the sauce into the yolks, then add the yolk mixture to the rest of the sauce and stir the custard over very low heat until the yolk thickens slightly. Cool the custard well. Add vanilla. Whip egg whites until stiff but not dry. Fold them lightly into the cooled chocolate mixture. Pour into greased soufflé dish and bake at 350°F about 20 minutes or until firm. Serve at once with whipped cream.

DINING OUT

Consumers are eating more than 20 percent of their meals away from home. Recent restaurant industry surveys estimate four of every ten restaurant meals are eaten in fast-food establishments. Americans spend 40 percent of their food dollars and consume roughly a third of their calories and total fat eating out.

Restaurants, cafeterias, pizza parlors, sandwich shops, and fast-food and convenience stores are not the only places to purchase prepared food. Supermarket take-out counters are gaining their market shares. The type of place you choose for dining away from home can affect the way you and the family eat.

Full-service restaurants, for instance, provide a greater variety and flexibility in preparation than do most fast-food eateries. You can ask restaurant waiters to have your food prepared without fat or salt, serve sauces on the side, or reduce your portion size. While they vary, supermarkets are limited in prepared food offerings.

Whatever source you choose for prepared foods, becoming a wise diner will help you control your choices as much as possible.

The American Heart Association (AHA) offers help for diet-conscious diners concerned about their fat and cholesterol intake. You can write to the AHA for their "Dine to Your Heart's Content" list of heart-conscious eateries whose offerings include low-fat, low-cholesterol menu items. To obtain a copy of the list of restaurants in your area, write to your local Heart Association.

Ordering a meal according to the government's dietary guidelines will also help you make wise menu choices. Think about what you've already eaten that day before going to the restaurant, so you will have a better idea of what to order.

Here are some tips for dining out gleaned from various sources, including the USDA's pamphlet *Eating Better when Eating Out and Using the Dietary Guidelines*, available at $1.50 for handling at the Consumer Information Center, Department 70, Pueblo, Colorado, 81009.

- If you order fish, poultry, or meat, ask to have them broiled, grilled, poached, or steamed, without added fat.
- Have skin removed from poultry, or do it yourself at the table.
- Order meat, fish, or poultry without sauce.
- Order plain meats, which are less caloric than stews.

- Ask for salad without the dressing, or have the dressing served on the side and use it sparingly, remembering that one tablespoon may contain 75 calories or more.
- Opt for lemon juice instead of salad dressing for salads.
- If you are served a large portion, eat half and take the remainder home in a doggy bag.
- Ask to have salt or monosodium glutamate omitted when the food is prepared.
- Ask if petite servings or half portions are available.
- Ask if low-fat or nonfat milk is available.
- Order fresh fruit for dessert instead of a rich cake, pastry, or pie.
- Order pastas with low-oil, low-salt sauces, such as marinara, clam, or vegetable sauces made with small amounts of olive oil.
- Pass the bread basket after taking one slice, or ask the waiter to remove the temptation altogether.
- Order hot soups; they take longer to eat, thus filling you up sooner.

BEFORE THE MEAL ARRIVES

- Go easy on potato chips, peanuts, or pretzels—fill up on raw vegetables instead.
- Avoid the dip if it's made with fatty cheese, cream cheese, sour cream, or mayonnaise.
- Order broth- or tomato-based soups instead of creamy soup made with cream and butter.
- Pass on crackers, which are high in fat and sodium.
- To limit alcohol intake, order fruit juice, mineral water, or spritzer.
- Be aware that words such as *homemade* and *fresh* do not necessarily mean low-fat or low-sodium.
- Be aware that terms such as *light* or *lite* may or may not mean that the food is lower in sodium and fat. Sometimes *light* simply means that the food or liquid is light in color.

AT THE SALAD BAR

- Load up on greens, fruits, and vegetables, but go easy on dressings and mayonnaise-based salads, such as potato, macaroni, or tuna salad.
- Choose lemon juice or vinegar instead of salad dressing.
- Be aware that one tablespoon of oil and vinegar or creamy dressing contains 100 calories or more.
- Use low- or reduced-calories dressings if available.

- Cut down on—or cut out—toppings that add calories, such as sour cream, cheese, bacon bits, olives, eggs, nuts, and croutons.
- Limit the use of soy sauce, steak sauce, catsup, mustard, pickles, and other high-sodium condiments.
- Use freshly ground pepper or an herb blend in place of salt.
- Choose vegetables that are nutrient-dense yet low in calories, such as beans, peas, carrots, broccoli, cauliflower, brussels sprouts, and spinach.
- Choose dark green leafy lettuces, which are higher in nutrients than light-colored lettuces.
- Vary the vegetables to ensure getting a wide variety of nutrients, especially hard-to-get minerals.

AT THE BREAKFAST COUNTER
- Avoid granola-type cereals made with excess amounts of sugar and fat.
- Order poached or boiled eggs instead of fried or scrambled eggs to reduce calories.
- Ask if scrambled eggs can be cooked in broth instead of fat, or if nonstick pans and/or vegetable spray can be used.
- Omelet add-ons, such as bacon, sausage, and cheese, add calories, fat, and cholesterol. Order vegetable omelets instead.
- Order ham or Canadian bacon instead of bacon and sausage; they are leaner.
- Avoid gravies, cream sauces, and Hollandaise, which add extra calories, fat, and sodium.
- To reduce calories and fat, avoid pancake toppings such as butter or margarine. Use syrup or jam sparingly. Instead, choose fruit toppings, such as berries, pineapple, or applesauce.
- Tomato and vegetable juice blends are higher in sodium than most fruit juices, so try to avoid them.
- Order low-fat and nonfat milk, which have the same nutrients, fewer calories, and less fat than whole milk.
- Avoid using dairy and nondairy creamers in tea and coffee, because they add high amounts of fat and calories. Some are made with coconut or palm oils, which are as high in saturated fats as animal fats.

AT THE FAST-FOOD COUNTER
- Choose regular sandwiches instead of double-decker sandwiches.
- Stick to plain sandwiches instead of those with bacon, sauces, cheese, and other added toppings.

- Avoid breaded, deep-fried fish and chicken sandwiches.
- Hold the cheese, tartar sauce, or mayonnaise on plain hamburgers.
- Order roast beef for a leaner option to most burgers.
- A quarter-pound burger with cheese contains 1,225 milligrams sodium, a regular-size order of fries has 150 milligrams sodium, and fried chicken has 800 milligrams sodium. To lower your sodium intake, avoid ordering these items.
- Choose a small rather than large order of fries.
- Have a salad instead of fries.

NUTRITIONAL ANALYSES OF SOME FAST FOODS

Fast Food	Calories	% Calories from Fat	Cholesterol Mg	Sodium Mg
Burger	290	40	45	435
with sauce	625	58	105	880
Chicken Nuggets	310	58	70	700
French fries	240	56	15	120
Milkshake	410	22	35	190
Apple Pie	280	48	5	400

AT THE SUPERMARKET

- Choose simple foods made without sauces.
- Make your own salad and go easy on the dressing.
- Choose plain fresh fruits and vegetables over creamy salads.
- Read labels or ingredient lists on frozen foods for sodium, fat, and cholesterol content.
- If you are eliminating salt, watch for terms such as smoked, pickled, barbecued, or marinated foods; foods in broth, or foods with soy sauce, Creole sauce, mustard sauce; or teriyaki. These foods are high in sodium.
- Be aware of terms that indicate high fat, such as buttered, buttery, fried, French fried, deep-fried, batter-fried, panfried and breaded, creamed, creamy, in cream sauce, in its own gravy, with gravy, pan gravy, Hollandaise, au gratin, in cheese sauce, scalloped, escalloped, rich, and pastry.

AT ETHNIC RESTAURANTS OR
FAST-FOOD EATERIES

- Try Japanese restaurants; they offer many low-fat, low-cholesterol dishes, such as sushi, sashimi, shabu-shabu, noodle soups, and poached dishes.
- Nouvelle Cuisine dishes are not necessarily low in fat, calories, cholesterol, or sodium, so ask how they are prepared.
- Choose meats, fish, or poultry that are roasted, broiled, grilled, or poached instead of fried or panfried.
- Be aware that high amounts of fat are often used in Chinese stir-fry dishes. Ask them to be prepared with less oil.
- Choose steamed vegetables, boiled noodles, steamed or poached fish, poultry, or lightly stir-fried meats at Chinese restaurants.
- Order pastas with simple sauces, such as tomato-based seafood sauces or vegetable sauces made with olive and garlic, in place of heavy meat or cream sauces.
- Most Mexican dishes are low in cholesterol if no lard is used, so do ask.
- Order tortillas, preferably corn, but eat them without butter.

SHOPPING SMART

Research by the USDA has shown that shoppers are concerned about links between diet and disease and are often confused by conflicting nutrition information. Making sound food choices at the marketplace is not easy.

The *Dietary Guidelines for Americans* can help give consumers a handle on shopping smart at the market.

The guidelines urge consumers to eat a variety of foods that provide enough essential nutrients and calories; to consume an adequate amount of starch and fiber; and to avoid too much fat, sugar, sodium, and alcohol.

Here are tips from the USDA that will help you make health-conscious choices with the guidelines in mind when you shop at the market counters.

PRODUCE SECTION

Stock up on fruits and vegetables that provide three to five servings of vegetables and two to four servings of fruit per day. Fruits and vegetables are good sources of vitamins A and C, as well as fiber. They are low in calories, sodium, and fat (except for coconuts, nuts, and avocados).

DAIRY COUNTER

Make sure you and your family eat two servings from the dairy group (milk, cheese, and yogurt) every day. Dairy foods are good sources of calcium and protein, but they also can be high in calories, fat, and sodium.

Skim and low-fat milk and plain low-fat yogurt provide the most calcium for the calories and fat. A cup of skim milk provides about the same amount of calcium as whole milk, but it has 60 fewer calories and 7 grams less fat.

Natural cheeses have higher calcium and lower sodium content than processed cheese, cheese foods, and spreads. For instance, an ounce of natural Cheddar contains less than half the sodium of an ounce of processed American cheese. However, low-fat and low-sodium cheeses are now available in both natural and processed varieties.

MEAT COUNTER

The USDA recommends 5 to 7 ounces of lean meat, the equivalent of two to three servings, in your daily diet. However, be sure to vary the diet with fish, poultry, beans, peas, nuts, seeds, or eggs.

Meats provide excellent sources of iron, zinc, and vitamin B6, which the

USDA has found to be below the RDA in 80 percent of American women's diets.

When purchasing beef, look for leaner cuts, such as sirloin, ground round, round, loin, or chuck (arm).

Purchase ground beef from leaner meat cuts such as sirloin and ground round. Ground chuck is leaner than regular ground beef.

Look for "Select" grade meat cuts, which are leaner than "Choice." "Choice" is leaner than "Prime."

Look for leaner pork cuts, such as tenderloin, center loin roast, chops, and ham.

Purchase poultry without skin. Light meat is leaner (it has fewer calories and less fat) than dark meat.

Avoid processed meats, such as hot dogs, bacon, sausages, and luncheon meats, because they tend to be high in fat and sodium. However, lower-sodium, low-fat processed meats are now widely available. Refer to Specialty Products List (p. 293).

BREAD AND CEREAL SHELF

Bread and cereal are important sources of complex carbohydrate, protein, iron, several B vitamins, and fiber.

Whole-grain breads are higher in fiber than those made with refined flours.

Check labels to see if cracked wheat, bulgur, oatmeal, whole cornmeal, whole rye, Scotch barley, or another ingredient is listed as the first ingredient on the label. So-called wheat bread may not be made from whole wheat. Bread that is brown in color does not necessarily contain whole wheat.

FROZEN FOOD COUNTER

Frozen foods may be high in calories, fat, sugar, and sodium, so check labels carefully before you buy.

SNACK RACK

Check labels of snack foods before you buy. Many are high in fats, cholesterol, calories, sugar, and sodium, while providing little or no nutritional benefit.

Nuts, chips, and pretzels are often high in salt content. Substitute salt-free counterparts whenever possible.

Rice cakes, crisp breads, matzo, melba toast, and saltines are lower in sodium and fat than most crackers.

EVERYDAY FOOD GUIDE

The Recommended Dietary Allowances (RDA) grew out of concern over the fitness—or lack of it—of military men during World War II.

A panel of nutrition experts, now known as the Food and Nutrition Board of the National Academy of Sciences, was summoned to define nutritional requirements. Those requirements became known as the RDA. The RDA undergoes alterations or additions every five years. The last revision was released in 1989 with minor changes. Two nutrients (Vitamin K and selenium) were added, and the RDA was increased for calcium for youngsters and Vitamin C for smokers.

However, the RDA has little meaning for the lay person, except in overall terms. For example, it takes a scientist or nutritionist to interpret the value of 1.5 milligrams riboflavin in terms of food intake.

To help translate the RDA into meaningful food recommendations, the USDA determined that adults need a minimum of two daily servings from the milk group, two from the protein-rich group, five or more from the vegetable and fruit group, and six or more from the bread and cereal group.

Children, however, need three, two, five, and six servings from the milk, meat, fruit and vegetable, and bread groups, respectively, and teenagers need even more—four, two, five, and six—to support their growing bodies. And like growing children, pregnant women need extra nutrients, especially from foods that provide protein, iron, and calcium. Pregnant teenagers need extra nutrients for their continued growth as well as that of their unborn child.

Finally, older people, especially women, must get enough nutrients to meet their increased needs for calcium, folic acid, Vitamin B12, riboflavin, and vitamins A and C, despite their lower energy needs. That's why it's important for older individuals to learn the value of nutrient density when making food choices.

The Everyday Food Guide will help you determine how much fat you and your family are eating so that less than 30 percent of the total calories consumed daily are derived from fat.

The serving size recommendations from the basic food groups (fruits and vegetables; whole grains and cereal; meat, fish, poultry, legumes, beans and eggs; milk, cheese, and yogurt) would supply a person with roughly 1,200 calories per day. However, the more energy you expend, the more you need to consume. This is even more true of athletes, pregnant women, and children, especially teenagers.

EVERYDAY FOOD GUIDE

This chart offers you a unique opportunity to look at the foods you eat to find out if you're getting the nutrients you need and eating less than 30 percent calories from fat.

The four-step process lets you personally choose foods that will help lower the total amount of fat you eat, which is associated with lowering saturated fat and cholesterol.

STEP 1: What Do You Eat?

On the blank line next to each food. write down the number of servings you've eaten of that food during the past 24 hours.

Consider the amount listed by each food as one serving, except in the meat group. A 5-ounce portion. the amount most adults eat, counts as two servings. Health experts recommend a 2- to 3-ounce portion per serving.

To score mixed foods, such as cheeseburgers, pizza, tacos, or frozen dinners, count the ingredients separately in each food group. For example, count a taco as a taco shell, hamburger meat, lettuce, tomato, and cheese. Many mixed foods contain more than 20 grams of fat.

STEP 2: Scoring For Fat

- Add your servings across each row. Record total in the Fat Score column.
- Multiply total servings by the number indicated.
- Write Fat Score in appropriate box.
- Add all Fat Scores and write total in box at bottom of column.
- Compare Fat Score (total grams) to Acceptable Fat Score chart.

STEP 3: Scoring For Nutrition

- Add your servings down each food group column. Record the total in the Nutrition Score boxes. Compare to the Recommended Servings.

	MILK AND MILK PRODUCTS Amounts listed = 1 serving	MEAT AND MEAT ALTERNATES 2-3 ounces = 1 serving 5 ounces = 2 servings	VEGETABLES AND FRUITS Amounts listed = 1 serving
FOODS WITH LITTLE OR NO FAT 0-1.4 grams per serving	— nonfat milk (1 cup) — nonfat yogurt (1 cup) — nonfat frozen yogurt (1 cup)	— dried peas & beans, cooked (1 cup) — shrimp, lobster (3 ounces)★ — scallops (3 ounces) — tuna, canned in water (3 ounces) — sole, broiled or baked (5 ounces)★	— green salad (1 cup) — vegetables, raw (1 cup) or cooked (½ cup) — fresh fruit (1 piece or ½ cup) — fruit juices (6 ounces) — dried fruits (¼ cup) — potato, baked or boiled (1) — tomato sauce (½ cup)
FOODS WITH SMALL AMOUNTS OF FAT 1.5-7 grams per serving	— low-fat milk, 1%, 2%, chocolate (1 cup) — low-fat yogurt, plain or with fruit (1 cup) — low-fat cottage cheese (1 cup) — low-fat or part-skim cheese (1 ounce) — frozen yogurt, ice milk (1 cup)	— tofu (½ cup) — beans, refried or baked (1 cup) — crab, clams (3 ounces)★ — tuna, canned in oil (3 ounces) — cod, trout, broiled or baked (5 ounces)★ — chicken, turkey, roasted, no skin (5 ounces)★	— coleslaw (½ cup) — vegetable soup (1 cup)
FOODS WITH MODERATE AMOUNTS OF FAT 7.1-14.9 grams per serving	— whole milk (1 cup) — cottage cheese, regular (1 cup) — cheese (1 ounce) — cream soup (1 cup)★ — milkshake (10 ounces) — pudding (1 cup) — ice cream (1 cup)★	— salmon, broiled or baked (5 ounces)★ — fried fish (5 ounces)★ — chicken with skin, roasted (5 ounces)★ — chicken or turkey bologna (2 ounces)★ — eggs (2)★ — lean beef, veal, lamb, ham, roasted or broiled, trimmed (5 ounces)★ — beef liver, fried (5 ounces)★	— hash brown potatoes (1 patty) — french fries (1 order)
FOODS WITH LARGE AMOUNTS OF FAT more than 15 grams per serving	— ice cream, rich (1 cup)★ — custard, baked (1 cup)★	— fried chicken with skin (5 ounces, 2 pieces)★ — hamburger, lean or regular (5 ounces, 2 patties)★ — pork roast (5 ounces)★ — luncheon meat, bologna, salami; beef or pork (2 ounces) — frankfurters; beef, pork, chicken, turkey (2)★ — pork or lamb chops (5 ounces, 2 small)★ — beef ribs, spareribs, corned beef (5 ounces)★ — peanut butter (2 tablespoons) — nuts (¼ cup) — sausage (2 ounces)	— potato salad (¾ C)★ — avocado (½)
NUTRITION SCORE Your Total Servings	☐ Recommended Servings: **At Least 2**	☐ Recommended Servings: **At Least 2**	☐ Recommended Servings: **4 or More**

Courtesy of Dairy Council of California

BREADS AND CEREALS	EXTRA FOODS	FAT SCORE
Amounts listed = 1 serving	Amounts listed = 1 serving	average grams of fat contained in each row
— cereal, cooked or dry (1 cup) — bread (1 slice) — soda or water crackers (5) — English muffin, bagel (½) — rice or pasta, cooked (½ cup) — corn tortilla (1) — hamburger or hot dog bun (½)	— mustard, catsup (1 tablespoon) — jelly, jam, honey (1 tablespoon) — syrup (3 tablespoons) — gelatin dessert (½ cup) — hard candy (6 pieces) — popcorn, plain airpopped (1½ cups) — wine, liquor (1 drink) — beer, soft drinks (12-ounce can) — reduced-calorie salad dressings (2 tablespoons) **ADD▶**	YOUR TOTAL SERVINGS ___ × 0 [0]
— roll (1) — muffin, biscuit (1) — flour tortilla, taco shell (1) — crackers (5) — pancakes (2) — waffles, frozen (2 squares)	— cream or creamer (1 tablespoon) — reduced calorie mayonnaise or margarine (1 tablespoon) — sherbet (½ cup) — pretzels (10) — cinnamon roll (1) — cookies (2) — olives (10) **ADD▶**	YOUR TOTAL SERVINGS ___ × 4 [ ]
— granola (½ cup) — croissant (1)	— sour or whipped cream (3 tablespoons) — cream sauces, gravy (¼) cup — margarine, butter, mayonnaise, oils (used in cooking or salads) (1 tablespoon) — bacon (3 slices) — cream cheese (1 ounce) — chocolate bar (1 ounce) — cake (1 piece) — doughnut (1) — potato, corn, tortilla chips (1 ounce) **ADD▶**	YOUR TOTAL SERVINGS ___ × 10 [ ]
Foods with a star ★ contain more than 50 milligrams of cholesterol per serving listed.	— salad dressing (2 tablespoons) — pie (1 slice) — onion rings (1 order) **ADD▶**	YOUR TOTAL SERVINGS × 20 [ ]
[ ] Recommended Servings: **4 or More**	No recommended amounts, but these foods are often high in fat and calories	TOTAL GRAMS OF FAT PER DAY [ ]

FIND YOUR ACCEPTABLE FAT SCORE

(go by your height even if your weight is different from the range indicated)

	Height (without shoes)	Desirable Weight (without clothes)	Calories Per Day (light activity)	Fat Score (grams/day)
WOMEN	5'1" 5'4" 5'7" 5'10"	101–130 110–142 122–154 134–169	1700–1900 1800–2000 1900–2100 2000–2200	57–63 60–67 63–70 67–73
MEN	5'6" 5'9" 6'0" 6'3"	121–154 133–167 145–182 157–197	2000–2300 2150–2450 2300–2650 2450–2850	67–77 72–82 77–88 82–95

SOURCE: Adapted from 1959 Metropolitan Desirable Weight Table, the basis for "Dietary Guidelines for Americans," 1985, USDA.

☐ My fat score is OK.

☐ My fat score is higher than I want it to be.

STEP 4: Planning Changes

A. To eat a more nutritious diet, make sure you're eating the recommended number of servings from each of the food groups.

• By eating the recommended number of servings, you're likely to bring your diet closer in line with recommendations to eat less than 30 percent of calories from fat.

• If you need to add foods, choose foods that will hold your fat score to acceptable levels.

B. To lower fat in your diet without compromising nutrition:

1. First consider making changes in the Extra Foods group. These foods provide few nutrients and are often high in fat and calories. Eat them less often and/or in smaller amounts.

• One-third of the fat in our diet comes from fats and oils added to foods, such as salad dressings, mayonnaise, and spreads.

2. To lower fat within the four food groups:

• Replace fatty foods in the bottom row with lower-fat foods from the middle to upper portions of the chart.

• Broil, steam, poach, BBQ, roast, or bake foods.

• Eat higher-fat foods less often and/or in smaller amounts.

Equally important, stay physically active!

Changes I'll Make	When

NUTRIENTS FOR HEALTH

Nutrients are chemical substances obtained from foods during digestion. They are needed to build and maintain body cells, regulate body processes, and supply energy.

About 50 nutrients, including water, are needed daily for optimum health. If one obtains the proper amount of the 10 "leader" nutrients in the daily diet, the other 40 or so nutrients will likely be consumed in amounts sufficient to meet body needs.

Nutrient	Important Sources of Nutrient	Provide energy
PROTEIN	Meat, Poultry, Fish Dried Beans and Peas Egg Cheese Milk	Supplies 4 calories per gram.
CARBOHYDRATE	Cereal Potatoes Dried Beans Corn Bread Sugar	Supplies 4 calories per gram. Major source of energy for central nervous system.
FAT	Shortening, Oil Butter, Margarine Salad Dressing Sausages	Supplies 9 calories per gram.
VITAMIN A (Retinol)	Liver Carrots Sweet Potatoes Greens Butter, Margarine	
VITAMIN C (Ascorbic Acid)	Broccoli Orange Grapefruit Papaya Mango Strawberries	
THIAMIN (B_1)	Lean Pork Nuts Fortified Cereal Products	Aids in utilization of energy.

One's diet should include a variety of foods because no *single* food supplies all the 50 nutrients, and because many nutrients work together.

When a nutrient is added or a nutritional claim is made, nutrition labeling regulations require listing the 10 leader nutrients on food packages. These nutrients appear in the chart below with food sources and some major physiological functions.

Some major physiological functions	
Build and maintain body cells	**Regulate body processes**
Constitutes part of the structure of every cell, such as muscle, blood, and bone; supports growth and maintains healthy body cells.	Constitutes part of enzymes, some hormones and body fluids, and antibodies that increase resistance to infection.
Supplies energy so protein can be used for growth and maintenance of body cells.	Unrefined products supply fiber—complex carbohydrates in fruits, vegetables, and whole grains—for regular elimination. Assists in fat utilization.
Constitutes part of the structure of every cell. Supplies essential fatty acids.	Provides and carries fat-soluble vitamins (A, D, E, and K).
Assists formation and maintenance of skin and mucous membranes that line body cavities and tracts, such as nasal passages and intestinal tract, thus increasing resistance to infection.	Functions in visual processes and forms visual purple, thus promoting healthy eye tissues and eye adaptation in dim light.
Forms cementing substances, such as collagen, that hold body cells together, thus strengthening blood vessels, hastening healing of wounds and bones, and increasing resistance to infection.	Aids utilization of iron.
	Functions as part of a coenzyme to promote the utilization of carbohydrate. Promotes normal appetite. Contributes to normal functioning of nervous system.

Courtesy of National Dairy Council, Rosemont, Illinois, © 1977.

Nutrient	Important Sources of Nutrient	Provide energy
RIBOFLAVIN (B$_2$)	Liver Milk Yogurt Cottage Cheese	Aids in utilization of energy.
NIACIN	Liver Meat, Poultry, Fish Peanuts Fortified Cereal Products	Aids in utilization of energy.
CALCIUM	Milk, Yogurt Cheese Sardines and Salmon with Bones Collard, Kale, Mustard, and Turnip Greens	
IRON	Enriched Farina Prune Juice Liver Dried Beans and Peas Red Meat	Aids in utilization of energy.

Some major physiological functions	
Build and maintain body cells	**Regulate body processes**
	Functions as part of a coenzyme in the production of energy within body cells. Promotes healthy skin, healthy eyes, and clear vision.
	Functions as part of a coenzyme in fat synthesis, tissue respiration, and utilization of carbohydrate. Promotes healthy skin, nerves, and digestive tract. Aids digestion and fosters normal appetite.
Combines with other minerals within a protein framework to give structure and strength to bones and teeth.	Assists in blood clotting. Functions in normal muscle contraction and relaxation, and normal nerve transmission.
Combines with protein to form hemoglobin, the red substance in blood that carries oxygen to and carbon dioxide from the cells. Prevents nutritional anemia and its accompanying fatigue. Increases resistance to infection.	Functions as part of enzymes involved in tissue respiration.

Courtesy of National Dairy Council, Rosemont, Illinois, © 1977.

WEIGHT CONTROL

In the seven dietary guidelines the surgeon general of the United States urges Americans to maintain a healthy weight and offers the following tips:

- Moderate intake of foods high in fat.
- Moderate intake of sugar.
- Moderate intake of alcohol.
- Eat a balanced diet from all five food groups—breads, cereal, and grains; fruits and vegetables; milk, cheese, and yogurt; and meat, eggs, poultry, and fish.
- Change eating habits that cost extra calories.
- Don't forget to exercise.

These basics are the same for everyone, but the strategy for losing weight is an individual matter that may require the assistance of a physician or dietitian. Check with your doctor if you plan to follow a low-calorie diet over a long period.

A few words about dieting: The surgeon general cautions against fad diets that promise quick weight loss. These diets can be dangerous. Diets that encourage little or no eating or promote heavy use of only one kind of food, or very low-calorie diets may cause health problems in the long run.

Another tip from the surgeon general: Don't be a "yo-yo." Most people who lose weight regain it, and if they lose it again, they regain it again. The repeated losing and regaining, called the "yo-yo syndrome," is dangerous. Losing and regaining weight repeatedly can increase the risk of heart disease. The trick is to achieve a healthy weight and maintain it for good.

Losing too much can be a problem, as well. Serious health problems, sometimes leading to death, can result from serious eating disorders, such as anorexia nervosa and bulimia, caused by refusing to eat; bingeing or gorging followed by vomiting; abusive use of laxatives or diuretics; or excessive exercise.

LIFE-STYLE

People whose life-styles include a dedication to fitness and health often have little problem with weight control. A healthy life-style involves sound eating habits, regular exercise and fitness, and nutrient awareness and education.

NUTRIENT AWARENESS

Whether you have five pounds or 20 pounds to lose, you have to use up more calories than you take in. That means you must reduce calories or increase activity—or do both.

To lose a pound a week, you must either decrease your calorie intake by 500 calories a day or burn up an extra 500 calories a day with more exercise.

However, knowing about the effect of nutrients will help you select foods that are less caloric yet higher in nutrients, so you do not shortchange your diet nutritionally. The Everyday Food Guide on p. 240 will help you plan your meals and make wise food choices.

The best approach is to choose a variety of foods from all food groups and go easy on foods that are especially high in fats and sugar, and alcoholic beverages.

A good rule of thumb is to remember that fats contain 9 calories per gram, carbohydrates 4 calories per gram, protein 4 calories per gram, and alcohol 7 calories per gram. So it makes sense to limit your intake of fat and alcohol and eat more foods high in complex carbohydrates (fruits, vegetables, and grains) as recommended in the *Dietary Guidelines for Americans*.

BREAD GROUP

- Avoid spreads high in fat and sugar.
- Eat cereals with little or no sugar.
- Be careful in choosing the sauces you put on rice and pasta.

FRUIT AND VEGETABLE GROUP

- Eat a variety of fruits.
- Don't add sugar to fruit.
- Go easy on butter, margarine, sauces, mayonnaise, sour cream, and other toppings.
- Avoid frying vegetables.

MEAT GROUP (MEAT, POULTRY, FISH, EGGS, PEAS, BEANS, TOFU)

- Use lean meats.
- Avoid sauced meats.
- Use poultry without skin.
- Avoid batter-frying, breading, or frying.
- Eat more fish.

- Broil, roast, simmer instead of frying or panfrying.
- Consider using low-fat protein-rich alternatives, such as eggs (preferably egg whites), dry beans, peas, and tofu.

MILK GROUP (MILK, CHEESE, YOGURT)
- Use skim or low-fat milk and cheeses.
- Use low-fat yogurt.
- Use yogurt instead of sour cream.

FATS
- Avoid baked cakes, cookies, and snack products made with excess fat and sugar.
- Avoid fatty snacks, such as chips, nuts, and coconut.
- Avoid deep-fried or breaded foods.
- Limit use of salad dressings, potato toppings, spreads, sauces, and gravies.
- Bake instead of frying potatoes.
- Bake instead of batter-frying meats.
- Avoid heavily marbled meats.
- Hold the mayo.
- Use ice milk or sherbet instead of ice cream made with butterfat.
- Hold the frosting on cakes and cookies.

ALCOHOLIC BEVERAGES
- Limit alcoholic beverages.
- Drink coolers, spritzers, and sparkling waters to cut down on hard liquors, wine, and beer consumption.

EATING BEHAVIOR

A change in eating behavior comes with a commitment to health and fitness.

You can unlearn poor eating habits by using some behavior modification techniques that have been proven to help individuals change eating habits for weight reduction and long-term maintenance.

Here is a list of such techniques developed by various behaviorists over the last 30 years:

- Establish one place in the house as your only dining spot.
- Eat slowly. Get into the habit of putting your fork down between bites.
- Completely chew food before taking another bite. The slower you eat, the less you will consume.

- Remove the serving dish from the table after everyone is served.
- Serve food in the kitchen. Food out of sight is out of mind.
- Serve yourself a single standard serving.
- Avoid eating while watching television. Unconscious eating can lead to overeating.
- Be especially aware of what you consume when you are bored, frustrated, or hungry.
- Engage in a pleasant activity, such as exercise, walking, or bicycling, to get your mind off of food.

PORTION CONTROL

Portion control is easy, as well as essential, to learn. The serving size information on our recipes will teach you the value and necessity of portion control. You might also check the Everyday Food Guide on p. 240 to get a realistic idea of what constitutes a serving in each food group. You can cut down on overeating by using little tricks, such as eating half the portion on your plate, saving desserts for between-meal snacks, drinking water during the meal, or eating slowly.

EXERCISE

Our staunch support of exercise has not diminished one bit over the last ten years. Today there is scientific proof that diet and exercise are really worth the effort.

Here are some of the benefits of exercise:

- Regular endurance-type activities, such as running, swimming, or brisk walking, are considered ideal for good cardiovascular health and weight control.
- Regular endurance-type exercise strengthens heart muscles and increases the flow of blood to the heart. Studies show that active people have fewer heart attacks than inactive people.
- Exercise releases tension and acts as a natural tranquilizer.
- Exercise promotes a feeling of well-being and self-esteem.

Check with your doctor before starting any exercise program. Set realistic goals, starting an activity or exercise slowly at first, then building up gradually to a vigorous daily workout.

Here are some tips from the USDA for adding exercise to your daily routine:

- Use the stairs rather than the elevator.
- Put more vigor into everyday activities.

- Take several one-minute stretch breaks during the day.
- Take a walk each day at lunchtime or after work.
- Attend an aerobics or slimnastics class.
- Develop a do-it-yourself home exercise program.
- Establish a regular weekly schedule for activities, such as swimming or tennis.
- Set up a daily routine of walking, bicycling, or jogging.
- Play basketball in a community gym or your backyard.
- Join an office, intramural, or community sports league.
- Go dancing or join a square-dance club.

CALCULATING BODY NEEDS

There are many ways to calculate body needs for ideal weight maintenance.

The average individual needs at least 1,200 nutrient calories (not just calories) for proper baseline nutrition and weight control. Needs differ with individuals, however, depending on activity levels, body type, intensity of activity, or even inactivity.

Most individuals who lead moderately active lives need roughly 15 calories per pound of weight, which means that if your ideal body weight is 130 pounds you can eat up to 1,950 calories a day to maintain your body weight. If, however, you are overweight, you will have to cut your calorie intake back and expend more energy to arrive at your ideal body weight. Since there are 3,500 calories in each pound of stored fat, you will need to consume 500 fewer calories each day until you arrive at your ideal weight.

Here is a formula that might be both fun and instructive in determining how you can maintain body weight.

For example:

130 lb. (present weight)

$\times 15$ (calories activity level per pound weight)

1,950 (calories needed to mainntain present weight)

-500 (calories daily to lose 1 pound per week*)

1,450 (maximum daily calories needed to lose 1 pound per week)

* For a two-pound weight loss per week, subtract 1,000 calories daily.

ACTIVITY VERSUS CALORIES

Total calories expended per hour varies with the activity, with one's body size, age, and sex, and with many other factors. This chart indicates *broadly* to what degree each activity affects total calories used per hour.

Most charts vary slightly in numbers, so think of the chart as a broad-based guide rather than a true indication.

Activity	Calories Expended per Hour
Competitive swimming, running, and other vigorous, intense sports	600
Jogging, swimming, dancing, skating	350 to 450
Walking, bicycling, golf, housework	250 to 300
Light household chores, driving	120 to 180
Lying down, sitting	70 to 100

NUTRIENT COUNTER

The Nutrient Counter is your reference encyclopedia of food values. Restricted dieters will find it an invaluable table for comparing fat, sodium, calories, and cholesterol. It is also an excellent tool for recipe modification and will help you become a nutrient-wise shopper and meal planner. (Figures shown represent average nutrient values. These references include standard error of the mean.)

Adapted from: Charles Frederick Church and Helen Nichols Church, *Food Values of Portions Commonly Used* (Philadelphia: J. B. Lippincott, 1975); Barbara Kraus, *The Dictionary of Calories and Carbohydrates* (New York: Grosset & Dunlap, 1973); Barbara Kraus, *The Dictionary of Sodium, Fats, and Cholesterol* (New York: Grosset & Dunlap, 1974).

NUTRIENT COUNTER FOR COMMON FOODS

Food and Description	Measure or Quantity	Calories	Sodium mg	Cholesterol mg	Fat in Grams		
					Total	Saturated	Unsaturated
A							
Alcohol (p. 272)		48	tr	0			
Almonds, unsalted	6 almonds	80	1	0	8.4	.1	8.3
Apple	1 medium	58	1	0	.8	--	--
Apple Juice, unsweetened	½ cup				tr	--	--
Apricot Jelly							
low calorie	1 tablespoon	5	tr	0	tr	--	--
regular	1 tablespoon	54	5	0	tr	--	--
Arrowroot	1 tablespoon	29	tr	0	.2	--	--
Artichoke, fresh	1 medium	44	30	0	.4	--	--
Asparagus							
fresh	5–6 spears	20	2	0	.1	--	--
Avocado	½ of 1 medium	185	4	--	18.4	--	--
B							
Baking Powder							
low sodium	1 teaspoon	6	tr	0	tr	--	--
regular	1 teaspoon	6	276	0	tr	--	--
Baking Soda	1 teaspoon	neg	1000	0	0	--	--
Bamboo Shoots	½ cup	27	--	0	.4	--	--
Banana	1 medium	101	2	0	.2	--	--
Bean Sprouts	½ cup	16	3	0	tr	--	--
Beef (p. 268)							
Blackberries							
fresh	½ cup	41	tr	0	.7	--	--
frozen, unsweetened	4 oz.	54	1	0	.3	--	--

Legend: tr = trace   neg = negligible   -- = figures unavailable

Food and Description	Measure or Quantity	Calories	Sodium mg	Cholesterol mg	Fat in Grams		
					Total	Saturated	Unsaturated
Blueberries							
fresh	½ cup	45	1	0	.8	--	--
frozen, unsweetened	4 oz.	45	--	0	.6	--	--
Bread							
rye	1 slice	70	128	0	.3	--	--
sourdough	1 slice	70	130	0	.7	--	--
white	1 slice	85	117	0	.7	--	--
whole wheat	1 slice	69	121	0	.6	--	--
Broccoli							
fresh	½ cup	20	18	0	.2	--	--
frozen	½ cup	24	19	0	.8	--	--
Brown Sugar Substitute	1 tablespoon	neg	tr	0	--	--	--
regular	1 tablespoon	48	tr	0	0		
Butter							
salted	1 tablespoon	100	147	36	11.3	6	5
unsalted	1 tablespoon	100	1	35	11.3	6	5
C							
Cabbage, fresh	1 cup, shredded	22	18	0	.2	--	--
Cantaloupes, fresh	¼ of 5" melon	30	12	0	.1	--	--
Capers, bottled	1 tablespoon	6	306	0	0		
Carrots							
fresh	1 large	21	24	0	.1	--	--
cooked	½ cup sliced	24	24	0	.2	--	--
Cashews, unsalted	6–8 nuts	84	21	0	4.9	.9	4

Food	Amount						
Catsup							
regular	1 tablespoon	18	263	0	tr	--	--
low sodium	1 tablespoon	19	4	0	tr	--	--
Cauliflower							
raw	½ cup	14	6	.1	--	--	--
frozen	½ cup	16	9	0	.2	--	--
Celery							
fresh	1 cup, diced	20	134	0			
stalk	1 large	7	50	0			
Cheese (p. 270)							
Chicken (p. 269)							
Chives, fresh	1 tablespoon	3	--	0	--		
Chocolate							
semisweet	1 ounce (1 square)	132	4	0	9.2	--	--
chocolate chips	1 ounce	137	4	0	9.2	--	--
	½ cup	431	18	0	22		
Cocoa	1 tablespoon	14	3	0	.7	--	--
chocolate wafer	1 wafer	20	29	0	.7	--	--
Coconut, shredded, unsweetened	1 tablespoon	42	1.21	0	3	--	--
Corn							
fresh	1 ear	70	tr	0	1	--	--
frozen	½ cup	74	1	0	1	0	--
Cornmeal	1 cup	540	1	0	4.1	0	4.1
Cornstarch	1 tablespoon	29	--	0	tr	--	--
Cranberries, fresh	½ cup	23	1	0	.4	--	--
Cranberry Juice, unsweetened	½ cup	24	5	--	--	--	--

Legend: tr = trace   neg = negligible   -- = figures unavailable

Food and Description	Measure or Quantity	Calories	Sodium mg	Cholesterol mg	Fat in Grams		
					Total	Saturated	Unsaturated
Cream Cheese	1 tablespoon	52	35	16	5.3	3.3	2
Crookneck Squash							
fresh	½ cup	13	1	0	.2	--	--
frozen	½ cup	24	3	0	--	--	--
Cucumbers	1 medium	16	6	0	.2	--	--
E							
Egg Substitute*	1½ ounce	40	70	0	5.6	--	--
Egg, white only	1 medium	16	48	0	tr	--	--
Egg, whole	1 medium	80	53	220	5	2	3
Eggplant	½ cup	25	2	0	.2	--	--
Endive, Belgian	1 head	20	14	0	--	--	--
F							
Fettuccini Egg Noodles, cooked	½ cup	100	2	25	1.2	--	--
Fish (p. 269)							
Flour							
all-purpose	1 tablespoon	29	tr	0	.1	--	--
whole wheat	1 tablespoon	29	tr	0	.1	--	--
whole wheat or all-purpose	1 cup	414	2	0	1.2	--	--
Fructose	1 tablespoon	48	0	0	0		
G							
Gelatin, unflavored	1 envelope	28	--	--	tr	--	
Graham Cracker	1 cracker	30	41	tr	.7	tr	--

Grapefruit							
fresh	½ medium	46	1	0	.1	--	--
canned, unsweetened	½ cup	45	1	0	.5	--	--
Grape Jelly, low calorie	1 tablespoon	15	tr	--	--	--	--
Grapes							
fresh	20	54	2	0	.2	--	--
canned, unsweetened	½ cup	58	5	0	.1	--	--
Green Beans							
fresh, cooked	½ cup	17	2	0	.1	--	--
frozen	½ cup	30	1	0	.1	--	--
Green Peppers	1 whole medium	31	8	--	.1	--	--
H							
Honey	1 tablespoon	61	1	0	0		--
Honeydew Melon	¼ of 5" melon	33	12	0	.3	--	--
Horseradish							
dried	1 teaspoon	--	tr	0	tr	--	--
fresh	1 ounce	25	2	0	tr	--	--
prepared	1 ounce	3	312	0	tr	--	--
L							
Lamb (p. 268)							
Lasagna Noodles, cooked	½ cup	100	1.8	--	2.4	--	--
Leeks, trimmed (4 to 5)	4 ounces	59	6	0	.3	--	--
Lemon Juice	2 tablespoons	27	1	0	0	--	--
Lettuce							
butter	¼ small head	14	9	0	.2	--	--
iceberg	¼ small head	14	9	0	.1	--	--
romaine	¼ small head	13	7	0	.2	--	--

* Nutrient count only for "Second Nature" egg substitute.

Legend: tr = trace neg = negligible -- = figures unavailable

Food and Description	Measure or Quantity	Calories	Sodium mg	Cholesterol mg	Total	Saturated	Unsaturated
Lima Beans							
fresh, cooked	½ cup	94	4	0	.4	--	--
frozen, cooked	½ cup	131	4	0	.2	--	--
Liqueurs (p. 272)							
M							
Mandarin Oranges,							
canned, unsweetened	½ cup	31	2	0	tr	--	--
Maple Syrup							
low-calorie	1 tablespoon	3	4	0	tr	--	--
regular	1 tablespoon	50	2	0	--	--	--
Margarine							
low-calorie	1 tablespoon	50	110	0	5.6	1	5
regular	1 tablespoon	101	138	0	11.3	3	9
Marmalade							
low-calorie	1 tablespoon	11	tr	0	0		
regular	1 tablespoon	60	tr	0	0		
Mayonnaise							
low-sodium	1 tablespoon	85	1	0	9	--	--
low-calorie*	1 tablespoon	25	--	--	--		
regular	1 tablespoon	101	84	10	11.2	2	9
Milk							
buttermilk	1 cup	88	318	5	.2	--	--
evaporated nonfat	½ cup	96	165	2	.5	--	--
nonfat	1 cup	80	126	5	.2	--	--
whole	1 cup	159	122	34	8.5	5	3.5
low-fat (2%)	1 cup	140	150	22	4.9	--	--

Mushrooms						
fresh	½ cup	10	5	0	.1	--	--
canned	½ cup	21	488	0	.1	--	--
Mustard						
dry	1 teaspoon	neg	1	0	tr	--	--
prepared	1 teaspoon	8	58	0	.4	--	--
Dijon	1 teaspoon	4	70	0	.2	--	--
N						
Noodles (egg), cooked	½ cup	100	1.5	25	2.4	.4	2
O						
Olive Oil	1 tablespoon	124	0	0	14	2	12
Onion						
green	1 small	11	1	0	.1	--	--
Spanish, white	1 medium	38	10	0	.1	--	--
Orange	1 medium	77	2	0	.3	--	--
Orange Juice, unsweetened	½ cup	56	1	0	.2	--	--
Orange Marmalade						
low-calorie	1 teaspoon	12	--	0	0		
regular	1 teaspoon	51	--	0	0		
P						
Papaya, fresh	½	44	4	0	.1	--	--
Pecans, unsalted	12 halves	96	tr	0	10	1	9
	½ cup chopped	357	tr	0	37		
Peaches						
fresh	1 medium	38	1	0	.1	--	--
canned, unsweetened	½ cup	38	2	0	.1	--	--
Pea Pods, fresh	½ cup	58	2	0	.2	--	--

* Nutrient count is only for "Hollywood Imitation Mayonnaise."
Legend: tr = trace   neg = negligible   -- = figures unavailable

Food and Description	Measure or Quantity	Calories	Sodium mg	Cholesterol mg	Fat in Grams		
					Total	Saturated	Unsaturated
Pears							
fresh	1 medium	90	3	0	.6	--	--
canned, unsweetened	½ cup	35	1	0	.2	--	--
Peas							
fresh	½ cup	58	1	0	.3	--	--
frozen	½ cup	57	115	0	.3	--	--
Pimiento, canned, drained	¼ cup	15	18	0	.1	--	--
Pineapple Juice, unsweetened	½ cup	66	1	0	.1	--	--
Pineapple							
fresh	1 slice	44	1	0	.2	--	--
canned, unsweetened	1 slice	33	.5	0	.5	--	--
crushed	½ cup	77	1	0	.1		
Pistachio nuts, shelled	30 nuts	88	--	0	33.3	3	30
Pork (p. 268)							
Potato, Russet	1 medium	76	3	0	.1	--	--
sweet	1 medium	115	12	0	.5		
Poultry (p. 269)							
Pumpkin, canned, unsalted	½ cup	41	1	0	.1	--	--
R							
Radishes	2–3	7	7	0	.1	--	--
Raisins	1 tablespoon	29	3	0	.1	--	--
Raspberries							
fresh	½ cup	41	1	0	.9	--	--
canned, water-packed	½ cup	41	1	0	.2	--	--

Rice							
brown, cooked	½ cup	135	--	0	.7	--	--
long grain, cooked	½ cup	87	--	0	.1	--	--
wild	½ cup	80	6	0	.6	--	13
S							
Safflower oil	1 tablespoon	124	0	0	14	1	13
Salt	1 teaspoon	0	2,325	0	0	--	
Sesame Seeds	1 tablespoon	80	6	0	8	--	
Sesame Seed Oil	1 tablespoon	124	0	0	5.1	--	--
Shallots	2 tablespoons, chopped	20	3	0	0		
Shellfish (p. 269)							
Sour Cream							
low-calorie	1 tablespoon	15	--	--	--		
regular	1 tablespoon	28	6	8	4.5	--	--
Soy Sauce, regular	1 tablespoon	6	1,200	0	.2		
Kikkoman Lite	1 tablespoon	10	300	0	0		
Spaghetti, cooked	½ cup	100	2	--	2.4	.4	2
Spinach							
fresh, raw	½ cup	8	12	0	.1	--	--
cooked	½ cup	18	19	0	.2		
frozen	½ cup	27	65	0	.3		
Squash							
crookneck, fresh	½ cup	13	1	0	.2	--	--
zucchini, fresh	½ cup	9	1	0	.1	--	--
zucchini, frozen	½ cup	20	3	0	.1	--	--
winter	4 ounces	46	1	0	.1	--	--

Legend: tr = trace   neg = negligible   -- = figures unavailable

Food and Description	Measure or Quantity	Calories	Sodium mg	Cholesterol mg	Total	Saturated	Unsaturated
Strawberries							
fresh	10	37	1	0	.7	—	—
frozen, unsweetened	4 ounces	25	1	0	.2	—	—
Sugar	1 tablespoon	48	0	0	0		
Sugar Substitutes							
Sucaryl	1 tablespoon	0	tr	0	0		
Sugar Twin	1 tablespoon	0	tr	0	0		
Sweet 'n Low	1 tablespoon	0	tr	0	0		
T							
Tartar Sauce	1 tablespoon	73	182	4	8	1	7
Tomatoes							
fresh	1 medium	22	4	0	.3	—	—
low-sodium, canned	1 medium	25	3	0	.2	—	—
plum, fresh	1 medium	11	2	0	.2	—	—
Tomato Juice							
regular, canned	½ cup	24	244	0	.1	—	—
low-sodium, canned	½ cup	20	3	0	.1	—	—
Tomato Puree							
regular, canned	1 cup	97	998	0	.5	—	—
low-sodium, canned	1 cup	88	14	0	.5	—	—
Tomato Sauce, canned	1 cup	80	1,296	0	tr	—	—
Tortilla,							
corn	1 medium	42	53	0	.6	—	—
flour, no lard	1 medium	150	225	0	4	—	—
Turkey (p. 269)							
Turnips, fresh	½ cup	20	33	0	.1		—

Fat in Grams column group covers Total, Saturated, and Unsaturated.

Food	Portion						
V							
Vanilla Wafers	1 wafer	17	12	0	.7	--	--
Veal (p. 268)							
Vegetable Oil	1 tablespoon	124	0	0	14.2	2.2	12
V-8 Juice,							
regular, canned	½ cup	20	414	0	tr	--	--
low-sodium, canned	½ cup	20	16	0	tr	--	--
W							
Walnuts,							
chopped, raw, unsalted	½ cup	377	2	0	36.6	--	33
Water chestnuts, canned	4 ounces	90	23	0	.2	--	--
Watermelon	½ cup	26	1	0	1.5	--	--
Wines (p. 272)							
Worcestershire Sauce	1 tablespoon	6	150	tr	tr	--	--
Y							
Yams, fresh	½ cup	115	.2	0	--	--	--
Yogurt							
fruit-flavored	1 cup	240	144	10	3.2	2	1
non-fat	1 cup	100	130	4	0	--	--
plain, made from partially skimmed milk	1 cup	122	116	18	3.9	2	2
plain, made from whole milk	1 cup	151	115	30	8.2	4	4
Z							
Zwieback Crackers	1 piece	31	6	0	.7	--	--

Legend: tr = trace   neg = negligible   -- = figures unavailable

NUTRIENT COUNTER FOR MEATS

Meat	Calories	Sodium mg	Cholesterol mg	Total Fat g
BEEF, lean only, select				
Chuck				
Blade Roast	202	56	90	10
Arm Pot Roast	175	56	86	6
Ground Beef, lean	321	56	74	16
(less than 22% fat)				
Rib				
Rib Roast Small End	172	56	67	8
Rib Steak	176	56	68	8
Loin				
Sirloin Steak	158	56	76	5
Porterhouse Steak,	185	56	68	9
choice				
Tenderloin Steak	170	56	71	7
T-bone Steak, choice	182	56	68	8
Flank				
Flank Steak, choice	176	56	57	9
Round				
Rump Roast	182	56	81	7
Top Round Steak	143	56	71	3
Bottom Round Steak	152	56	66	6
Tip Roast	153	56	69	5
VEAL	166	75	100	6
PORK				
Loin				
Sirloin Roast, lean only	177	60	73	9
Loin Chops, lean only	165	60	68	7
Tenderloin, lean only	133	60	67	4
Smoked Ham				
Whole	135	1,028	48	6
LAMB				
Shoulder				
Blade Chop	179	66	78	10
Rib Chop	183	66	80	9
Leg Whole	162	66	76	7

NOTE: All quantities are 3-ounce cooked servings.

Courtesy of the United States Department of Agriculture, Handbook No. 813, 1990.

Meat	Calories	Sodium mg	Cholesterol mg	Total Fat g
FISH				
Codfish	78	70	50	tr
Haddock	79	61	60	tr
Halibut	100	60	50	1
Mackerel (Pacific)	160	80	40	7
Perch	95	77	60	2
Pike	93	51	78	1
Red Snapper	97	50	40	2
Salmon	119	64	54	4
Sole	73	73	60	7
Swordfish	106	127	83	3
Trout	195	52	50	11
Tuna,				
unsalted, water-packed	127	41	20	1
salted, canned in oil	288	800	20	21
SHELLFISH				
Abalone	105	301	85	1
Clams	82	80	40	2
Crab	81	266	59	2
Lobster	91	210	85	2
Oyster	66	73	50	1
Scallops	82	160	50	tr
Shrimp	91	158	141	1
POULTRY				
Chicken, dark meat				
(no skin)	112	83	59	3.3
(with skin)	177	63	82	5.6
Chicken, light meat				
(no skin)	101	83	59	1.3
(with skin)	154	46	63	3.3
Turkey, dark meat				
(no skin)	143	80	67	5
(with skin)	223	122	109	15
Turkey, light meat				
(no skin)	119	44	55	1
(with skin)	189	47	86	12

NOTE: All quantities are 3-ounce servings (100 grams).

Courtesy of the United States Department of Agriculture, *Composition of Foods,* Agricultural Handbook No. 8, 1963.

NUTRIENT COUNTER FOR CHEESES

Note: All quantities are 1 ounce unless otherwise indicated.

Cheese	Calories	Sodium mg	Cholesterol mg	Fat in Grams		
				Total	Saturated	Unsaturated
Blue	100	396	21	8.15	5.30	2.85
Brick	105	159	27	8.41	5.32	3.09
Brie	95	178	28	7.85	--	--
Camembert	85	239	20	6.88	4.33	2.55
Cheddar	114	176	30	9.40	5.98	3.42
Colby	112	171	27	9.10	5.73	3.37
Cottage, creamed (1 cup)	217	850	31	9.47	5.99	3.48
Cottage, 2% low fat (1 cup)	203	918	19	4.36	2.76	1.60
Cottage, 1% low fat (1 cup)	164	918	10	2.30	1.46	.84
Cottage, dry curd (1 cup)	123	19	10	.61	.40	.21
Cream Cheese	99	84	31	9.89	6.23	3.66
Edam	101	274	25	7.88	4.98	2.90
Feta	75	316	25	6.03	4.24	1.79
Gouda	101	232	32	7.78	4.99	2.79
Gruyère	117	95	31	9.17	5.36	3.81

Limburger	93	227	26	7.72	4.75	2.97
Monterey Jack	106	152	--	8.58	--	--
Mozzarella, part skim	80	106	22	6.12	3.73	2.39
Muenster	104	178	27	8.52	5.42	3.10
Parmesan, grated	129	528	22	8.51	5.41	3.10
grated (1 tablespoon)	31	88	--	1.7	--	--
Provolone	100	248	20	7.55	4.82	2.73
Ricotta, whole milk (1 cup)	428	207	124	31.93	20.41	11.52
Ricotta, part skim milk (1 cup)	340	307	76	19.46	12.12	7.34
Romano	110	340	29	7.64	--	--
Swiss	107	74	26	7.78	5.04	2.74
Pasteurized Process						
American	106	406	27	8.86	5.58	3.28
Swiss	95	388	24	7.09	4.55	2.54
Swiss Cheese Food	92	440	23	6.84	--	--
American Cheese Spread	82	381	16	6.02	3.78	2.24
Low-Sodium Cheeses						
American	110	10	--	9	--	--
Gouda	110	10	--	9	--	--

Courtesy of the United States Department of Agriculture, *Composition of Foods*, Agricultural Handbook No. 8, 1963.

ALCOHOL EXCHANGE LIST

Everyone should be aware of alcohol's effect on the body. Alcohol not only is high in calories (about 140 calories per 2 ounces) but also tends to lower the sugar levels in the blood rather than elevate them. Diabetics and hypoglycemics who must avoid rises in insulin must control their intake of alcoholic beverages and should be advised by their physicians or dietitians on their use.

The Alcohol Exchange List is designed to help plan alcohol intake carefully. It lists the alcoholic calories of commonly consumed alcoholic beverages in normal servings with appropriate bread and fat exchanges.

Beverages	Amount	Calories	Exchange
Distilled			
Gin, Rum, Vodka, Whiskey	1 ounce	70	2 fat exchanges
Brandy	1 ounce	73	1 bread exchange
Cognac	1 ounce	73	1 bread exchange
Liqueurs			
Cordial-Anisette	1½ ounces	74	1 bread exchange
Apricot Brandy	1 ounce	86	1 bread exchange
Benedictine	1 ounce	112	1 bread exchange
Crème de Menthe	1 ounce	94	1 bread exchange
Curaçao	1½ ounces	84	1 bread exchange
Wine			
Port	3½ ounces	84	1 bread exchange ½ fat exchange
Dry Sherry	2 ounces	84	⅓ bread exchange 1½ fat exchanges
Champagne, extra dry	3 ounces	87	½ bread exchange 1 fat exchange
Dubonnet	3 ounces	96	½ bread exchange 1½ fat exchanges
Madeira	3 ounces	120	1 bread, 1 fat
Dry Marsala	3 ounces	124	2 bread exchanges 2 fat exchanges
Sweet Marsala	3 ounces	182	2 bread exchanges ½ fat exchange
Muscatel	4 ounces	158	1 bread exchange 2 fat exchanges
Dry Red Wine	3 ounces	64	1 bread exchange
Sake	3 ounces	75	½ bread exchange ½ fat exchange
Dry Vermouth	3½ ounces	112	1½ bread exchanges
Sweet Vermouth	3½ ounces	151	1½ bread exchanges ½ fat exchange
Dry White Wine	3 ounces	74	1 bread exchange
Beer	12 ounces	151	1 bread exchange 2 fat exchanges

OMEGA-3 FATTY ACIDS IN SELECTED SEAFOODS

This chart will help you compare omega-3 fatty acid concentration levels in some of the more popular fish we eat in the United States.

Food	Omega-3 Fatty Acids (grams)	Cholesterol (milligrams)
Bass, fresh water	0.3	59
Cod, Atlantic	0.3	43
Halibut, Pacific	0.5	32
Mackerel, Atlantic	2.6	80
Perch, white	0.4	80
Salmon, pink	0.1	54
Snapper, red	0.2	63
Tuna, albacore	1.5	54
Trout, lake	2.0	48
Crab, Alaska king	0.3	93
Shrimp, Atlantic brown	0.3	142
Clam, soft shell	0.4	72
Oyster, Pacific	0.6	50
Sardines, in oil	1.7	—
Salmon, red	1.3	—
Cod, baked	0.3	50
Haddock, baked	0.2	70
Fish Sticks & Fillets (frozen and breaded)	.15	—

Note: All quantities are 3.5-ounce servings (100 grams).

Adapted from Hepburn, F. N., et al., *Journal of the American Dietetic Association* 86 (1986):794.

FIBER CONTENT IN FOODS

Common servings of foods containing water-insoluble dietary fiber are shown below. Increase your intake by including fiber from all sources. Foods from the meat and dairy group are not good fiber sources. Foods that are good sources of fiber are usually low in fat.

Serving Size	Grams of Dietary Fiber
Breads	
1 medium bran muffin	3
1 slice whole-wheat bread	2
1 slice white bread	1
1 slice pumpernickel	1
1 slice rye	1
1 slice raisin bread	1
4 squares saltines	0
Cereals and Pastas	
1 ounce Fiber One	12
1 ounce All-Bran	9
1 ounce Bran Flakes	4
1 ounce Raisin Bran	4
1 ounce Fruit & Fiber	4
1 ounce Cheerios	2
1 ounce Oatmeal	2
1 ounce Grape Nuts	2
1 cup popcorn	2
1 cup whole-wheat pasta	5
½ cup cooked brown rice	<1
½ cup cooked white rice	<1
½ cup egg noodles	0
Cooked Legumes	
½ cup kidney beans	9
½ cup baked beans	7
½ cup navy beans	5
½ cup pinto beans	5
½ cup lentils	2
Vegetables	
½ cup cooked frozen peas	4
1 medium baked potato (with skin)	4
½ cup cooked broccoli tops	3
½ cup cooked young carrots	3
½ cup cooked corn	3
½ medium avocado	2
½ cup cooked green beans	2
½ cup cooked brussels sprouts	2

Serving Size	Grams of Dietary Fiber
½ cup cooked egg plant	2
½ medium cooked sweet potato	2
½ raw cabbage	2
½ cup raw bean sprouts	1
1 medium dill pickle	1
½ cup mashed potatoes	1
10 medium French fries	1
½ tomato	1
1 stalk raw celery	<1
6 slices raw cucumber	<1
2 rings green pepper	<1
½ cup raw onions	<1

Fruits and Nuts

3 dried figs	7
¼ cup almonds	5
3 dried prunes	4
1 medium apple (with skin)	3
1 medium banana	3
½ cup blackberries	3
5 dates	3
1 medium nectarine, with skin	3
1 medium peach with skin	3
¼ cup roasted peanuts	3
1 cup strawberries	3
¼ cantaloupe	2
10 medium olives	2
1 medium orange	2
2 tablespoons peanut butter	?
1 medium tangerine	2
¼ cup chopped walnuts	2
1 medium apricot	1
10 large cherries	1
½ grapefruit	2
½ cup pineapple	1
2 tablespoons raisins	1
2 medium plums	<1
½ cup orange juice	0

VEGETABLE OIL–FAT COMPARISON

Current recommendations suggest that fat intake should not be below 30 percent of your total calories. Saturated fatty acids should account for less than 10 percent of your calorie intake, polyunsaturated should account for 10 percent of the calories, and your intake of monounsaturated fatty acids should range between 10 and 15 percent of your calorie intake. Here is a chart to help you compare the fat content of various foods. It also shows you other sources of monounsaturated fatty acids besides olive oil. The chart gives the fatty acid and cholesterol contents per tablespoon of selected oils, spreads, and salad dressings.

Food	Calories	Fat	Monounsaturated Fat (gm)	Polyunsaturated Fat (gm)	Saturated Fat (gm)	Cholesterol (mg)
OILS						
Coconut	120	13.6	0.8	0.2	11.8	—
Corn	120	13.6	3.3	8.0	1.7	—
Olive	119	13.5	9.9	1.1	1.8	—
Palm	120	13.6	5.0	1.3	6.7	—
Peanut	119	13.5	6.2	4.3	2.3	—
Rapeseed	120	13.6	7.6	4.5	0.9	—
Sunflower	120	13.6	1.6	10.1	1.2	—
Soybean (Hydrogenated)	120	13.6	5.9	5.1	2.0	—
SPREADS						
Butter	108	12.8	3.6	0.6	7.5	33
Margarine (hard stick)	102	11.4	1.2	1.8	9.1	—
Margarine (corn, soft tub)	102	11.4	4.5	4.5	2.1	—

Food	Calories	Fat	Monounsaturated Fat (gm)	Polyunsaturated Fat (gm)	Saturated Fat (gm)	Cholesterol (mg)
DRESSINGS						
Blue Cheese	77	8.0	1.9	4.3	1.5	n/a
Italian	69	7.1	1.7	4.1	1.0	—
Thousand Island	59	5.6	1.3	3.1	0.9	2
Mayonnaise (soy)	99	11	3.1	5.7	1.6	8
Miracle Whip	57	4.9	1.3	2.6	0.7	4
FOOD						
Sole, poached	91	0.5	0.2	0.3	0.5	50
Haddock, poached	91	0.5	0.1	0.3	0.1	60
Cod, poached	84	0.7	0.1	0.4	0.2	50
Salmon, poached	149	11.6	5	3.3	3.2	54
Chicken Breast, broiled	171	4.6	2.2	0.7	1.6	63
Beef roast, lean sirloin	258	8.5	4.3	0.4	3.8	67
Beef brisket	286	22.4	11.4	1.0	10	83

SPICES, HERBS, AND WINES

No more excuses. There have never been more fresh herbs available than there are today.

Fresh basil varieties, tarragon, rosemary, thyme, sage, garlic, Italian parsley, oregano, and dill no longer are considered exotic. They are as commonplace in today's home cuisine as spices you find on the shelf.

Light Style recipes give you an idea of how fresh herbs and spices can be incorporated into saltless dishes for flavor enhancement. You can also concoct your own flavor combinations using the suggestions in our spice and herb chart in this chapter.

Some tips about using herbs and spices:

- As a general rule, spices should be added toward the end of cooking, as the flavor of ground spices is imparted immediately.
- The flavor of fresh herbs takes longer to release, so they are added early in cooking.
- Whole spices are best added to slow-simmering dishes. They can be tied in cheesecloth bags for steeping while sauces and soups simmer.
- The aroma and flavor of seeds, as well as the dishes to which they are added, can be enhanced by toasting the seeds.
- Whole dried leaves impart superior flavor when they are ground or pulverized just before being added to foods.
- It's best to replenish your supply of herbs and spices at least once every six to eight months, to give your cooked foods the best flavor possible.
- Store fresh herbs as you would any fresh green, whether you wrap them in a damp cloth or in plastic wrap. Packages should be closed airtight after opening to prevent too-rapid deterioration.
- Pot your own herbs for year-round supplies—it's much less expensive, too.

USES OF SPICES AND HERBS

Spice	Uses
Allspice	Pot roast, fish, eggs, pickles, sweet potatoes, squash, fruit.
Anise Seed	Cookies, cakes, breads, candy, cheese, beverages, pickles, beef stew, stewed fruits, fish.
Basil	Tomatoes, noodles, rice, beef stew, pork, meat loaf, duck, fish, veal, green or vegetable salad, eggplant, potatoes, carrots, spinach, peas, eggs, cheese, jelly.

Spice	Uses
Bay Leaf	Soups, chowders, pickles, fish, pot roast, variety meats, stews, marinades.
Caraway Seed	Green beans, beets, cabbage, carrots, cauliflower, potatoes, sauerkraut, turnips, zucchini, goose, lamb, pork, spareribs, beef or lamb stew, marinades for meats, cake, cookies, rice, rye bread.
Cardamom	Baked goods, pickles, grape jelly, puddings, sweet potatoes, squash, fruit soups.
Cayenne Pepper	Meat dishes, spaghetti, pizza, chicken, fish, eggs, cheese, vegetables, pickles.
Celery Seed	Potato salad, fruit salad, tomatoes, vegetables, stuffings, pickles, breads, rolls, egg dishes, meat loaf, stews, soups. Celery powder may be used in any of the above.
Chili Powder	Tomato or barbecue sauces, dips, egg dishes, stews, meat loaf, chicken, marinades for meats, cheese, bean casseroles, corn, eggplant.
Cinnamon	Beverages, bakery products, fruits, pickles, pork, ham, lamb or beef stews, roast lamb, chicken.
Cloves	Fruits, pickles, baked goods, fish, stuffings, meat sauces, pot roast, marinades for meats, green beans, Harvard beets, carrots, sweet potatoes, tomatoes. Used whole to stud ham, fruit, glazed pork, beef.
Curry Powder	Curried beef, chicken, fish, lamb, meatballs, pork, veal, eggs, dried beans, fruit, dips, breads, marinades for meats.
Dill Seed	Pickles, pickled beets, salads, sauerkraut, green beans, egg dishes, stews, fish, chicken, breads.
Fennel Seed	Egg dishes, fish, stews, marinades for meats, vegetables, cheese, baked or stewed apples, pickles, sauerkraut, breads, cakes, cookies.
Garlic	Tomato dishes, soups, dips, sauces, salads, salad dressings, dill pickles, meat, poultry, fish stews, marinades, bread.
Ginger	Pickles, conserves, baked or stewed fruits, vegetables, baked products, beef, lamb, pork, veal, poultry, fish, beverages, soups, oriental dishes.
Mace	Baked products, fruits, meat loaf, fish, poultry, chowder, vegetables, jellies, pickles, breads.
Marjoram	Lamb, pork, beef, veal, chicken, fish, tomato dishes, carrots, cauliflower, peas, spinach, squash, mushrooms, broccoli, pizza, spaghetti, egg dishes, breads, soups.
Mint	Punches, tea, sauces for desserts, sauces for lamb, mint jelly, sherbet, vegetables, lamb stew, lamb roast.
Dry Mustard	Egg and cheese dishes, salad dressings, meat, poultry, vegetables.

Spice	Uses
Mustard Seed	Cucumber pickles, corned beef, coleslaw, potato salad, boiled cabbage, sauerkraut.
Nutmeg	Hot beverages, puddings, baked products, fruits, chicken, seafood, eggs, vegetables, pickles, conserves.
Onion Powder	Dips, soups, stews, all meats, fish, poultry, salads, vegetables, stuffing, cheese dishes, egg dishes, breads, rice dishes.
Oregano	Tomatoes, pasta sauces, pizza, chili con carne, barbecue sauce, vegetable soup, egg and cheese dishes, onions, stuffings, pork, lamb, chicken, fish.
Paprika	Beef, pork, veal, lamb, sausage, game, fish, poultry, egg dishes, cheese dishes, vegetables lacking color, pickles.
Parsley	Soups, coleslaw, breads, tomato and meat sauces, stuffings, broiled or fried fish, meats, poultry.
Pepper: Black	Meats, poultry, fish, eggs, vegetables, pickles.
Cayenne	Meats, soups, cheese dishes, sauces, pickles, poultry, vegetables, spaghetti sauce, curried dishes, dips, tamale pie, barbecued beef and pork.
White	White or light meats, vegetables.
Poppy Seed	Pie crust, scrambled eggs, fruit compotes, cheese sticks, fruit salad dressings, cookies, cakes, breads, noodles. Sprinkle over top of fruit salads, vegetables, breads, cookies and cakes.
Poultry Seasoning	Stuffings, poultry, veal, meat loaf, chicken soup.
Rosemary	Lamb, poultry, veal, beef, pork, fish, soups, stews, marinades, potatoes, cauliflower, spinach, mushrooms, turnips, fruits, breads.
Saffron	Baked goods, chicken, seafood, rice, curries.
Sage	Stuffings for poultry, fish, and other meats, sauces, soups, chowders, poultry, fish, beef, pork, veal, marinades, lima beans, onions, eggplant, tomatoes, cheese, potatoes.
Sesame Seed	Sprinkle on canapes, breads, cookies, casseroles, salads, noodles, soups, vegetables. Add to pie crust, pie fillings, cakes, cookies, dips, stuffings.
Tarragon	Sour cream sauces, casseroles, marinades, pot roasts, veal, lamb, poultry, fish, egg dishes.
Thyme	Meat, poultry, fish, vegetables.
Turmeric	Cakes, breads, curried meats, fish, poultry, egg dishes, rice dishes, pickles.
Vanilla	Baked goods, beverages, puddings.

Adapted from The United States Department of Agriculture Research Service, Consumer and Food Economics Institute.

WINES

The *Light Style* approach to cooking relies heavily on the effective use of herbs and spices to enhance the flavor of dishes without salt. Wines can also be used to add flavor to food.

Light Style treats wine as a seasoning. A little goes a long way—after all, we want to enhance, not mask, flavors.

You may be wondering about the alcohol content in foods made with wine, especially in a book that downplays alcohol consumption. But the calories are negligible when spirits are used in small amounts; there are about 64 calories in 3 ounces of red wine, or 11 calories per tablespoon. In addition, when cooking with wine, heat causes some of the alcohol to evaporate. Research studies show that the longer food cooks, the more alcohol burns off.

However, if you are on a sodium-restricted diet, avoid so-called cooking wines, as they are higher in sodium than regular wines.

Here are some tips we'd like to pass along about cooking with wines:

- A touch of wine adds flavor to fish or fowl.
- Wine brings out the rich flavor of sauces, stews, or soups.
- Wines serve as a natural tenderizer for meats when used as a marinade.
- As a basting sauce, wine does wonders to bring out the flavor of meat.
- A small amount of wine will do the trick when used as extract would be in sweet dishes and fruit.
- Add wine last to sauces, soups, or stews.
- Use white wine when cooking with vegetables, fish, or fowl and red wine in dishes with red meats and game.
- Red or white wine can be added to tomato sauces for added flavor.
- Learn the art of reducing sauces with wines by first simmering them with onions or other vegetables until the wine is almost absorbed, then adding other liquids, such as broth, tomato sauce, or creams.

TABLE OF EQUIVALENTS

Item	Substitution
Artificial Sweeteners (Sugar Substitutes) (Not effective in baking) Sugar Twin:	
1 teaspoon	= 1 teaspoon sugar
Aspartame:	
1 teaspoon	= 2 teaspoons sugar
Sugar Twin, Brown:	
1 teaspoon	= 1 teaspoon sugar
Sweet 'N Low:	
1/10 teaspoon	= 1 teaspoon sugar
1/3 teaspoon	= 1 tablespoon sugar
1 teaspoon	= 1/6 cup sugar
1 1/2 teaspoons	= 1/4 cup sugar
3 teaspoons	= 1/2 cup sugar
6 teaspoons (2 tablespoons)	= 1 cup sugar
Adolph's Sugar Substitute:	
2 shakes of jar	= 1 rounded teaspoon sugar
1/4 teaspoon	= 1 tablespoon sugar
1 teaspoon	= 1/4 cup sugar
2 1/2 teaspoons	= 2/3 cup sugar
1 tablespoon	= 3/4 cup sugar
4 teaspoons	= 1 cup sugar
Sucaryl (Liquid Sweetener):	
1/8 teaspoon	= 1 teaspoon sugar
1/2 teaspoon	= 4 teaspoons sugar
3/4 teaspoon	= 2 tablespoons sugar
1 1/2 teaspoons	= 1/4 cup sugar
3 teaspoons (1 tablespoon)	= 1/2 cup sugar
Fructose	
1/2 teaspoon	= 1 teaspoon sugar
1 1/2 teaspoons	= 1 tablespoon sugar
2 tablespoons	= 1/4 cup sugar
1/4 cup fructose	= 1/2 cup sugar
6 tablespoons	= 3/4 cup sugar
1/2 cup	= 1 cup sugar

TABLE OF SUBSTITUTIONS

The Table of Substitutions is your tool for modifying recipes accurately.

It contains the conversions for regular and artificial sweeteners (if you need to use them), herbs and spices, and several staple ingredients commonly used in *Light Style* recipes.

Although we do not encourage the use of artificial sweeteners and have removed any mention of them from the original recipes, we list them for those who are medically advised to use them or prefer them. They are, however, not recommended for use in baked dishes.

We do not necessarily endorse commercial egg substitute, but we do give it as a substitution only if you prefer using it to using the homemade version or egg whites, as suggested in our recipes. Just remember to take into account sodium and preservative content when using commercial egg substitute.

TABLE OF SUBSTITUTIONS

Item		Substitution or Equivalent
Baking Powder		
1 teaspoon	=	1 teaspoon baking soda + ½ teaspoon cream of tartar
Baking powder, low-sodium		
1½ teaspoons	=	½ teaspoon baking powder

Recipe: Your druggist can make low-sodium baking powder for you by using the following formula. This formula yields about 4½ ounces.

Potassium bicarbonate	39.8 grams
Cornstarch	20.0 grams
Tartaric acid	7.5 grams
Potassium bitartrate	56.1 grams

Item		Substitution or Equivalent
Carob powder		
3 tablespoons powder + 2 tablespoons water	=	1 ounce unsweetened chocolate
Chocolate		
1 square, 1 ounce	=	4 tablespoons grated
Chocolate, unsweetened		
1 ounce	=	3 tablespoons cocoa + 1 tablespoon low-calorie margarine
Chocolate, unsweetened		
1 ounce + 1 tablespoon sugar	=	1⅔ ounces semisweet chocolate
Cream, heavy whipping		
1 cup	=	2 cups whipped
Eggs		
1	=	3 tablespoons egg substitute
1 medium egg white	=	1½ tablespoons
9 medium egg whites	=	1 cup
1 egg yolk	=	1 tablespoon
1 egg yolk	=	1 tablespoon egg substitute
Flours (for thickening)		
1 tablespoon	=	1½ teaspoons cornstarch or arrowroot
Fruits		
Apples, 1 pound, 4 small	=	3 cups sliced or chopped
Apricots, 1 pound, 6 to 8	=	2 cups chopped
Bananas, 1 pound, 4 medium	=	2 cups mashed
Berries, 1 pint	=	2 cups
Cantaloupe, 2 pounds	=	3 cups diced
Grapes, Concord, ¼ pound, 30	=	1 cup
Grapes, Thompson seedless, ¼ pound, 40	=	1 cup
Honeydew melon, 2 pounds	=	3 cups diced

Item	Substitution or Equivalent
Lemon, 1	= 1 to 3 tablespoons juice 1 to 1½ teaspoons grated zest
Mangoes, 1 pound, 2 average	= 1½ cups chopped
Nectarines, 1 pound, 3 average	= 2 cups chopped
Orange, 1 medium	= 6 to 8 tablespoons juice 1 tablespoon grated zest ¾ cup sectioned
Peaches, 1 pound, 4 medium	= 2 cups sliced or chopped
Pears, 1 pound, 4 medium	= 2 cups sliced or chopped
Pineapple, 3 pounds, 1 medium	= 2½ cups chopped
Prunes, 1 pound, cooked and drained	= 2 cups
Tangerines, 1 pound, 4 average	= 2 cups sectioned
Watermelon, 10 to 12 pounds, 1 average	= 20 to 24 cups cubed
Gelatin 1 envelope (¼ ounce)	= 1 tablespoon
Honey 1 cup	= 1¼ cups sugar + ¼ cup liquid
Margarine 1 cube (¼ pound)	= ½ cup or 8 tablespoons
Milk, nonfat evaporated, chilled, 1 cup	= 2 cups whipped
Nuts, shelled	
Almonds, ½ pound	= 2 cups
Almonds, 42 chopped	= ½ cup
Almonds, 4 ounces, blanched, slivered	= 1 cup
Brazil nuts, ½ pound	= 1½ cups
Peanuts, ½ pound	= 1 cup
Pecans, ½ pound	= 2 cups
Pistachios, 1 pound	= 3⅔ cups
Walnuts, ½ pound	= 2 cups
Walnuts, 15 chopped	= ½ cup
Yeast	
Active dry, 1 package	= 1 tablespoon
Compressed, 1 cake	= 1 package active dry
Yogurt plain, 1 cup	= 1 cup buttermilk

METRIC CONVERSION TABLES

FLOUR AND SUGAR MEASUREMENTS

To measure flour, spoon it into a cup and, with the edge of a knife blade, level it off even with the cup lip.

Flour measurements	Ounces	Nearest equivalents
1 tb	¼ oz	7½ g
¼ c; 4 tb	1¼ oz	35 g
⅓ c; 5 tb	1½ oz	50 g
½ c	2½ oz	70 g
⅔ c	3¼ oz	100 g
¾ c	3½ oz	105 g
1 c	5 oz	140 g
1¼ c	6 oz	175 g
1⅓ c	6½ oz	190 g
1½ c	7½ oz	215 g
2 c	10 oz	285 g
3½ c	16 oz; 1 lb	454 g
3¾ c	17½ oz	500 g

Sugar measurements	Ounces	Nearest equivalents
1 tsp	⅙ oz	5 g
1 tb	½ oz	12–15 g
¼ c; 4 tb	1¾ oz	50 g
⅓ c; 5 tb	2¼ oz	65 g
½ c	3½ oz	100 g
⅔ c	4½ oz	125 g
¾ c	5 oz	145 g
1 c	7 oz (6¾ oz)	190–200 g
1¼ c	8½ oz	240 g
1⅓ c	9 oz	245 g
1½ c	9½ oz	275 g
1⅔ c	11 oz	325 g
1¾ c	11¾ oz	240 g
2 c	13½ oz	380–400 g

LIQUID MEASURE CONVERSIONS

Cups and spoons	Liquid ounces	Approximate metric term	Approximate centiliters	Actual milliliters
1 tsp	⅙ oz	1 tsp	½ cl	5 ml
1 tb	½ oz	1 tb	1½ cl	15 ml
¼ c; 4 tb	2 oz	½ dl; 4 tb	6 cl	59 ml
⅓ c; 5 tb	2⅔ oz	¾ dl; 5 tb	8 cl	79 ml
½ c	4 oz	1 dl	12 cl	119 ml
⅔ c	5⅓ oz	1½ dl	15 cl	157 ml
¾ c	6 oz	1¾ dl	18 cl	178 ml
1 c	8 oz	¼ l	24 cl	237 ml
1¼ c	10 oz	3 dl	30 cl	296 ml
1⅓ c	10⅔ oz	3¼ dl	33 cl	325 ml
1½ c	12 oz	3½ dl	35 cl	355 ml
1⅔ c	13⅓ oz	3¾ dl	39 cl	385 ml
1¾ c	14 oz	4 dl	41 cl	414 ml
2 c; 1 pt	16 oz	½ l	47 cl	473 ml
2½ c	20 oz	6 dl	60 cl	592 ml
3 c	24 oz	¾ l	70 cl	710 ml
3½ c	28 oz	⅘ l; 8 dl	83 cl	829 ml
4 c; 1 qt	32 oz	1 l	95 cl	946 ml
5 c	40 oz	1¼ l	113 cl	1134 ml
6 c; 1½ qt	48 oz	1½ l	142 cl	1420 ml
8 c; 2 qt	64 oz	2 l	190 cl	1893 ml
10 c; 2½ qt	80 oz	2½ l	235 cl	2366 ml
12 c; 3 qt	96 oz	2¾ l	284 cl	2839 ml
4 qt	128 oz	3¾ l	375 cl	3785 ml
5 qt		4¾ l		
6 qt		5½ l (or 6 l)		
8 qt		7½ l (or 8 l)		

To convert
Ounces to milliliters: Multiply ounces by 29.57
Quarts to liters: Multiply quarts by 0.95
Milliliters to ounces: Multiply milliliters by 0.034
Liters to quarts: Multiply liters by 1.057

OUNCES TO GRAMS

Ounces	Convenient equivalent	Actual weight
1 oz	30 g	28.35 g
2 oz	60 g	56.7 g
3 oz	85 g	85.05 g
4 oz	115 g	113.4 g
5 oz	140 g	141.8 g
6 oz	180 g	170.1 g
8 oz	225 g	226.8 g
9 oz	250 g	255.2 g
10 oz	285 g	283.5 g
12 oz	340 g	340.2 g
14 oz	400 g	396.9 g
16 oz	450 g	453.6 g
20 oz	560 g	566.99 g
24 oz	675 g	680.4 g

To convert
Ounces to grams: Multiply ounces by 28.35
Grams to ounces: Multiply grams by 0.035

SELECTED MEASUREMENTS

Low-Calorie Margarine, Margarine, or Butter			
1 teaspoon	=	⅙ ounce	or 5 grams
1 tablespoon	=	½ ounce	or 15 grams
½ cup (1 stick)	=	4 ounces	or 115 grams
1 cup (2 sticks)	=	8 ounces	or 230 grams
2 cups (4 sticks)	=	1 pound	or 454 grams
Nuts (chopped) 1 cup	=	5 ounces	or 155 grams

POUNDS TO GRAMS AND KILOGRAMS

Pounds	Convenient equivalent	Actual weight
¼ lb	115 g	113.4 g
½ lb	225 g	226.8 g
¾ lb	340 g	340.2 g
1 lb	450 g	453.6 g
1¼ lb	565 g	566.99 g
1½ lb	675 g	680.4 g
1¾ lb	800 g	794 g
2 lb	900 g	908 g
2½ lb	1125 g	1134 g
3 lb	1350 g	1360 g
3½ lb	1500 g	1588 g
4 lb	1800 g	1814 g
4½ lb	2 kg	2041 g
5 lb	2¼ kg	2268 g
5½ lb	2½ kg	2495 g
6 lb	2¾ kg	2727 g
7 lb	3¼ kg	3175 g
8 lb	3½ kg	3629 g
9 lb	4 kg	4028 g
10 lb	4½ kg	4536 g
12 lb	5½ kg	5443 g
14 lb	6¼ kg	6350 g
15 lb	6¾ kg	6804 g
16 lb	7¼ kg	7258 g
18 lb	8 kg	8165 g
20 lb	9 kg	9072 g
25 lb	11¼ kg	11,340 g

SPECIALTY FOODS

An extraordinary array of low-sodium, -fat, and -calorie foods lines market shelves today. The products listed here include the newest products on the market and brands that we have found to be the lowest in calories, fat, and sodium for the *Light Style* recipes.

However, the list is not an endorsement of the products, but a practical solution for those whose medical needs dictate their use. We strongly advise the use of ingredients that are not processed whenever possible.

The Food and Drug Administration requires nutrition labels for foods that make a nutritional claim, such as "low-fat" or "cholesterol free," and foods that have had nutrients added. Manufacturers may voluntarily include nutrition labels as part of their packaging.

Label information on processed and canned foods can be of great help in evaluating the product before you buy it. Labels may be helpful in making choices because they list ingredients in descending order of amount, with the top five indicating the largest amounts. If the label, for instance, lists fat, sugar, or salt as the first ingredient, you will know that the ingredient predominates. Labels also show the serving size, number of servings per container, and calories, protein, carbohydrates, fat, and sodium per serving. They also give the percentages per serving of the United States RDA of protein, five vitamins, and two minerals, and sometimes additional vitamins, minerals, and cholesterol.

Nutritional information is provided per serving, so check to see how many servings are contained in the package and whether the serving size given is actually the amount you eat.

A few precautionary comments:

- Watch for special claims, such as "lite" or "low-salt," and check the amounts on the label or the ingredients list to ensure that the claim is justified.
- Be aware of disguised phrases or words that describe sugar, such as corn syrup, molasses, honey, sorbitol, fructose, and maltose.
- Look for the following words, which indicate saturated fat content: lard, animal fat, animal shortening, hydrogenated chicken/beef/pork fat, meat fat, butter, butter fats, whole milk solids, cream, and dairy fats.
- Watch for these ingredients, which contain sodium: baking powder, baking soda, soy sauce, monosodium glutamate, and sea salt.
- Most canned foods contain high levels of salt, so check all packaged food labels for salt content.

- Low-calorie toppings have no specific food value, but we have listed them for those who must restrict fat intake. Another idea is to make your own topping, using our recipe, Heavenly Whipped Topping (p. 184).

SPECIALTY PRODUCTS

The products listed are brands that we have found to be lowest in sodium, fat, cholesterol, and calories, and, in our opinion, highest in flavor compared to all others. This list, however, is not an endorsement of these products.

Sources for Special Products

Supermarket Savvy Brand-Name Food List
A 14-page list of the healthier foods, by brand name.
P.O. Box 25
Addison, TX 75001

General Mills Products
General Mills Chemical Corp.
Dietetic Specialties
4620 West 77 Street
Minneapolis, MN 55435

Lifetime Food Co., Inc.
Lifetime natural cheeses
426 Orange St.
Sand City, CA 93955

ENER-G Foods, Inc.
P.O. Box 24723
Seattle, WA 98124-0723

Product	Brand Name	Where Distributed	Comment
Cheeses			
Cheeses reduced in fat, cholesterol, and sometimes calories	Lifetime, Dormans Light, Kraft Light, Weight Watchers, Natural, New Holland	Supermarkets	
Goat milk cheese	Laura Chenel, Chevre, Feta	Supermarkets and specialty cheese shops.	Equivalent in fat to skim milk cheese.
Condiments			
Low-sodium baking powder	Cellu	Supermarkets and health food stores.	
Low-sodium catsup	Heinz	Supermarkets	
Low-sodium chili sauce	Cellu	Supermarkets	
Low-sodium mustard	Cellu Feather weight	Health food stores and supermarkets	
Low-sugar jelly and jams	Smucker's, Kerns	Supermarkets and gourmet shops	Manufacturers vary. Look for the pure fruit jams.
Low-calorie, low-cholesterol mayonnaise	Kraft, Best Foods, Weight Watchers	Supermarkets	
Light cream cheese		Supermarkets	Brand names vary from state to state.
Light sour cream		Supermarkets	Read labels. Beware of coconut and palm oils.

Product	Brand Name	Where Distributed	Comment
Low-calorie margarine; Light margarine	Fleischmann's, Mazola, Weight Watchers, Imperial, Parkay	Supermarkets	Look for 50 calories or less per tablespoon.
Low-calorie salad dressing	Richard Simon's, Kraft, Wishbone, Walden Farms, Bernsteins	Supermarkets	Comes in a spray bottle.
Hot Sauce	Tabasco, McHenny Company	Supermarkets	
Low-sodium Soy Sauce	Kikkoman	Supermarkets	
Worcestershire Sauce	French's	Supermarkets	
Gelatin, flavored, low-calorie	Jello, D-Zerta	Supermarkets	Made with Nutra-sweet.
Herb Blends	Mrs. Dash, Parsley Patch	Supermarkets	Remember to look for added salt.
Egg Substitute Second Nature, Egg Beaters	Avoset Food Corporation	Supermarkets	
Fish, canned	Iris, Star-Kist, Cellu, Chicken of the Sea	Supermarkets	
Hot dogs, lite	Hebrew National	Supermarkets	Kosher, all-beef.

Food	Brand	Where to Buy	Notes
Ice cream, American Dream	Dreyers	Supermarkets	Low-fat, cholesterol-free ice cream.
Luncheon meats	Oscar Meyer	Supermarkets	
Nuts Unsalted Nuts Raw Nuts	Planters	Supermarkets	
Peanut Butter	Laura Scudder, Ralph's Old Fashion	Supermarkets	Nonhydrogenated.
Peanut Butter, unsalted	Peter Pan	Supermarkets	
Nondairy Whipped Toppings	Presto Foods Dream Whip D-Zerta Whip Bird's Eye Dieter's Gourmet		
Pastas	Pasta Mama	Gourmet shops	No added eggs (most pasta is eggless).
Spaghetti Sauce	Conca D'Oro	Gourmet shops	No added sugar or salt. Made with olive oil.
Stocks Beef, Chicken, and Fish	Cellu, Perfect Addition	Health food stores Supermarkets	Frozen food section.
Vegetable Spray	Pam	Supermarkets	Prevents food from sticking. It contains only 2 calories and comes in a variety of flavors.

Product	Brand Name	Where Distributed	Comment
Yogurt, frozen	Dreyers	Supermarkets	
Vegetables			
low-sodium canned	Hunt's, Delmonte, Cellu, Feather-Weight	Supermarkets	Brand names vary in different states.
frozen	Green Giant, Bird's Eye	Supermarkets	
Tomato juice, low-sodium	V8	Supermarkets	
Low-sodium tomato paste	Cellu, Feather-Weight, Hunt's		
Equipment			
The Victor Grill	Let's Get "Cookin'"	4643 Lakeview Cyn. Dr. Westlake Village, CA 36191 (818) 991–3940	Allows you to barbecue on the stove top.
Cameron Smoker Cooker	Let's Get "Cookin'"	4643 Lakeview Cyn. Dr. Westlake Village, CA 36191 (818) 991–3940	The smoker brings out the salt flavor in food without having to add salt.
Spanet Roaster	Let's Get "Cookin'"	4643 Lakeview Cyn. Dr. Westlake Village, CA 36191 (818) 991–3940	
Joyce Chin Peking Pan	Let's Get "Cookin'"	4643 Lakeview Cyn. Dr. Westlake Village, CA 36191 (818) 991–3940	A wok cooker that you don't have to add oil to.

GLOSSARY

Calorie: A unit of heat measurement, or in terms of food, a measure of energy value of food.

Cholesterol: A fatlike waxy substance manufactured by the body and present in animal fats, oils, blood, bile, nerves, and all cells of the body. It is manufactured naturally by the body and also comes from foods we eat. The main dietary sources of cholesterol are foods of animal origin, such as liver, egg yolks, dairy products, most meats, shellfish, and some foods high in saturated fats. These lipids may undergo a chemical change and eventually may turn into fatty deposits. There is no cholesterol in foods of plant origin, such as vegetables, fruit, grains, and nuts. Buildup of cholesterol in the arteries has been associated with heart disease. Cholesterol is, however, important to the regulation of some body functions and as a precursor of vitamin D, sex hormones, adrenal hormones, and bile acids necessary for proper fat absorption.

Coronary Artery: Those arteries that supply blood to the heart muscles.

Coronary Artery Disease (Atherosclerosis): A condition caused by deposits, including cholesterol, which may decrease the inside diameter of the arteries and interfere with blood circulation.

Decalcification: Dissipation or loss of calcium from the bones, caused either by malabsorption of calcium or an inadequate supply of calcium in the diet, or binding of calcium by very large amounts of some fibers (phytates) in food, or inactivity.

Deficiency Disease: A disease resulting from an inadequate supply of nutrients needed by the body to function healthfully.

Diabetic Exchange: For diabetics who need to carefully calculate carbohydrates, fat, and protein intake to avoid sudden rises in blood sugar levels, the American Diabetes Association has devised a list of foods in which specific amounts are approximately equal in calories and nutrients as in the amounts of protein, carbohydrates, and fat. The list is divided into six main groups, or exchanges, for easy calculation: milk, vegetable, fruit, bread, meat, and fat.

Enriched: Foods to which nutrients have been added in amounts sufficient to restore those in the unprocessed state, as in bread enriched with iron, thiamin, and niacin to replace nutrients lost in the processing of the wheat.

Essential Fatty Acids: These are polyunsaturated and occur most abundantly in vegetable oils, such as corn oil. The body can neither manufacture them nor do without them. Fatty acids are essential for growth and certain body functions in infants and adults, as well.

Fiber: A complex carbohydrate, generally defined as the part of the plant material that cannot be digested and absorbed in the bloodstream. There are two types of fiber: water-soluble and water insoluble. Water-insoluble fiber is found in wheat bran, corn bran, breads and cereals, and fruits and vegetables. Insoluble fiber is thought to be responsible for helping to reduce the risk of colon cancer and promote regularity, and it aids in the treatment of diverticulosis. Water-soluble fibers are found in oat bran, figs, dried beans (kidney, pinto, lima, and navy), black-eyed peas, carrots, green peas, and corn. Zucchini and broccoli have some soluble fiber as do bananas, apples, pears, and oranges. This type of fiber is thought to help lower blood cholesterol levels.

Fortified: Foods to which nutrients have been added in amounts sufficient to make the total content larger than that contained in the unprocessed state. Vitamin D, for example, is used to "fortify" milk.

Glucose: A single sugar occurring in fruit, honey, and sugar, and metabolized by most cells of the body. Starch, a complex carbohydrate, breaks down to glucose.

Hemoglobin: A protein in the blood that contains iron and carries oxygen from the lungs to the tissues.

Hydrogenation: Combination of unsaturated fatty acids with hydrogen to form saturated fatty acids.

Hyper- (prefix): Excess.

Hypercholesterolemia: Abnormally high levels of blood cholesterol.

Hyperlipidemia: Abnormally high levels of blood triglyceride.

Hyperlipoproteinemia: Abnormally high levels of blood lipoprotein.

Hypertension: Abnormally high blood pressure.

Hypo- (prefix): Deficiency.

Insulin: A hormone made in the pancreas that lowers levels of blood glucose by stimulating its conversion into glycogen (starch). Insulin also promotes fat storage.

Lipid: A term used to cover all water-insoluble fats and fatlike substances, such as triglycerides, lipoproteins, steroids, cholesterol, and phospholipids. Includes oils, butter, margarine, etc.

Lipoproteins: There are two main types, both of which contain protein, cholesterol, and phospholipid. High density or alpha lipoproteins (HDL) contain a higher proportion of phospholipids and protein. Low density or beta lipoproteins (LDL) contain a higher proportion of cholesterol. Too much LDLs have been associated with buildup of cholesterol, which can cause heart attacks.

Malnutrition: An imbalance between the body's supply of nutrients and the body's demand for nutrients.

Metabolism: The chemical changes that go on in the body as food is converted into body tissue.

Monounsaturated Fatty Acids: A fat present in olive, peanut, avocado, rapeseed oils. Research indicates that monounsaturated fats are helpful in reducing levels of LDL (low-density lipoprotein) cholesterol in the blood, and, as a result, may help reduce the risk of heart disease. Refer to the Vegetable Oil–Fat Comparison Chart on p. 276.

Nutrients: Individual chemical substances in foods that are used to nourish the body.

Omega-3 Fatty Acids: A polyunsaturated fat found primarily in deep-sea salt-water fish. Tuna and salmon are two of the best sources of omega-3 fatty acids. Health professionals believe that just two to three servings of fish a week may help reduce the risk of heart disease. Refer to the chart on p. 273 for omega-3 concentration levels in fish.

Osteoporosis: Occurs when bone loss is so excessive that bones fracture under everyday common stresses. According to the experts, the best way to prevent or treat osteoporosis is to increase your consumption of calcium-rich foods, exercise, moderate your protein intake, and avoid excess caffeine and alcohol. Milk and other dairy foods are the major sources of calcium in the United States. The best way to assure an adequate intake of calcium is to eat a wide variety of foods from the four food groups. By improving their diet and exercising regularly, young women may be able to prevent osteoporosis from developing later in life.

Plaque: A material deposited in arteries containing lipids, among other substances.

Polyunsaturated Fatty Acids: Generally, these are oils in their natural states and are of vegetable origin. Most vegetable oils are polyunsaturated, such as safflower, sunflower, corn, soybean, and cottonseed oils. The exceptions are coconut and palm oil.

RDA: The Recommended Dietary Allowances developed by the Food and Nutrition Board of the National Academy of Sciences during World War II is a table of nutrients in varying amounts for each age group considered as standards for optimal health.

Risk Factor: An inherent or environmental factor that is associated with increased incidences of coronary heart disease but is not necessarily the cause.

Saturated Fatty Acids: Saturated fats are usually of animal origin and solid at room temperature. Foods high in saturated fats include heavily marbled and fatty meat, whole milk and cream, cheese made from whole milk, and chocolate. The body also makes its own fat from excess food and this fat is predominantly saturated. Because coconut oil is a highly saturated vegetable fat, it also falls in the saturated fat category. Some foods, however, are higher in saturated fats than others.

Snack Foods: A loose definition of foods broadly considered to be of minimal nutritional value. These foods are generally high in sugar and/or fat content, such as potato chips, candy, and soft drinks.

Sodium: An essential mineral for life of humans, animals, and plants. Sodium occurs naturally in many foods, but the principal source in the diet of humans is sodium chloride—ordinary table salt—of which sodium is one of the constituents. Sodium is important for many body functions, including temperature regulation. When excess sodium cannot be excreted by the body, it causes water retention, which puts a strain on various body organs. High sodium intake has also been associated with high blood pressure, and the reduction of dietary sodium has been shown to reduce blood pressure.

Sucrose: Ordinary cane sugar. A disaccharide, sucrose consists of two molecules, one each of glucose and fructose.

BIBLIOGRAPHY

American Dietetic Association. "Comments made at Surgeon General's Report/Editorial Briefing." 25 October 1988.

American Institute for Cancer Research. *Dietary Guidelines to Lower Cancer Risk.* AICR Information Series, 1982. Dairy Council of California. *Calcium Update,* 1988.

Beef Board and Beef Council. *Meal Styles.* Fresno: Beef Board and Beef Council, 1988.

Church, Charles Frederick, and Helen Nichols Church. *Food Values of Portions Commonly Used.* Philadelphia: J. B. Lippincott Company, 1975.

Dairy Council of California. *Food for a Healthy Heart.* Sacramento: Dairy Council of California, 1989.

Goodhart, R., and M. Shils, eds. *Modern Nutrition in Health and Disease.* Philadelphia: Lea & Febiger, 1973.

Information Services. *Composition of Foods.* Agriculture Handbook No. 8. Washington, DC: United States Government Printing Office, 1976–1990.

Lawler, Marilyn, and Corinne H. Robinson. *Normal and Therapeutic Nutrition.* New York: Macmillan Company, 1977.

Lempert, Philip. The Lempert Report, "Fast Food and Nutrition." Montclair, New Jersey: Consumers Insights, 1 November 1989.

National Dairy Council. *Guide to Good Eating.* Nutrition Source Book. Rosemont, Illinois: National Dairy Council, 1977.

Nutrition and the MD, vol. 12, no. 12, December 1986; vol. 13, no. 98, September 1987; vol. 15, no. 1, January 1989.

"Osteoporosis." *Consumer Report,* 1984, p. 76.

Science News Magazine, vol. 136, 1989, p. 344.

Tufts University. "Fiber's Role in Food and Fitness." *Diet and Nutrition Newsletter,* July 1985.

United States Department of Agriculture. Human Nutrition.

United States Department of Agriculture. *Dietary Guidelines for Americans,* Second Edition. Washington, DC: United States Government Printing Office, 1985.

United States Department of Agriculture. "Dietary Guidelines for Americans," *Home and Garden*, no. 232, April 1986.

United States Department of Agriculture. "Eating Right the Dietary Guidelines Way." *USDA News Feature*. 10 July 1989.

RECIPE INDEX

Albondigas Soup, 27

APPETIZERS
Appetizer Artichokes, 17
Champagne Meatballs, 17
Chicken Pacifica, 18
Crab Dip, 14
Guacamole, 15
Marinated Mushrooms, 148
Melon with Port, 19
Pears Alexander, 202
Pizza, 19
Pizza Canapés, 20
Scallops Dejonghe, 20
Seafood Cocktail, 21
Seafood Dip, 15
Sirloin Teriyaki, 22
Skinny Dip, 16
Stuffed Cherry Tomatoes, 23
Stuffed Mushrooms, 22
Tortilla Salad, 24

APPLES
Apple-Onion Stuffing, 93
Applesauce, 178
Apple Sizzle Crêpes, 208
Apple-Stuffed Pork Chops, 109
French Apple Tart, 196
Waldorf Salad, 155

Apricot Ice Cream, 207
Artichokes, Appetizer, 17

ASPARAGUS
Asparagus Picante, 127
Steamed Asparagus, 127

Autumn Salad, 155

AVOCADO
Avocado-Orange Salad, 151
Avocado Salad, 142
Guacamole, 15

Baklava, 191
Barbecued Chicken, 83
Basil Dressing, 161

BEANS
Green Beans Amandine, 131
Savory Green Beans, 135

Béchamel Sauce (White Sauce), 167

BEEF
Beef Brochette, 99
Beef Stock, 37
Beef Tacos, 99
Champagne Meatballs, 17
Chateaubriand, 100
Chinese Beef with Pea Pods, 101
Roast Beef au Jus, 102
Sirloin Teriyaki, 22
Steak Diane, 103
Steak Dijon, 103
Steak Oscar, 104
Tournedos Rossini, 104
Vienna Dip, 102

BERRIES
Berries on Ice, 205
Berry Bowl, 200
Chilled Berry Soup, 35

BEVERAGES
Bloody Mary, 214
Breakfast Shake, 215
Eggnog, 215
Herb Tea, 216
Ice Ring, 217
Mimosa Cocktail, 216
Persian Refresher, 217
Sparkling Punch, 217
Sunrise Punch, 218
Virgin Mary, 215
Virgin Spritzer, 219
Wine Spritzer, 218
Yogurt Smoothie, 219

Biscuits, Cloud, 43
Blender Béarnaise, 169
Bloody Mary, 214
Blossom Peach Salad, 154
Bouquet Garni, 181

BREADS
Bread Sticks, 46
Cloud Biscuits, 43
Corn Bread, 44
French Bread, 46
Garlic Bread, 45
Mexican Bread Pudding, 197
Oat Bran Muffins, 44
Pizza, 19
Pizza Canapés, 20
Ramona's Rolls, 48
Ramona's Whole-Wheat Bread, 47

Breakfast Shake, 215
Broccoli alla Romana, 128
Buttermilk-Cucumber Dressing, 161

CABBAGE
Coleslaw De Luxe, 145
Gingham Salad, 148

California Cheesecake, 192
California Quiche, 56
California Salad, 152
California Tostada, 143
Candied Sweets (potatoes), 137
Cannelloni, Kathy's, 115
Cannelloni Noodles, 115
Cantaloupe Crab Boats, 153

CARROTS
Carrots à l'Orange, 128
Minted Baby Carrots, 132

Catsup, 182

CAULIFLOWER
Cauliflower in Lemon Sauce, 129
Orange-Cauliflower Salad, 149
Tomato-Cauliflower Salad, 150

Champagne Meatballs, 17
Chantilly Potatoes, 137
Chateaubriand, 100
Cheesecake, California, 192

CHICKEN
Barbecued Chicken, 83
California Tostada, 143
Chicken alla Marsala, 85
Chicken Cashew, 84
Chicken Marengo, 84
Chicken-Mushroom Sauté, 88
Chicken Oriental, 89
Chicken Pacifica, 18
Chicken Piccata, 90
Chicken Soup Klara, 28
Chicken Stock, 38
Chicken-Stuffed Papaya, 153
Chicken Tarragon, 90
Chinese Chicken Salad, 144
Enchiladas Suiza, 86
Lemon Chicken, 87
Oven-Fried Chicken, 91

Chilled Berry Soup, 35
Chilled Crookneck Soup, 36
Chinatown Soup, 28
Chinese Beef with Pea Pods, 101
Chinese Chicken Salad, 144
Chinese Stir-Fry Pork, 110
Chinese Stir-Fry Vegetables, 129

CHOCOLATE
    Chocolate Crumb Crust, 194
    Chocolate Mousse Pie, 193
    Chocolate Soufflé, 209
    Cholesterol-Free Substitute, 183

Citrus Compote, 200
Classic Sole, 69
Cloud Biscuits, 43
Coffee Ice, 206
Coleslaw De Luxe, 145

CONDIMENTS AND SPECIALTY
    RECIPES
    Bouquet Garni (fresh or dried), 181
    Catsup, 182
    Cholesterol-Free Egg Substitute, 183
    Cranberry Sauce, 179
    Cream Cheese, 185
    Dijon Mustard, 182
    Fresh Cranberry Relish, 183
    Heavenly Whipped Topping, 184
    Herb Blend, 184
    Ice Ring, 217
    Low-Calorie Margarine (whipped), 185
    Seafood Cocktail Sauce, 186
    Soy Sauce, 187
    Tartar Sauce, 187

Confetti Rice, 120
Consommé Madrilène, 29

COOKIES
    Oatmeal Cookies, 199
    Peanut Butter Cookies, 199
    Snowdrop Cookies, 198

CORN BREAD
    Corn Bread, 44
    Herb-Corn Bread Stuffing, 95

Cornish Game Hens with Herb-
    Corn Bread Stuffing, 95
Court Bouillon, 72

CRAB
    Cantaloupe Crab Boats, 153
    Chinatown Soup, 28
    Crab Dip, 14

Crab-Stuffed Sole, 75
Crêpes St. Jacques, 61
Seafood Cocktail, 21
Seafood Dip, 15

CRANBERRIES
    Cranberry Sauce, 179
    Fresh Cranberry Relish, 183

Cream Cheese, 185
Creamed Spinach, 130
Creamy Garlic Dressing, 162

CRÊPES
    Apple Sizzle Crêpes, 208
    Blueberry Cheese Blintzes, 64
    Crêpes Divan, 60
    Crêpes Florentine, 61
    Crêpes St. Jacques, 61
    Feather Crêpe Cups, 64
    Feather Crêpes, 63
    Feather Wheat Crêpes, 63
    Fruit in Crêpe Baskets, 209
    Peach Crêpes, 208
    Ratatouille Crêpes, 62
    Strawberry Crêpes, 208

Crookneck Soup, Chilled, 36
Crookneck Squash, Herbed, 131

CRUSTS
    Chocolate Crumb Crust, 194
    Graham Cracker Crumb Crust, 192
    Pie Crust, 196
    Quiche Crust, 56

CUCUMBERS
    Buttermilk-Cucumber Dressing, 161
    Cucumbers in Yogurt, 145
    Scandinavian Cucumbers, 150

Curry Mayonnaise, 180

DESSERTS
    Apple Sizzle Crêpes, 208
    Applesauce, 178
    Apricot Ice Cream, 207
    Baklava, 191
    Berries on Ice, 205
    Berry Bowl, 200
    California Cheesecake, 192
    Chocolate Crumb Crust, 194
    Chocolate Mousse Pie, 193
    Chocolate Soufflé, 209
    Citrus Compote, 200
    Coffee Ice, 206
    Cold Pumpkin Soufflé, 195
    French Apple Tart, 196
    Fruit in Crêpe Baskets, 209

Graham Cracker Crumb Crust, 192
Heavenly Whipped Topping, 184
Lemon Soufflé, 210
Lemon Topping, 193
Melon Baskets, 205
Melon with Port, 19
Meringue Shells, 204
Mexican Bread Pudding, 197
No-Bake Fruit Cake, 197
Oatmeal Cookies, 199
Papaya with Lime, 201
Peach Crêpes, 208
Peach Ice Cream, 207
Peach Melba, 202
Peaches Galliano, 201
Peanut Butter Cookies, 199
Pears Alexander, 202
Pie Crust, 196
Pineapple in Rum, 203
Pineapple Sauce, 177
Snowdrop Cookies, 198
Strawberries in Meringue, 203
Strawberries Romanoff, 204
Strawberry Crêpes, 208
Strawberry Ice, 206
Strawberry Ice Cream, 207
Strawberry Sauce, 181
Strawberry Soufflé, 211
Vanilla Ice Cream, 207

DIJON
    Dijon Mustard, 182
    Steak Dijon, 103

Dilly Trout in a Pouch, 70

DIPS
    Crab Dip, 14
    Curry Mayonnaise, 180
    Drawn Margarine, 170
    Guacamole, 15
    Seafood Cocktail Sauce, 186
    Seafood Dip, 15
    Skinny Dip, 16
    Tartar Sauce, 187
    Vinaigrette, 165

DRESSINGS
    Basil Dressing, 161
    Buttermilk-Cucumber Dressing, 161
    Creamy Garlic Dressing, 162
    Green Goddess Yogurt Dressing, 162
    Herb Dressing, 163
    Lemon Dressing, 163
    Low-Calorie Russian Dressing, 166

DRESSINGS (*con't*)
Orange Blossom Dressing, 164
Oregano Dressing, 164
Rice Vinegar Dressing, 165
Vinaigrette, 165

EGGPLANT
Ratatouille, 134
Ratatouille Crêpes, 62

EGGS
Chocolate Soufflé, 209
Eggnog, 215
Egg Substitute (cholesterol free), 183
Frittata, 51
Lemon Soufflé, 210
Mushroom Soufflé, 54
Omelet, variations:
Cheese, 52
Florentine, 52
Frittata, 51
Herb, 51
Oriental, 53
Spanish, 53
Supreme, 53
Quiche, variations:
California, 56
Zucchini, 57
Spinach Soufflé, 55

Enchiladas Suiza, 86
Endive-Watercress Salad, 146

Fabulous Salad, 147
Feather Crêpe Cups, 64
Feather Crêpes, 63
Feather Wheat Crêpes, 63
Fettuccini Alfredo, 116

FISH
Cantaloupe Crab Boats, 153
Classic Sole, 69
Crab-Stuffed Sole, 75
Crêpes St. Jacques, 61
Dilly Trout in a Pouch, 70
Fish Stock, 38
Grilled Salmon, 80
Lime-Laced Lobster Tails, 78
Lobster Bisque, 32
Marine Kebabs, 71
Picnic Lobster, 78
Poached Sea Bass, 71
Sauce Velouté, 176
Scallops Dejonghe, 20
Scallops in Cider, 79
Scallops Marcus, 79
Seafood Cocktail, 21
Seafood Dip, 15

Sole Amandine, 72
Sole Meunière, 77
Sole Veronique, 74
Swordfish Piquant, 73
Whitefish à la Port, 76

Florentine Omelet, 52
French Apple Tart, 196
French Bread, 46
French Onion Soup, 30
French Provincial Sauce (Brown Sauce), 171
Fresh Cranberry Relish, 183
Frittata, 51

FRUIT
Apple-Onion Stuffing, 93
Applesauce, 178
Apple Sizzle Crêpes, 208
Apple-Stuffed Pork Chops, 109
Apricot Ice Cream, 207
Autumn Salad, 155
Avocado-Orange Salad, 151
Avocado Salad, 142
Berries on Ice, 205
Berry Bowl, 200
Blossom Peach Salad, 154
California Salad, 152
Cantaloupe Crab Boats, 153
Chicken-Stuffed Papaya, 153
Chilled Berry Soup, 35
Citrus Compote, 200
Cranberry Sauce, 179
French Apple Tart, 196
Fruit in Crêpe Baskets, 209
Holiday Salad, 157
Lemon Soufflé, 210
Lemon Topping, 193
Melon Baskets, 205
Melon with Port, 19
Orange-Cauliflower Salad, 149
Papaya with Lime, 201
Peach Crêpes, 208
Peach Ice Cream, 207
Peach Melba, 202
Peaches Galliano, 201
Pears Alexander, 202
Pineapple Sauce, 177
Pineapple in Rum, 203
Strawberries in Meringue, 203
Strawberries Romanoff, 204
Strawberry Crêpes, 208
Strawberry Ice, 206
Strawberry Ice Cream, 207
Strawberry Sauce, 181
Strawberry Soufflé, 211
Sunshine Salad, 156
Waldorf Salad, 155

GAME
Cornish Game Hens with Herb-Corn Bread Stuffing, 95

Garlic Bread, 45
Gazpacho Andaluz, 36
Gingham Salad, 148
Graham Cracker Crumb Crust, 192

GREEN BEANS
Green Beans Amandine, 131
Savory Green Beans, 135

Green Goddess Yogurt Dressing, 162
Guacamole, 15

Hearty Minestrone, 31
Heavenly Whipped Topping, 184
Herb Blend, 184
Herb–Corn Bread Stuffing, 95
Herb Dressing, 163
Herb Omelet, 51
Herb Tea, 216
Herbed Crookneck Squash, 131
Herbs and Spices, 279
Holiday Salad, 157
Hollandaise, Mock, 180

ICE CREAM
Apricot, 207
Peach, 207
Strawberry, 207
Vanilla, 207

ICES
Coffee Ice, 206
Strawberry Ice, 206

Italian Meat Sauce, 172
Italian Tomato Sauce, 173

Kathy's Cannelloni, 115
Kebabs, Marine, 71

LAMB
Irish Stew, 105
Roast Leg of Lamb with Pineapple Sauce, 106

Lasagna, 117
Leek and Potato Soup, 33

LEMON
Lemon Chicken, 87
Lemon Dressing, 163
Lemon Soufflé, 210

LEMON (*con't.*)
Lemon Spinach, 132
Lemon Topping, 193

LOBSTER
Lime-Laced Lobster Tails, 78
Lobster Bisque, 32
Picnic Lobster, 78

Low-Calorie Margarine
(whipped), 185
Low-Calorie Russian Dressing,
166

Madeira Sauce, 175
Margarine, Drawn, 170
Margarine, Low-Calorie
(whipped), 185
Marinara Sauce, 174
Marinated Mushrooms, 148
Marine Kebabs, 71
Mayonnaise, 179
Mayonnaise, Curry, 180

MEATS
Albondigas Soup, 27
Apple-Stuffed Pork Chops,
109
Beef Brochette, 99
Beef Tacos, 99
Champagne Meatballs, 17
Chateaubriand, 100
Chinese Beef with Pea Pods,
101
Chinese Stir-Fry Pork, 110
Irish Stew, 105
Lasagna, 117
Mexican Pork Stew, 110
Pork with Sage, 111
Roast Beef au Jus, 102
Roast Leg of Lamb with
Pineapple Sauce, 106
Steak Diane, 103
Steak Dijon, 103
Steak Oscar, 104
Tournedos Rossini, 104
Veal Abel, 106
Veal alla Marsala. *See* Chicken
alla Marsala
Veal Bourguignonne, 107
Veal Parmigiana, 108
Veal Piccata. *See* Chicken
Piccata
Venetian Veal, 108
Vienna Dip, 102

Mediterranean Salad, 149
Melon Baskets, 205
Melon with Port, 19
Menus, 222
Meringue Shells, 204

Mexican Bread Pudding, 197
Mexican Pork Stew, 110
Mimosa Cocktail, 216
Minted Baby Carrots, 132
Mock Hollandaise, 180
Mornay Sauce, 172
Mousse, Chocolate Pie, 193
Mushroom Sauté, 133
Mushroom Soufflé, 54
Mushroom, Tomato Salad, 151
Mushrooms, Marinated, 148
Mushrooms, Stuffed, 22

Noodles, Cannelloni, 115
Noodles Simplice, 118
Nutrient Counter, 256–271

OMELETS
Cheese, 52
Florentine, 52
Frittata, 51
Herb, 51
Omelet Supreme, 53
Oriental, 53
Spanish, 53

Orange, Avocado Salad, 151
Orange Blossom Dressing, 164
Orange-Cauliflower Salad, 149
Oregano Dressing, 164
Oriental Omelet, 53
Oven-Fried Chicken, 91
Oven-Fried Potatoes, 138

Papaya and Chicken Salad. *See*
Chicken-Stuffed Papaya
Papaya with Lime, 201
Parmigiana, Veal, 108

PASTA
Cannelloni Noodles, 115
Chicken Pasta Al Pesto, 119
Fettuccini Alfredo, 116
Kathy's Cannelloni, 115
Lasagna, 117
Noodles Simplice, 118
Spaghetti with Italian Meat
Sauce, 118

Pea Pods, Chinese Beef with,
101
Pea Soup, 33

PEACHES
Peach Crêpes, 208
Peach Ice Cream, 207
Peach Melba, 202
Peaches Galliano, 201

Peanut Butter Cookies, 199
Pears Alexander, 202
Peas and Pods, 133

Persian Refresher, 217
Piccata, Chicken (or Veal), 90
Picnic Lobster, 78
Pie Crust, 196
Pineapple in Rum, 203
Pineapple Sauce, 177
Pizza, 19
Pizza Canapés, 20
Poached Sea Bass, 71
Pommes Parisienne, 138

PORK
Apple-Stuffed Pork Chops,
109
Chinese Stir-Fry Pork, 110
Mexican Pork Stew, 110
Pork with Sage, 111

POTATOES
Candied Sweets, 137
Chantilly Potatoes, 137
Oven-Fried Potatoes, 138
Pommes Parisienne, 138
Potato and Leek Soup, 33
Potatoes Nicoise, 140
Potatoes Vegetarian, 139

POULTRY
Barbecued Chicken, 83
Chicken alla Marsala, 85
Chicken Cashew, 84
Chicken Marengo, 84
Chicken-Mushroom Sauté, 88
Chicken Oriental, 89
Chicken Pacifica, 18
Chicken Piccata, 90
Chicken Stock, 38
Chicken-Stuffed Papaya, 153
Chicken Tarragon, 90
Chinese Chicken Salad, 144
Cornish Game Hens with
Herb–Corn Bread Stuffing,
95
Crêpes Divan, 60
Enchiladas Suiza, 86
Lemon Chicken, 87
Oven-Fried Chicken, 91
Roast Turkey with Royal
Glaze, 92
Turkey Divan, 92
Turkey Stock, 38
Turkey Tetrazzini, 94

Pudding, Mexican Bread, 197

PUNCH
Sparkling, 217
Sunrise, 218

QUICHES
California, 56
Quiche Crust, 56
Zucchini, 57

Ramona's Rolls, 48
Ramona's Whole-Wheat Bread, 47
Ratatouille, 134
Ratatouille Crêpes, 62

RICE
  Confetti Rice, 120
  Rice Pilaf, 120
  Rice Vinegar Dressing, 165
  Saffron Rice, 121
  Spanish Rice, 121
  Steamed Rice, 122
  Wild Rice Skillet, 122

Roast Beef au Jus, 102
Roast Leg of Lamb
  with Pineapple Sauce, 106
Roast Turkey with Royal Glaze, 92
Rosewater Syrup, 191

Saffron Rice, 121

SALADS
  Autumn Salad (gelatin), 155
  Avocado-Orange Salad, 151
  Avocado Salad, 142
  Blossom Peach Salad, 154
  California Salad, 152
  California Tostada, 143
  Cantaloupe Crab Boats, 153
  Chicken-Stuffed Papaya, 153
  Chinese Chicken Salad, 144
  Coleslaw De Luxe, 145
  Cucumbers in Yogurt, 145
  Endive-Watercress Salad, 146
  Fabulous Salad, 147
  Gingham Salad, 148
  Holiday Salad (gelatin), 157
  Marinated Mushrooms, 148
  Mediterranean Salad, 149
  Melon Baskets, 205
  Orange-Cauliflower Salad, 149
  Pears Alexander, 202
  Scandinavian Cucumbers, 150
  Sunshine Salad (gelatin), 156
  Tomato-Cauliflower Salad, 150
  Tomato-Mushroom Salad, 151
  Tortilla Salad, 24
  Waldorf Salad, 155
  Walnut-Fig-Spinach Salad, 158

SANDWICHES
  California Tostada, 143
  Vienna Dip, 102

SAUCES AND CONDIMENTS
  Applesauce, 178

Béchamel Sauce (White Sauce), 169
Blender Béarnaise, 169
Bouquet Garni, 181
Catsup, 182
Chicken or Turkey Gravy, 170
Cranberry Sauce, 179
Cream Cheese, 185
Curry Mayonnaise, 180
Dijon Mustard, 182
Dill Sauce, 188
Drawn Margarine, 170
French Provincial Sauce
  (Brown Sauce), 171
Fresh Cranberry Relish, 183
Heavenly Whipped Topping, 184
Herb Blend, 184
Italian Meat Sauce, 172
Italian Tomato Sauce, 173
Low-Calorie Margarine, 185
Madeira Sauce, 175
Marinara Sauce, 174
Mayonnaise, 179
Mock Hollandaise, 180
Mornay Sauce, 172
Pineapple Sauce, 177
Sauce Abel, 176
Sauce Velouté, 176
Seafood Cocktail Sauce, 186
Soy Sauce, 187
Spanish Sauce, 174
Strawberry Sauce, 181
Suiza Sauce, 86
Tarragon Sauce, 177
Tartar Sauce, 187

Savory Green Beans, 135
Scallops Dejonghe, 20
Scallops in Cider, 79
Scallops Marcus, 79
Scandinavian Cucumbers, 150
Sea Bass, Poached, 71

SEAFOOD
  Cantaloupe Crab Boats, 153
  Classic Sole, 69
  Crab Dip, 14
  Crab-Stuffed Sole, 75
  Crêpes St. Jacques, 61
  Dilly Trout in a Pouch, 70
  Fish Stock, 38
  Lime-Laced Lobster Tails, 78
  Lobster Bisque, 32
  Marine Kebabs, 71
  Picnic Lobster, 78
  Poached Sea Bass, 71
  Scallops Dejonghe, 20
  Scallops in Cider, 79
  Scallops Marcus, 79

Seafood Cocktail, 21
Seafood Cocktail Sauce, 186
Seafood Dip, 15
Sole Amandine, 72
Sole Meunière, 77
Sole Veronique, 74
Swordfish Piquant, 73
Whitefish à la Port, 76

Shredded Zucchini, 135
Sirloin Teriyaki, 22
Skinny Dip, 16
Snowdrop Cookies, 198

SOUFFLÉS
  Chocolate, 209
  Cold Pumpkin, 195
  Lemon, 210
  Mushroom, 54
  Spinach, 55
  Strawberry, 211

SOUPS AND STOCKS
  Albondigas Soup, 27
  Beef Stock, 37
  Chicken Soup Klara, 28
  Chicken Stock, 38
  Chilled Berry Soup, 35
  Chilled Crookneck Soup, 36
  Chinatown Soup, 28
  Consommé Madrilène, 29
  Court Bouillon, 72
  Fish Stock, 38
  French Onion Soup, 30
  Gazpacho Andaluz, 36
  Hearty Minestrone, 31
  Lobster Bisque, 32
  Pea Soup, 33
  Potato and Leek Soup, 33
  Turkey Stock, 38
  Vegetable Soup, 34
  Veal Stock, 37

Soy Sauce, 187
Spaghetti with Italian Meat
  Sauce, 118
Spanish Omelet, 53
Spanish Rice, 121
Spanish Sauce, 174
Sparkling Punch, 217
Spices and Herbs, 279

SPINACH
  Creamed Spinach, 130
  Crêpes Florentine, 61
  Gingham Salad, 148
  Lemon Spinach, 132
  Spinach Soufflé, 55

STEAK
  Steak Diane, 103
  Steak Dijon, 103

STEAK (*con't*)
Steak Oscar, 104
Tournedos Rossini, 104

Steamed Asparagus, 127
Steamed Rice, 122
Stocks. *See* Soups and Stocks

STRAWBERRIES
Strawberries in Meringue,
203
Strawberries Romanoff, 204
Strawberry Crêpes, 208
Strawberry Ice, 206
Strawberry Ice Cream, 207
Strawberry Sauce, 181
Strawberry Soufflé, 211

Stuffed Cherry Tomatoes, 23
Stuffed Mushrooms, 22

STUFFINGS
Apple-Onion Stuffing, 93
Herb-Corn Bread Stuffing, 95

Suiza Sauce, 86
Sunshine Salad, 156
Swordfish Piquant, 73
Syrup, Rosewater, 191

TARRAGON
Chicken Tarragon, 90
Tarragon Sauce, 177

Tartar Sauce, 187

TOMATOES
Italian Tomato Sauce, 173
Stuffed Cherry Tomatoes, 23
Tomato-Cauliflower Salad,
150
Tomato-Mushroom Salad, 151
Tomato Puree, 175

Tortilla Salad, 24
Tournedos Rossini, 104
Trout, Dilly in a Pouch, 70

TURKEY
Roast Turkey with Royal
Glaze, 92
Stock, 38
Turkey Crêpes Divan, 60

Turkey Divan, 92
Turkey Tetrazzini, 94

Vanilla Ice Cream, 207

VEAL
Veal Abel, 106
Veal alla Marsala. *See* Chicken
alla Marsala
Veal Bourguignonne, 107
Veal Parmigiana, 108
Veal Piccata. *See* Chicken
Piccata
Veal Stock, 37
Venetian Veal, 108

VEGETABLES
Appetizer Artichokes, 17
Asparagus Picante, 127
Broccoli alla Romana, 128
Candied Sweets (potatoes),
137
Carrots à l'Orange, 128
Cauliflower in Lemon Sauce,
129
Chantilly Potatoes, 137
Chilled Crookneck Soup, 36
Chinese Stir-Fry Vegetables,
129
Coleslaw De Luxe, 145
Creamed Spinach, 130
Crêpes Florentine, 61
Cucumbers in Yogurt, 145
Endive-Watercress Salad, 146
Fabulous Salad, 147
French Onion Soup, 30
Gingham Salad, 148
Green Beans Amandine, 131
Herbed Crookneck Squash,
131
Lemon Spinach, 132
Marinated Mushrooms, 148
Mediterranean Salad, 149
Minted Baby Carrots, 132
Mushroom Sauté, 133
Mushroom Soufflé, 54
Orange-Cauliflower Salad,
149
Oriental Omelet, 53
Oven-Fried Potatoes, 138
Pea Soup, 33

Peas and Pods, 133
Pommes Parisienne, 138
Potato and Leek Soup, 33
Potatoes Vegetarian, 139
Potatoes Nicoise, 140
Ratatouille, 134
Ratatouille Crêpes, 62
Savory Green Beans, 135
Scandinavian Cucumbers,
150
Shredded Zucchini, 135
Spinach Soufflé, 55
Steamed Asparagus, 127
Stuffed Cherry Tomatoes, 23
Stuffed Mushrooms, 22
Tomato-Cauliflower Salad,
150
Tomato-Mushroom Salad, 151
Vegetable Soup, 34
Venetian Veal, 108
Vinaigrette, 165
Virgin Mary, 215
Whipped Butternut Squash,
136
Zucchini Oregano, 136

Vienna Dip, 102
Virgin Spritzer, 219

Waldorf Salad, 155
Whipped Butternut Squash, 136
Whitefish à la Port, 76
Wild Rice Skillet, 122
Wine Spritzer, 218

Yams, Candied Sweets, 137

YOGURT
Cucumbers in Yogurt, 145
Green Goddess Yogurt
Dressing, 162
Skinny Dip, 16

ZUCCHINI
Frittata, 51
Quiche, 57
Shredded Zucchini, 135
Zucchini Oregano, 136